D1131285

BERG'S *WOZZECK*

BERG'S

WOZZECK

HARMONIC LANGUAGE
AND DRAMATIC DESIGN

JANET SCHMALFELDT

YALE UNIVERSITY PRESS
NEW HAVEN AND LONDON

Published with assistance from the
Louis Stern Memorial Fund.

Designed by Sally Harris
and set in Times Roman type by Graphic Composition, Inc.
Printed in the United States of America by
The Murray Printing Company,
Westford, Mass.

Library of Congress Cataloging in Publication Data

Schmalfeldt, Janet, 1945–
  Berg's *Wozzeck*: harmonic language and dramatic design.
  Bibliography: p.
  Includes index.
  1. Berg, Alban, 1885–1935. Wozzeck. I. Title.
II. Title: Wozzeck.
MT100.B57S35 1983   782.1'092'4   82–10896
ISBN 0–300–02710–9

10 9 8 7 6 5 4 3 2 1

For my mother
in memoriam

CONTENTS

PREFACE

At a time when atonal composition was still largely confined to the production of short works and miniatures, Alban Berg's decision to compose a full-length atonal opera on the subject of Georg Büchner's fragmentary and disturbingly revolutionary *Woyzeck* showed great courage. The outcome of that decision—*Wozzeck*—stands today as one of the greatest works in the history of opera, one whose brilliant orchestration alone can ravish even those listeners who are otherwise not fond of twentieth-century music and make an impact never to be forgotten. With this study, I join the many writers about music for whom *Wozzeck* has had an irresistible appeal.

In his 1929 *Wozzeck*-lecture, Berg himself provided the ground plan for later studies of the opera. Whereas these have presented generally reliable information on such issues as forerunners of the work, its genesis and reception, its leitmotivic scheme, its large formal design, the diversity of formal, harmonic, and orchestrative procedures employed, the composer's subtle treatment of the vocal parts, his "constructive" rhythms, and the relationship of Berg's *Wozzeck* to Büchner's *Woyzeck*, only one large-scale attempt has been made to describe those elements of pitch organization that provide the basis for harmonic contrast and continuity. I refer to the work of George Perle, whose contribution I discuss in my introductory chapter. A technical approach to the question of the harmonic organization of *Wozzeck* would be premature were it not for the more general studies of Perle and earlier writers. Thanks to these, it will now be appropriate, first, to establish which pitch structures serve as fundamental components of the harmonic language and, second, to set forth as the central issue an examination of the interaction of harmonic language with dramatic design.

Decisions about fundamental harmonic features presuppose a systematic preliminary investigation of all pitch-structural components of the opera. That such an investigation has not been previously attempted may relate to the fact that only recently have analysts of atonal music recognized the need for sharing well-developed criteria as bases for the comparison and classification of pitch structures. Elementary pitch-class set-theoretic principles have provided one response to this need. I propose to demonstrate that essential yet hitherto unexplored aspects of Berg's harmonic procedure in *Wozzeck* can be uncovered by means of the pitch-class set-analytical method. This demonstration yields a view of the harmonic design differing significantly from earlier studies. It will be shown that Berg's expansion of nineteenth-century leitmotivic procedure is manifested in the extraordinary interpenetration of motivic-dramatic plan and harmonic design: Berg introduces the fundamental elements of his harmonic vocabulary as pitch-structural components of easily recognizable motivic shapes; in addition, he then permits these pitch structures to recur in contexts that free them from dependence upon motives, such that they may now create their own referential networks in association with specific characters and dramatic issues.

Since pitch-class set-theoretic concepts will be familiar to many but not all readers, my study begins with an exposition of the historical development of pitch-class set theory, within which basic definitions are introduced in preliminary application to excerpts from *Wozzeck*. I proceed with an introduction to primary pitch materials of the opera, as projected (1) in a series of cadential and initial structures that articulate the formal divisions of Act I/Scene 1, and (2) in association with prominent motivic-thematic components of the work. Consideration of the formal design of Büchner's play in relation to Berg's plan for the first act prepares the way for a survey of those pitch materials that reinforce the centrality of the character Wozzeck by serving as the pervasive pitch-structural components of the opera. Wozzeck's pitch-structural "family" will then be juxtaposed with pitch materials associated with Marie. I conclude by summarizing the essential vocabulary of the harmonic language of *Wozzeck* in terms of the interaction of three distinct set-complex "families" that underscore a central dramatic issue—the conflict between Wozzeck and Marie.

In light of the recent publication of two major studies on Alban Berg, a brief statement about the chronology of my own project is now in order. My work is the outcome of analysis and research begun in earnest around 1973 and completed in the form of a doctoral dissertation in December 1978. With the appearance shortly thereafter of Douglas Jarman's *The Music of Alban Berg* (Jarman 1979), I was pleased to discover that Jarman and I had independently made a number of similar observations about *Wozzeck*; the opportunity to acknowledge these as well as to clarify points where Jarman and I diverge gave a fresh impetus to the task of revising my manuscript for publication. The second study, George Perle's *The Operas of Alban Berg, Vol. I: "Wozzeck"* (Perle 1980), appeared just after my revisions had been completed. As with Jarman's work, I regard the availability of Perle's new publication as propitious. Three of its six chapters—the three most relevant to my own project—have been adapted with minimal changes from the three previously published articles listed in my bibliography under Perle 1967a, 1967b, and 1971. I can hope that Perle's book will thus have drawn renewed attention to issues that play a major role in the pages to follow.

The publication of Perle's *The Operas of Alban Berg, Vol. I* also relates indirectly to the fact that a number of my ideas as well as aspects of my interpretation of ten of the musical examples in the present volume have already appeared in print. I refer here to a review of Perle's book published in the *Journal of the American Musicological Society* by Martha MacLean Hyde (Hyde 1981). This reviewer became familiar with my work in her capacity as one of the original readers of my dissertation; she subsequently asked my permission to consult my study in the preparation of her critique.

I am deeply indebted to the European American Music Distributors Corporation, sole representatives of all rights in the United States and in Canada, for permission to reproduce excerpts from the following:

Alban Berg, *Wozzeck* (Vienna: Universal Edition, 1931; copyright renewed 1958 by Universal Edition), vocal score.

———, *Wozzeck* (Vienna: Universal Edition, 1926; English translation, London: Alfred A. Kalmus, 1952; copyright renewed 1954 by Helene Berg), orchestral score.

———, Sonata Op. 1 (Berlin-Lichterfelde: Schlesinger'sche Buch- u. Musikhdlg., 1926; copyright renewal 1954 by Helene Berg).

Unless otherwise indicated, translations from the German are my own in consultation with friends and with reference to published translations. I most gratefully acknowledge Daniel Wilson's assistance in this area.

Especially in the final stages of this project, I might have lost sight of the end were it not for the generous support of many friends and colleagues. Among these, Robert Jones read three of my chapters with the utmost care, responded to innumerable questions about stylistic details, offered a remarkable range of valuable suggestions, and prepared the index. Professors Jeffrey Sammons and Roslyn Belkin gave expert critical attention to my material on Georg Büchner; Bo Alphonce offered thoughtful responses to the content of chapters 1 and 2; Eric Regener and Kenneth Milkman provided criticisms and clarifications concerning set-theoretic issues; typist Lucy Felicissimo helped to make the final preparation of my manuscript the happiest of experiences; Lisa Dahlgren worked with me through long hours of proofreading; and the unconditional support of my family gave me courage to finish what I had undertaken. Finally, with Allen Forte, I have known the privilege of having at once a very special teacher, an extraordinary friend, and a superbly conscientious advisor.

To Allen Forte, to all the others whose help I have received, to my longstanding friends from New Haven days, and to my colleagues at McGill University, I extend my deepest thanks.

1 INTRODUCTION

Pitch-Class Set Theory: Historical Perspective

While the central subject of this study is Alban Berg's *Wozzeck*, the primary analytical method to be employed finds its basis in the development of what I shall call pitch-class set theory. In the hope that my readers may include not just those who are interested in the analytical method but also those who are simply drawn to the opera, I have set forth the material of this chapter with the following intentions. First, for the reader who is not familiar with set-theoretic concepts, my introduction is provided to make my own analysis of the opera intelligible without preliminary recourse to other texts. In an effort to engage the reader's interest in new analytical methods, stress has been placed on their historical development, interpreted as a response to fundamental analytical problems posed by the new music of this century. It is hoped that on the basis of information introduced here, the reader will wish to proceed to my study of *Wozzeck* with the promise that technical explanations will continue to be provided at the moment they are needed. Second, for those who know the theoretical literature and have worked with set-theoretic concepts, the forthcoming material will serve to place my own work in a perspective determined by the course of past and current theoretical concerns. Finally, to those who have played a role in the development surveyed, I ask that this introduction be regarded as a grateful acknowledgment of contributions from which my own work has grown.

Theoretical interest in the abstract properties of nontriadic pitch materials coincides with the emergence of new modes of musical expression at the turn of the century.[1] That interest grew stronger with the development of the twelve-tone idea in Vienna, introduced in publications between 1920 and 1926 by J. M. Hauer (1883–1959)[2] and formulated as a compositional method after

1

1922 in the music of Arnold Schoenberg.[3] From the long list of writings about the twelve-tone method that Schoenberg's work spawned,[4] the entries of two authors will be mentioned for their historical significance in the development of atonal theory before 1945. The first of these is Anton Webern's *Der Weg zur neuen Musik* (translated as *The Path to the New Music*, 1963), originating from two series of lectures that he delivered in 1932 and 1933; Webern's purpose was to show how twelve-tone composition is the natural and necessary outcome in the "organic" development, or "path," of Western music from Gregorian chant to Schoenberg. Second, Ernst Krenek's early writings (see Krenek 1937, 1939, 1940, 1943) are representative of efforts to explore new possibilities for the extension of the dodecaphonic system.

It must be stressed that theoretical as well as compositional interest in new pitch combinations was by no means unique to the Viennese or to twelve-tone devotees. In the United States, presumably as early as 1919, Henry Cowell discussed chords composed of major and minor seconds—"tone clusters" whose theoretical justification rested on Schoenberg's premise that dissonances derive from the nature-given higher partials of the overtone series.[5] In Germany in 1937, the firm of Schott published Paul Hindemith's attempt to construct an acoustically based theory that would provide an explanation for any tone structure available within the equal-tempered system.[6] In France in 1944, Olivier Messiaen described seven "new" symmetrically constructed scale structures that he called "modes of limited transposition."[7] These composers and others were in certain cases independently providing different explanations for pitch structures that today might be described as identical in respect to *total interval content*.

As we proceed, I shall trace the development of the notion of total interval content and provide a formal definition. For now, the total interval content of a pitch collection can be described in general terms as the totality of intervals (equated with their inversions) that obtain between each pitch and every other pitch in the collection. Messiaen's *mode* 5, presented as the scale pattern C♮-D♭-F♮-F♯-G♮-B♮ in Messiaen 1944 (vol. 1, p. 55; vol. 2, ex. 347) has the same total interval content as the chord on Hindemith's Table of Chord-Groups spelled C♮-F♯-G♮-C♯-D♮-G♯, which is classified with those chord-types "containing one or more minor seconds or major sevenths or both—one or more tritones subordinate" (Hindemith 1937, revised translated ed. 1945, appended table). Likewise, the total interval content of Hauer's *trope* 38 (C♮-C♯-E♭-F♯-G♮-A♮; see Eschman 1945, 2d ed. 1968, p. 86) is identical with the total interval content of Messiaen's "truncated" *mode* 2 (C♮-E♭-F♮-F♯-A♮-B♮; Messiaen 1944, vol. 1, p. 55; vol. 2, ex. 341). Nicolas Slonimsky labels a scale pattern with again the same total interval content as a "tritone progression," derived from "equal division of one octave into two parts," with "interpolation of two notes" (Slonimsky 1947, pp. 1–2).[8] This smattering of names, "chord-types," and descriptions is meant to illustrate the absence of agreement on criteria for comparing and classifying pitch combinations. Total interval content is just one of any number of criteria that might have been agreed upon. By 1945 the need for a more systematic treatment of pitch combinations and transformations had become apparent.

Without question the most far-reaching response to that need has been the development of the concept of *pitch-class set*. As applied to the twelve-tone row, this concept emerged with the notion of the *ordered twelve-tone set*, introduced by Milton Babbitt in 1946.[9] Babbitt's outstanding contribution was to recognize that the well-known concept of *group* in mathematics may be effectively used as a model for the representation of the twelve-tone system, since the rules of formation and transformation within the latter are sufficiently analogous to those of the former:

> . . . the twelve-tone system, like any formal system whose abstract model is satisfactorily formulable, can be characterized completely by stating its elements, the stipulated relation or relations among these elements, and the defined operations upon the so-related elements. Such a characterization, though explicitly presented in verbal form at the earliest stage of the twelve-tone development, is likewise easily and explicitly inferable as the maximum procedural intersection among the "classical" twelve-tone works of Schoenberg, Webern, and Berg. [Babbitt 1960, pp. 246–47.]

On the one hand, the elements of the twelve-tone system are "'traditional' ones, both insofar as they are pitch classes with class membership defined by octave equivalence, and as there are twelve such pitch classes . . . " (ibid., p. 247). On the other hand, the twelve-tone system diverges from systems of the past most significantly in that "relations are defined entirely by the imposition of a total linear ordering upon the pitch classes, thus defining a twelve-tone 'set' (designated: S)" (ibid., p. 247).[10]

In the ground-breaking exposition quoted below, Babbitt explains why and how the ordered twelve-tone set will be represented in numerical notation:

> . . . compositional transposition, traditionally, implies contour preservation, a consideration that is, literally, meaningless in defining transposition as a twelve-tone operation, since contour is a function of the

registral specification of the elements, and registral choice is as undefined by the structure of a set as is duration, intensity, timbre, or any of
the other attributes necessarily associated with a compositional representation of a set; as a result, a set cannot be stated in musical notation
without the additional qualification that each pitch sign be taken to signify the total pitch class a member of which it denotes. Since such a
qualification only too easily leads to but another confusion of systematic
principle with compositional permissive ("a tone may be stated in any
octave"), it is both safer and more efficient to represent a twelve-tone
set in numerical notation, by an ordered number couple succession, the
first member of the couple signifying order position in S ("order number"), the second signifying the "pitch number" of the pitch class. The
initial pitch class of S is denoted by the couple (0,0), and is taken as the
origin of the coordinate system for both order and pitch numbers, both
of which range over the integers 0 — 11 inclusive, each integer appearing once and only once as an order number and a pitch number. In the
case of order numbers, this represents the fact that twelve and only twelve
pitch classes are involved: in the case of pitch numbers, this is the arith-
metical analogue of octave equivalence (congruence mod. 12).*

---

*Two numbers, a and b, are said to be "congruent mod. 12" if, and only if, $a - b =$
$k.12$ where k is an integer (including zero). [Ibid., p. 248.]

The reader will note that Babbitt's exclusive concern here is the *ordered*
twelve-tone set; accordingly, Babbitt assigns as "pitch number" the numerical
symbol 0 to the first pitch class of any ordered twelve-tone set and gives to
each successive pitch class in the series the positive numerical value mod 12
that represents its intervallic distance in number of semitones "above" the
first pitch class of the series.

Babbitt's conception of the ordered twelve-tone set can be applied in the
more general context of the *unordered pitch-class set containing twelve or
fewer than twelve distinct elements*. Like the twelve-tone concept, this broader
concept can be exemplified most efficiently by translating the twelve pitch
classes into numerical notation. But since with unordered pitch collections
the "first" pitch class no longer necessarily serves as a point of reference,
Babbitt's "moveable-do" approach to the assignment of the number 0 can be
modified in favor of a "fixed-do" approach that is intentionally arbitrary and
non-connotative but has mnemonic value. If with Babbitt we accept as ax-

ioms the notion of octave equivalence and the corresponding notion of en-harmonic equivalence, we may permanently assign the labels 0, 1, 2, . . . , 11 to the universal set of twelve pitch classes U as follows:[11]

$$
\begin{array}{c}
\underbrace{\text{B}\sharp\ \ \text{D}\flat\flat}\ \text{etc.} \\
\text{U:}\quad
\begin{array}{cccccccccccc}
\text{C}\natural & \text{C}\sharp & \text{D}\natural & \text{D}\sharp & \text{E}\natural & \text{F}\natural & \text{F}\sharp & \text{G}\natural & \text{G}\sharp & \text{A}\natural & \text{A}\sharp & \text{B}\natural \\
0 & 1 & 2 & 3 & 4 & 5 & 6 & 7 & 8 & 9 & 10 & 11
\end{array}
\end{array}
$$

Since two pitches that are octave-equivalent are congruent (mod 12) in the sense defined by Babbitt, these labels may be considered as *pitch-class integers mod 12*,

> or better, because it avoids all possible confusion, "residues modulo 12."
> An "integer" to a mathematician is an ordinary counting number: after counting to 11, one continues on to 12, 13, etc. In contrast, the residues modulo 12 (or "mod 12") have a circular structure: if one continues past 11, one returns to 0. [Lewin 1977a, p. 29.]

(In common with current practice, the assignment to pitch classes of residues mod 12, or pitch-class integers mod 12 (abbreviated *pc integers*), as shown above will remain fixed throughout this study.[12])

Now, in the formulation of procedures for the analysis of atonal music that may or may not be serial, a central notion will be the unordered pitch-class set. The *unordered pitch-class set* (abbreviated *pitch-class set*, or *pc set*) is an unordered collection of distinct elements, all of which must belong to the universal set U (0, 1, 2, . . . , 11); that is to say, an unordered pitch-class set must contain all the elements of U or be a subset of U. We shall say that for two sets A and B, B is a *subset* of A if and only if every element of B is an element of A. If B is a subset of A, this is to say that B "is included in" A (notated B ⊂ A) and A "includes" B (notated A ⊃ B); the relationship be-tween A and B thus described is the *inclusion relation*.

At this point it may be useful to summarize the series of conceptual steps we have taken thus far. We implicitly began by making a distinction between pitch collection (or pitch combination) and *pitch-class collection*, a collec-tion in which each element is regarded as a representative of one of the twelve pitch classes. There we examined Babbitt's specific kind of *ordered pitch-class collection*, the *ordered twelve-tone set*. Then we arrived at the concept of the *unordered pitch-class set*, now defined simply as an unordered collection of distinct pitch classes (i.e., no duplicates). We shall hereafter examine unordered pitch-class sets by translating their elements into pitch-class integers.

Before continuing with our survey of the development of pitch-class set theory, it will be well to introduce certain *canonical transformations*, or *operations*, on pc sets, ordered or unordered, which will grow increasingly important in the forthcoming discussion. To begin, I shall offer a definition for *pitch-class* (pc) *interval*: a pc interval measures the directed distance from one pitch class to another; thus where a and b are pc integers, the pc interval from a to b will be b − a (mod 12). For example:

the pc interval from D♮ (pc2) to F♯ (pc6) is $6 - 2 = 4$;

the pc interval from F♯ (pc6) to D♮ (pc2) is $2 - 6 = -4 \equiv 8$ (mod 12);

the pc interval from B♮ (pc11) to C♮ (pc0) is $0 - 11 = -11 \equiv 1$ (mod 12).

(The triple-barred equal sign has the standard meaning of mathematical congruence.) It follows that there are 12 distinct pc intervals, ranging in value from 0 to 11.

Now the operation *transposition* can be defined as follows: pc set B will be said to be *transpositionally related* to pc set A if sets A and B are not identical but contain the same number of elements and if there is some integer t, representing some pc interval, that when added (mod 12) to each element of set A will yield a distinct element in set B. For example:

A: pcs 0, 1, 2
B: pcs 10, 11, 0

The non-identical sets A and B above are transpositionally related, since each set contains three elements and since there is an integer t that when added (mod 12) to each element of A yields a corresponding element of B; the value of t, the pc interval of transposition, or transposition operator, is 10.

In the system as defined so far, the residue 0 (mod 12) functions as an identity element with respect to the operation of addition of pc integers.[13] Hence it is possible to define an *inverse relation*. Two pc integers will be said to be *inverse-related* if their sum is the identity element, that is, if their sum is 12 [$\equiv 0$ (mod 12)]. With the following pairs of pc integers, then, each element of the pair will be regarded as the *inverse* of the other element:

$$0 \leftrightarrow 0$$
$$1 \leftrightarrow 11$$
$$2 \leftrightarrow 10$$
$$3 \leftrightarrow 9$$
$$4 \leftrightarrow 8$$
$$5 \leftrightarrow 7$$
$$6 \leftrightarrow 6$$

The notion of an inverse relation has a precedent in the traditional tonal-based concept of *harmonic inversion of intervals*—inversion based on octave equivalence, such that, for example, a minor second, the distance of 1 semitone between two pitch classes, is considered inverse-related to the major seventh (the distance of 11 semitones) formed by the same two pitch classes. From the historical viewpoint the pitch-class set-theoretic concept of inversion moreover finds a direct origin in the technique of the strict inversion of melodic contour, wherein the precise intervallic distance from each pitch to the next in the given melodic series will be preserved but reversed in direction. Since the concept of inversion has been thus traditionally associated with the interval rather than with the pitch class, the idea of inverse-related pc integers lacks elegance, to say the least, because it rubs against our intuitive understanding of the inversion process. In short, the notion of inverse-related pc integers calls for further explanation.

For the purpose of accommodating nontonal compositional technique, it has become conventional to extend the tonal concept of harmonic inversion by bringing it into association with transposition as follows: the distance between any two pcs that is a minor second (pc interval 1) will be considered inverse-related to the distance between any two pcs that is a major seventh (pc interval 11); likewise the major second (pc interval 2) will be inverse-related to the minor seventh (pc interval 10), and so on. This is to say that the list of paired elements displayed above may be used to represent *inverse-related pc intervals* as well as inverse-related pc integers. The concept of inverse-related pc intervals permits a reduction of the 12 intervals to 6 *interval classes*, as will be discussed shortly.

Now note that the value of the pc interval from the identity element pc0 to a given pitch class will always *be equal to* the pc integer that represents that given pitch class. Thus, for example, the value of the pc interval from pc0 to pc11 is 11, and the value of the pc interval from pc0 to pc1 is 1; moreover, as stated above, pc intervals 1 and 11 are now understood as inverse-related.

On the basis of this correspondence between pc interval and pc integer, it is possible to demonstrate the operation *inversion* by means of an integer model without denying the role of the interval. Thus the following demonstration is offered, one whose pragmatic value will best serve our purpose in this study.

One pc set will be *inversionally related* to another if both sets contain the same number of elements and if to each element in the first set there corresponds its inverse element in the second:

A: pcs 0, 1, 3
B: pcs 0, 11, 9

In other words, an inversionally related form B of set A can be obtained simply by converting each pc integer of set A into its inverse-related pc integer as shown above.

Finally, bringing together the operations of transposition and inversion, we can say that pc sets of the same number of elements may be related by inversion followed by transposition. Among the following sets A, B, and C, sets A and B are inversionally related, and sets B and C are transpositionally related:

A: pcs 4, 5, 7
B: pcs 8, 7, 5
C: pcs 9, 8, 6

Set C may now be regarded as related to set A by inversion followed by transposition. Note that "whereas transposition does not imply prior inversion, inversion always implies subsequent transposition, even if it is the trivial case $t = 0$" (Forte 1973a, p. 9).

At the appropriate points in the historical survey that will now be resumed, the notions of transpositionally related and inversionally related pc sets will be reexamined in connection with the process of mapping and the concept of normal order. These preliminary definitions will suffice for the moment.

Especially in the United States the influence of Babbitt's twelve-tone set theory was both immediate and long-range. For the twelve-tone theorist, the concept of the ordered twelve-tone set provided the generality necessary for the definition of transformation and invariance characteristics associated with the operations described above (see Rothgeb 1966).[14] Once those general attributes of twelve-tone sets had been established (Babbitt 1960, 1961), the particular transformational properties of hexachords (source sets) could be examined (Rochberg 1955, 1959; Martino 1961; Babbitt 1961), and wide-ranging observations could be made about combinatoriality (Martino 1961; Babbitt 1961, 1973–74, 1976; Morris and Starr 1977, 1978); "segmental association" (Lewin 1962); invariance (Alphonce 1974); "inversional balance" (Lewin 1968); the all-interval series (Bauer-Mengelberg and Ferentz 1965; Cohen 1972–73; Morris and Starr 1974); order transformation (Lewin 1966; Rothgeb 1967); multiple order functions (Winham 1964; Howe 1965; Batstone 1972; Morris and Starr 1974); and the generation of multiple-order-function twelve-tone rows (Morris 1977).[15] Although analysis of the early twelve-tone literature has been a point of departure for many twelve-tone theorists, a major concern has been the presentation of new technical resources for the contemporary composer; to a certain extent, then, the concept of set with its ramifications has served a "prescriptive" function (e.g., see especially Wuorinen 1979).

For the theorist whose domain is the analysis of non-serial atonal music, the formal set relations of inclusion as well as the operations of transposition, inversion, intersection, and complementation (the latter two will be discussed in chapter 2) have provided a much-needed basis for comparing pitch-class collections of any number of pitch classes to determine relatedness according to specified criteria for similarity. In this area, Howard Hanson's *Harmonic Materials of Modern Music* (1960)—a study that did not explicitly utilize the set model—constituted an important breakthrough in the analysis of pitch combinations but also exemplified the need for a systematically defined hierarchy of relationships.

Like Hindemith (1937) and, more recently, George Perle (1954), Hanson sought a classification for all pitch-class collections within the twelve-pitch-class system. Hanson proposed that one must identify the "structure" of a pitch combination by calculating what I have described earlier as its total interval content (Hanson does not use this term); it happens that his criterion for the identification of pitch combinations guarantees the identification of all pc sets that are related by transposition or inversion followed by transposition as defined above. In this sense, then, Hanson's list, unlike earlier lists of pitch-class collections, may be described as complete without duplications.

In several other respects as well, Hanson's work touched upon issues that became of increasing concern after 1960. To the "young composer," Hanson recommended his interval-calculation procedure as a kind of "chemical analysis" that would reveal the fundamental attributes of new sonorities.[16] His symbological scheme for displaying the "analysis" of a given pitch combination produces a primitive version of the ordered array, introduced for the same purpose in 1961 by Donald Martino and in 1964 by Allen Forte, whose *interval vector* is an ordered array that displays the total interval content of a pc set (see below). The role of the interval vector as one criterion for the definition of an equivalence relation among pitch-class sets will be examined as we proceed.[17] Hanson uses the term "involution" to describe the inversion relation; he may have been the first to describe those "sonorities which have the same components [i.e., the same total interval content] but which are not involutions one of the other, although each has its own involution" (Hanson 1960, p. 22). In the same year (1960) David Lewin published a description of these special pc sets; known as the *Z-related* sets in Forte's theory, these will play a crucial role in the discussion to follow.

To summarize, Hanson provided one means with which to answer a fundamental question one might want to ask when comparing any two pitch combinations of the same number of distinct pitch classes, namely: Can these pitch combinations be described as "similar" in some specifically defined structural sense? Without a sufficiently general and systematic methodology, Hanson was not prepared, however, to pursue the next question: In what ways might two pitch combinations that do *not* contain the same number of distinct pitch classes be related? The penultimate chapter of *Harmonic Materials* and the large diagram that accompanies the text represent an impressive first attempt to show "the projection and interrelation of sonorities in equal temperament"—relationships by inclusion in set-theoretic terms (see above). The diagram bears a graphic resemblance to Forte's set-complex table (see table 1, p. 235). Although the diagram accommodates representations for all of the distinct collections of two to ten pitch classes, it in fact shows only which collections with n distinct pitch classes are related by inclusion to which collections of $n + 1$ and $n - 1$ distinct pitch classes. Thus if the reader wishes to learn, for instance, which tetrachords are included in which hexachords, he must trace this information on the diagram through "connecting" pentachords, assuming the transitive property that:

$$\text{if } A \subset B \quad \& \quad B \subset C, \quad \text{then } A \subset C$$

where A, B, and C are distinct pitch-class sets.

The most problematic aspect of Hanson's work is the fact that his analysis of the origin and construction of pitch combinations is unsystematic to the extent that in many cases several analytical representations are offered for the same "sonority."[18] Finally, although Hanson illustrates new sonorities by means of an eclectic selection of excerpts from the twentieth-century repertoire, he does not attempt to develop an analytical method; the reader is left to make his own steps in that direction.

George Perle knew Babbitt's work and acknowledges Babbitt's contribution with special reference to the technical vocabulary that he himself employs in *Serial Composition and Atonality: An Introduction to the Music of Schoenberg, Berg, and Webern* (1962). Like Babbitt and those others upon whose work Babbitt has had direct influence, Perle uses the twelve-tone system as his frame of reference. Significantly, a major portion of his text concerns the examination of technical procedures employed in the classic dodecaphonic works of the three Viennese composers. Here as well as in his articles about *Wozzeck* (Perle 1967a, 1967b, 1971), a characteristic attribute of Perle's work is his departure from "formidable diagrams, graphs, and mathematical formulas" (Perle 1962, p. vii) and his concern for detailed analysis of the function of the set in relationship to motivic and structural features of particular compositions (e.g., thematic formations; rhythmic-motivic transformation; changes of texture, register, and timbre; simultaneities; phrase groups and larger formal units). Perle's separate treatments of "'free' atonality" and "nondodecaphonic serial composition" are important because of their uniqueness in 1962[19] but limited at the outset by his premise that in the development toward the twelve-tone system, "'free' atonality" represents an early stage that "precludes by definition the possibility of a statement of self-consistent, generally applicable compositional procedures" (Perle 1962, p. 9).

Assuming that there will be no hierarchical structuring of small and large pitch combinations, Perle explains the organization of the non-serial atonal composition in terms of "microcosmic" three- to four-note sets,[20] called *basic cells*, which are statable as chords or melodic figures or as combinations of both. Like the ordered twelve-tone set, the basic cell has a "fixed intervallic content" and may appear in transformations by inversion or transposition or, if ordered, by retrograde or retrograde inversion as well; it may also be expanded "through association with independent details" (p. 9).

Perle recognizes at least two "phases," or "styles," of atonal composition. The first is represented by works such as Schoenberg's *Klavierstück* Op. 11/1, in which "specific harmonic and melodic details are stabilized at definite pitch levels as referential formations of overall significance" (p. 19). The second includes works governed by the "principle of nonrepetition" (p. 23), composed in the so-called athematic style—"a kind of musical stream of consciousness wherein the thread of continuity is generated by momentary association" (p. 19); thus in Schoenberg's *Erwartung* Op. 17 and in his *Sechs kleine Klavierstücke* Op. 19, as well as in Berg's *Vier Stücke* Op. 5 and in Webern's *Vier Stücke* Op. 7,

> microcosmic elements are transposed, internally reordered, temporally or spatially expanded or contracted, and otherwise revised, in a fluctuating context that constantly transforms the unifying motive itself. [P. 19.]

For these works the term "athematic" is just as inappropriate as "all-thematic," since

> any aspect of a musical idea—melodic contour, harmonic formation, texture, dynamics, rhythm, even the octave position of an individual note—may serve as the momentary referential basis of a nonliteral re-statement. [P. 23.]

On the one hand, the atonal work may generally be characterized by a "total interpenetration of harmonic and melodic elements" (p. 24); on the other hand, there are "independent harmonic entities," "*arbitrarily selected*" [emphasis my own], which cannot be explained by the concept of the basic cell or by "any other single concept" (p. 25).

Faithful to this point of view, Perle is successful in describing the "refractory" nature and the apparently intentional ambiguities of the "'free' atonal" idiom. His viewpoint can be challenged, however, on grounds that he himself provides in his treatment of a consummate "'free' atonal" work—*Wozzeck*. With his notion of "aggregates of basic cells," whose application to Act II/Scene 1 of *Wozzeck* (Perle 1967a, pp. 223–39) I shall discuss in chapter 4 below, Perle moves toward the position that collections of more than three to four pitch classes play a constructive role in the "'free' atonal" style. Subsequent studies by other theorists (to be discussed below) have yielded abundant evidence in support of this position, and these studies further call into question the already dubious assumption that the "'free' atonal" composer feels free to select harmonic elements in an arbitrary fashion without reference to a broader organizational scheme.

In "A Theory of Set-Complexes" (1964) Allen Forte published the first systematic formal exposition of set-theoretic concepts in application to the analysis of nonserial atonal compositions. This article was to be regarded as the introduction to a more fully developed theory of set relations that appeared in 1973 under the title *The Structure of Atonal Music*. One very crucial change of definition (see below), several important amplifications, and considerable clarification of analytical procedure by means of musical examples render Forte's 1973 publication the more significant reference not only for the present survey of his work but also for the detailed application of his theory that will be undertaken in the course of this study.

In *The Structure of Atonal Music* (1973a) as well as in the 1964 article and elsewhere (see Forte 1972, 1973b, 1974b, 1978a, 1978b), Forte is concerned specifically with the large-scale organization of pitch structures in compositions drawn from an international repertory of non-serial atonal works written for the most part between 1908 and 1925. Thus on the one hand, while examples from Schoenberg, Webern, Stravinsky, and Berg appear most frequently, Busoni, Bartók, Ives, Ruggles, Scriabin and Varèse are also represented; on the other hand, discussion of the twelve-tone works of these and other composers as well as of more recent atonal compositions is excluded.

Fundamental to Forte's theory is the conviction that the analyst who wishes to investigate the pitch organization of an atonal work must have a reliable technical apparatus with which to identify relationships among pitch combinations of structural significance within the work. Forte's position in respect to "the structure" of atonal music in general (see below) is of utmost importance to an understanding of his theory, and the study of *Wozzeck* undertaken here can be regarded as an effort to probe that position. For the moment I shall treat Forte's work simply as a direct response to the need for a systematically formulated criterion by which to define a fundamental relationship two or more pitch combinations might share—an *equivalence relation*. Here the reader will be assisted by an introduction to three concepts that will be basic to the present undertaking: the *interval vector*, *normal order*, and *prime form*.

Hanson's "chemical analysis" of the total interval content of pitch combinations would have provided a satisfactory criterion for equivalence were it not for the fact that, as described earlier in Hanson's terms, the twelve-pitch-class system accommodates a special group of distinct pitch-class sets within which pairs of sets have the same "analysis" (i.e., the same total interval content) but are not related one to another by transposition or inversion followed by transposition. As a means of illustrating this fact, we may begin by choosing one of those special pairs of pc sets and examining the total interval content of each of its members.

Example 1 shows the twice-stated pitch combination ⎣C♮-A♮-B♮-F♮⎦, identifiable in this setting as one of the Doctor's themes from *Wozzeck*.[21]

Example 1. Act II/Scene 2: mm. 171–73.

The total interval content of this pitch combination can be tabulated as follows:

1. Replace the letter name for each pitch class with the appropriate pc integer (residue mod 12):

C♮	A♮	B♮	F♮
0,	9,	11,	5

2. Calculate the pc interval from each pc integer to every other pc integer in the set:

   0, 9, 11, 5
   ⎣ 9 ⎦
   ⎣ 11 ⎦
   ⎣ 5 ⎦
   ⎣ 2 ⎦
   ⎣ 4 ⎦
   ⎣ 6 ⎦

3. Assign each pc interval and its inverse to the same *interval class* (abbreviated ic) as follows:

   ic1 contains pc intervals 1 and 11
   ic2 contains pc intervals 2 and 10
   ic3 contains pc intervals 3 and 9
   ic4 contains pc intervals 4 and 8
   ic5 contains pc intervals 5 and 7
   ic6 contains pc interval 6 (which is its own inverse)

In taking this step, we follow Hanson (see note 16) in reducing the 12 distinct pc intervals to 6 interval classes.

$$0, 9, 11, 5$$

$(9 \rightarrow)$ ⌊ic3⌋

$(11 \rightarrow)$ ⌊ic1⌋

⌊ic5⌋

⌊ic2⌋

⌊ic4⌋

⌊ic6⌋

We may now more concisely display the results of our analysis by constructing an ordered array, within which the leftmost number will always be the number of occurrences of interval class 1, the next number to the right will always be the number of occurrences of ic2, etc. We construct the array by counting the number of occurrences of each interval class and placing that number in the appropriate column. If an interval class is not represented in the set, the entry 0 (zero) will be placed in the appropriate column:

Number of occurrences of: ic ic ic ic ic ic

1 2 3 4 5 6

[1 1 1 1 1 1]

An ordered array that serves as a representation of the total interval content of a pc set—that is, the "distribution of ic occurrences associated with a given set" (Teitelbaum 1965, p. 78)—will be called an *interval vector*, after Forte (1964, p. 140). The interval vector for the set of pitch classes that compose the Doctor's theme at Example 1 is therefore [111111].

The interval vector format is such that with a glance it is possible to ascertain certain basic properties of the pc set. For instance, the interval vector [111111] shows that the 4-note collection featured in the Doctor's theme is one form of what has been called an *all-interval tetrachord* (the name signifies that each of the 6 interval classes is represented at least once).

Now, if we were to place each of the 552 distinct collections of 4 pitch classes into a *class of pc sets* in which membership is based upon relationship under transposition or inversion as described earlier, we would obtain 29 distinct 4-element classes of sets, or *set-types*. Of those 29 set-types, there are only two set-types in which all 6 interval classes are represented at least once. So far the reader knows, then, that the pc set represented in the Doctor's theme at Example 1 must be a member of one of those two set-types. Let us now examine another passage associated with the Doctor.

Example 2 is excerpted from the one scene of *Wozzeck* that is dominated by the Doctor. (At the moment shown in Example 2 the Doctor is haranguing Wozzeck on the subject of man's "freedom" of will to exert self-control.)

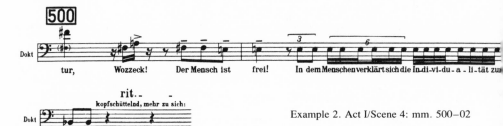

Example 2. Act I/Scene 4: mm. 500–02

Using the procedure outlined above, we shall calculate the interval vector of the pc set F#-A♮-E♮-B♭, represented here:

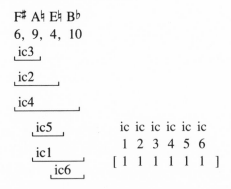

Since the total interval content of the pc set from Example 2—represented by the vector [111111]—is exactly the same as that of the pc set from Example 1, we should now want to know whether these two pc sets are the same set-types—that is, whether one of the two sets associated with the Doctor is transpositionally or inversionally related to the other. In the discussion that ensues, it will be shown that this is not the case. Hanson would have recognized that fact but was not prepared to display it clearly.[22] To Forte, whose first concern was to formulate a general, non-biased, and absolutely precise criterion for distinguishing the structure of one pitch combination from that of any other, the problem of deciding whether pairs of pc sets of the kind shown in Examples 1 and 2 are essentially similar (on the basis of identical interval content) or essentially different (on the basis of set-types defined by the transposition and inversion relationships) was initially important and later crucial in his choice of criterion for a definition of equivalence. The problem posed by these special pairs of sets can be further clarified by reference to the notion of *normal order*, introduced by Babbitt in 1961.

The normal order of a pitch-class set may be conceived as the most tightly compressed arrangement of pitch classes within a pc collection—the arrangement with the smallest intervallic span. Given a set of *n* elements in some order, there are *n circular permutations* of that set, each permutation formed by placing the first (leftmost) element of the set last (farthest to the right). An easy method for calculating the normal order of a set is outlined below:

1. Each of the circular permutations of the set is displayed in its *ascending numerical order*. (This means that 12 will be added to the first element of each permutation each time that element is placed in the last position to form the next permutation.) Accordingly, the pitch collection C♮-A♮-B♮-F♮ from Example 1 is:

   a) translated into integer (mod 12) notation: 0, 9, 11, 5;
   b) placed in ascending order: 0, 5, 9, 11;
   c) and permuted as follows: 1: (0, 5, 9, 11)

                                      2: (5, 9, 11, 12)

                                      3: (9, 11, 12, 17)

                                      4: (11, 12, 17, 21)

2. Now the *normal order* will be *that permutation in ascending order with the least difference determined by subtracting the first integer from the last*:

	Difference between first and last integer:
1: (0, 5, 9, 11)	11
2: (5, 9, 11, 12) →	7
3: (9, 11, 12, 17)	8
4: (11, 12, 17, 21)	10

The arrow signals the fact that the second permutation produces the least difference—that is, the smallest intervallic span—between first and last integers; of the four permutations, the second permutation is the "most tightly compressed" intervallic arrangement and will therefore be regarded as the normal order of the set.[23]

The concept of normal order provides nothing more than a systematic means of arranging the pc integers of a set so that the set can be easily compared with any other pc set of the same number of elements that has been submitted to the same procedure. The goal of the comparison is to determine whether sets are transpositionally or inversionally related. So far the concept of normal order provides a convenient means of determining whether two pc sets are transpositionally related: by aligning any two sets in normal order, we can easily ascertain whether there is some value of t that, when added to each element of one set, generates the corresponding element of the other set. In order to facilitate comparison of sets that may be inversionally related, we will now need to extend the normal-order procedure to include the notion of *best normal order*; a best normal order will be defined on the basis of a comparison of two sets which we already know to be inversionally related. Once a best normal order among transpositionally and inversionally related sets has been established, that order can be used as a convenient canonical point of reference for the comparison of any two pc sets.

Accordingly, using the normal order (5, 9, 11, 12) of the pitch combination C♯-A♮-B♭-F♮, let us now examine an inversionally related form of this set. It has become conventional to use the mathematical process of *mapping* as a model for the processes of both inversion and transposition. Given the fixed correspondence of inverse-related pc integers displayed earlier, the rule of correspondence *I* maps each element of a given set A onto its inverse, producing an inverted form of set A that we shall call set B. Accordingly, the inverted form B of our set A (5, 9, 11, 12) will be:

$$I$$

A		B
5	→	7
9	→	3
11	→	1
12	→	0

It can be seen that inversion of a pitch-class set that is in normal order produces a set that is in *descending order*; in other words, the normal order of the inverted set B above is obtained by reading the integers from the bottom to the top of the column.

For the purpose of simplifying a comparison of sets A and B, we shall now transpose both the original set A in normal order and its inverted form B in normal order so that the first integer of each is 0; that is, we will subtract the value (mod 12) t of the first integer of each set, now interpreted as a pc interval, from itself and from all remaining integers of the set (with set B the trivial case $t=0$ obtains):

$$\text{A: } 5, 9, 11, 12 \quad \text{B: } 0, 1, 3, 7$$
$$0, 4, \;\; 6, \;\; 7 \qquad\;\; 0, 1, 3, 7$$

Now it can be observed that although the difference between first and last integers of set A remains the same as that of set B,

A: 0, 4, 6, 7   B: 0, 1, 3, 7

   ⌞_7_____⌟   ⌞_7_____⌟

the inversion process effects an internal reversal of the pc intervals formed by adjacent pcs:

A: 0, 4, 6, 7   B: 0, 1, 3, 7

   ⌞_4_⌟   ⌞_1_⌟

     ⌞_2_⌟   ⌞_2_⌟

       ⌞_1_⌟   ⌞_4_⌟

and a consequent change in comparison to set A of the difference between the first integer and the next-to-last integer of set B:

A: 0, 4, 6, 7   B: 0, 1, 3, 7

    ⌞_6_____⌟   ⌞_3_____⌟

The difference between first integer and second integer ($= 1$) of set B is *less* than the difference between first and second integers ($= 4$) of set A; as inverted permutation of set A, set B provides an arrangement in which the smallest pc interval is that formed by the first pitch class and the second pitch class. For the comparison of pc sets that, like sets A and B, are related by inversion, Forte presents the following extension of the procedure for determining normal order:

If the least difference of first and last integers is the same for any two permutations, select the permutation with the least difference between first and second integers. If this is the same, select the permutation with the least difference between the first and third integers, and so on, until the difference between the first and the next to last integers has been checked. If the differences are the same each time, select one ordering arbitrarily as the best normal order. [Forte 1973a, p. 4.]

Since set B (0,1,3,7) is the permutation with the least difference between first and second integers, we select set B as that form of the original pitch-class set from Example 1 which is in *best normal order*.

Finally, from the notion of best normal order we move to the notion of *prime form*, used by Martino (1961) and defined by Forte (1973a, pp. 4–5) as *that form of a pitch-class set which is in normal order (or best normal order) and whose first integer is 0*. Set B (0, 1, 3, 7) is in best normal order, and its first integer is 0; set B is therefore a prime form.

With the concepts of normal order and prime form, we arrive at an arbitrary but uniform method for comparing pitch combinations—a method which supplements that provided by the concept of interval vector: while the latter supplies a representation of the total interval content of a pitch-class set, the former provides a convenient and reliable procedure for determining whether two sets can be mapped onto each other, that is, whether two pc collections are transpositionally or inversionally related.

We are now prepared to resume our comparison of the pitch-class sets from Examples 1 and 2. Were the set from Example 2 in fact a transposed or inverted form of the set from Example 1, then the prime form for each set would be the same; in other words, if the second set in normal order could be mapped onto the first set under transposition or inversion followed by transposition for some value of t, then the prime form of the second set would be identical to that of the first. Clearly the simplest way to determine whether our two sets are transpositionally or inversionally related is to calculate the prime form of the set from Example 2 and compare it with the prime form (0,1,3,7) of the set from Example 1:

Set from Ex. 2:	F♯ A♮ E♮ B♭	
translated into integer (mod 12) notation:	6, 9, 4, 10	
placed in ascending order:	4, 6, 9, 10	Difference between first and last integer:
permuted:	1: (4, 6, 9, 10)	→ 6
	2: (6, 9, 10, 16)	10
	3: (9, 10, 16, 18)	9
	4: (10, 16, 18, 21)	11

selection of normal		
order:	4, 6, 9, 10	
inverted:	4 → 8	
	6 → 6	
	9 → 3	
	10 → 2	

normal order of set
from Ex. 2 and its

inverted form:	4, 6, 9, 10	2, 3, 6, 8
transposed to level 0	0, 2, 5, 6	0, 1, 4, 6
and compared:	2	1

selection of best nor-
mal order in prime
form: 0, 1, 4, 6

Our calculation displays the promised evidence that the set from Example 2 does *not* have the same prime form as that of the set from Example 1; the former is therefore not transpositionally or inversionally related to the latter, even though both sets have the same total interval content.

The fact that there are other pairs of set-types in the twelve-pitch-class system which share this kind of relationship has created a unique problem in the search for a satisfactory criterion by which to define an equivalence relation for pc sets of the same number of elements. Subsequent to a formal description of the special set-pairs published by David Lewin in 1960, Allen Forte chose to distinguish these from other set-types by assigning to them the label *Z-related*. In his 1964 article, Forte made no further distinction between one member of a Z-related pair and the other; concomitantly, he proposed that two pitch-class sets can be regarded as equivalent if they have the same total interval content (see Forte 1964, p. 143). Thus Forte followed Martino (1961) in regarding Z-related sets of the same number of elements to be equivalent, and he arbitrarily selected one member of each pair of these set-types as a prime form, with the other member as a special variant. In response to Forte's 1964 article, John Clough rejected Forte's equivalence relation on the grounds that it contradicts in some cases "our intuitive notions of pitch-set similarity"; Clough proposed several alternatives, stressing that an equivalence based on inversion and transposition has the advantage of being "a simple venerable concept, of preeminent musical relevance" (Clough 1965, pp. 163, 165). A debate on the subject ensued (see Forte 1965; Howe 1965), and since the publication of Forte's 1973 text, in which a new definition for equivalence is posited, the general question of equivalence criteria has again been raised (see reviews of Forte's text by Browne [1974], Benjamin [1974], Regener [1974], and Howe [1974–75]; David Lewin's 1977b article marks the point where the issue of equivalence begins to recede in favor of investigations within the broader domain of generalized similarity relations among pc sets).

Between 1964 and the publication of Forte's text in 1973, two aspects of his work led Forte to reassess his definition of the equivalence relation. First, with continued analysis it became evident to him that a characteristic structural feature of the atonal repertoire is the prominence of Z-related set-pairs in contexts where each member of a pair is given its own structural and aural identity but also placed in association with its Z-correspondent by registral, textural, rhythmic, motivic, dramatic, or other means. An instance of this kind of association has been demonstrated above: we investigated two temporally remote melodic statements from *Wozzeck* whose respective 4-element pitch structures, while by no means identical, are Z-related and are further connected by their association with the Doctor. Second, an even stronger argument for reassessing the question of whether Z-related set-types should be regarded as equivalent arose in the development of Forte's theory of set complexes, introduced in 1964 and presented with several refinements and a large number of extensions in 1973. The notion of *set complex* is an extension of the concepts of inclusion and complementation. Complementation will play an important role in my study of *Wozzeck* and will be formally introduced in chapter 2. The set complex will be featured only in my summary statements about the opera, for which reason a presentation of the concept will be reserved for the final chapter. It suffices here to remind the reader that the inclusion relation describes the relation between a set and its subset.

Now, despite the fact that members of Z-related set-pairs have the same total interval content (i.e., the same interval-class structure), the distinct pitch-class structure of each member, exemplified by its unique prime form, yields a distinct *subset structure* with respect to subsets whose number of elements is greater than 2; thus a pitch-class set that is a subset of one member of a Z-related set-pair may be, however will not necessarily be, a subset of its Z-correspondent. But logically, where the equal sign below represents some defined equivalence between pc sets (such as equivalence based on identical total interval content),

$$\text{if set } A \subset \text{ set } B \text{ \& set } B = \text{ set } C, \text{ then set } A \subset \text{ set } C.$$

Since this statement is not always true when sets B and C are respective members of Z-related set-pairs, then either the definition of equivalence on

the basis of total interval content or a general property of the inclusion relation—its transitivity—is called into question. Less formally, members of Z-
related set-pairs have their own "families" of subsets as well as their own
unique and in some cases remarkable structural properties, without the recognition of which important local and long-range relationships among pitch
combinations may be overlooked.

For these formal and analytical reasons Forte reached the decision that Z-
related sets of the same number of elements should not be regarded as equivalent. This of course meant that identical total interval content could not
provide the general criterion for equivalence. But since members of Z-related
set-pairs may be distinguished from each other by their unique prime forms,
the problem of accommodating the Z-related set-pairs in a general theory of
set relations is solved in using the relation by transposition or inversion (represented by the identical prime form) as the basis for equivalence. Accordingly, in the 1973 text we have the following definition:

> Two pitch-class sets will be said to be equivalent if and only if they are
> reducible to the same prime form by transposition or by inversion fol-
> lowed by transposition. [Forte 1973a, p. 5.][24]

The proposal of a definition for equivalence that is general for all available
pitch-class collections is a step that, however controversial or even modest it
may seem today, can be regarded as at least temporarily conclusive in respect
to that long-range development toward the systematic comparison of pitch
combinations which has been surveyed above. For Forte, the redefinition of
an equivalence relation has at the same time represented a first step in the
expansion of set-theoretic principles toward a comprehensive model of relations among pitch combinations. The product of that expansion is Forte's
theory of set complexes.

At the very least, by reducing the 4096 (2^{12}) unordered sets available in
the twelve-pitch-class system to 232 set-types of 2 to 10 elements, where a
set-type can now be defined as a class of sets whose members are equivalent
under transposition and/or inversion, Forte provides a well-defined basis for
determining *whether or not, or to what extent*, the pitch organization of an
atonal composition achieves comprehensibility and coherence on the basis of
recurrences of pitch combinations of the same number of pitch classes that
share the same systematically determined fundamental structural properties.
With the very title of his text—*The Structure of Atonal Music*—Forte places
his own position on the line: for Forte, the most fundamental aspect of the
so-called atonal idiom is its exhibition of pitch-structural relationships that
can be revealed by the set-structural relationships he defines. Among these,

the notions of inclusion, complementation, invariance, and, finally, the set complex were conceived to provide a means of examining more elaborate networks of relationships within the atonal composition—relationships among pc sets that do not have the same number of elements. Here, for the first time in the development of analytical methods for atonal music, Forte attempts to provide a convincing measure of the means whereby local and intermediate levels of pitch organization in the atonal work cohere in relationship to the very largest context of which they are components—the work as a whole.

Considerations Leading to the Choice of Wozzeck for This Study

My own study of *Wozzeck* has been undertaken with the conviction that Forte's theory of unordered pitch-class sets and set complexes represents a critical point in the development of an understanding of non-serial atonal composition. Judging from responses to the theory in the forms of thoughtful critical evaluations (see Browne 1974; Regener 1974; Benjamin 1974, 1979); interpretation (Beach 1979); elaborations and extensions (see Teitelbaum 1965; Gilbert 1970a, 1974; Chrisman 1971, 1977; Chapman 1978, 1981); applications in the analysis of single works (e.g., see Gilbert 1970; Wittlich 1974, 1975; Parks 1980, 1981) as well as groups of works by individual twentieth-century composers (e.g., see Neumeyer 1976 on Hindemith; Baker 1977 on Scriabin; Hyde 1977, 1980a, 1980b on the twelve-tone works of Schoenberg); and, finally, alternative generalizations of criteria for similarity relations among pc sets (Regener 1974; Lewin 1977b, 1979–80a, 1979–80b; Morris 1979–80; Rahn 1979–80; Lord 1981), my conviction is shared by others.[25] My own response to the theory is also a response to specific published and unpublished criticisms of the theory (see especially Benjamin 1974): that is, I am convinced that if the notions of set and set complex are to have long life as models for the interpretation of atonal compositions, it will be because these concepts not only provide explanations for the choice of pitch combinations in the atonal work but also shed light on the relationship of pitch organization to other aspects of the atonal work—its formal architecture, its rhythmic-motivic organization, and textual or other extramusical dimensions it might have.

Although the question of the interaction of pitch organization with formal structure has by no means been ignored by Forte,[26] a detailed investigation of pitch-structural relationships that span large formal units or movements of an extended atonal work did not fall within the scope of his 1973 publication.[27] Forte's brief but cogent remarks about *Wozzeck* in his *Structure of*

Atonal Music, my own fascination with both the opera and the play, and, finally, my curiosity about the functional and dynamic role pitch-organizational features of the opera might play in relationship to formal and dramatic elements—these have served as my point of departure.

Historical as well as analytical considerations have figured in my choice of Alban Berg's *Wozzeck* as the subject of a set-theoretic study. *Wozzeck* (completed in short score by October 1921) is the longest atonal work predating twelve-tone composition, and it is the first full-length atonal opera. Its composition coincided with the maturing of Berg's pre-dodecaphonic idiom. Today the work is regarded as a landmark in the development of the Viennese atonal style.

These facts gain significance in light of Berg's own comments, delivered prior to a performance of *Wozzeck* in Oldenburg in 1929—some fifteen years after he had begun the work. Here Berg observes that he had made the decision to compose *Wozzeck* at a time when atonal composition was still very much confined to the production of short forms and miniatures:

> . . . I was confronted with a new problem, at least from the harmonic point of view: How do I achieve the same degree of closure [completeness], the same compelling musical unification, without the previously tried-and-true means of tonality and without the formal creative possibilities based upon it? Completeness not only in the small forms of scenes . . . but also, and this was the hard part, unification in the large forms of individual acts and in the overall architecture of the work as a whole? [In Redlich 1957a, p. 312; my translation.][28]

While it is a fact, on the one hand, that in 1929 as well as later (see Berg 1936) Berg expresses his distaste for the term "atonal," on the other hand it cannot be stressed too strongly that he proceeds without the slightest ambiguity to describe the so-called atonal style as a style that "*relinquished tonality* [emphasis my own] and with it one of the strongest and most widely proven means of building small as well as very large forms" (ibid., p. 311).[29]

The Oldenburg lecture must have been an extraordinary event. With candor no less remarkable because it was intended to be persuasive, Berg managed to demonstrate some of the ways in which he succeeded in solving the "new problem." (Not only did he himself play many excerpts from the piano-vocal score, he also arranged to have others performed by the Oldenburg orchestra.) The demonstration was subsequently repeated by the composer preceding performances of *Wozzeck* elsewhere throughout Germany. Berg's notes for the lecture were adapted under his supervision and published by

Willi Reich as a "guide" to the opera in 1931. Though the original lecture was not published in its entirety until 1957 (Redlich 1957a), it served, thanks to Reich, as the basis for many of the commentaries about *Wozzeck* that appeared after 1930 (see Reich 1931, 1963; Redlich 1957b; Jouve and Fano 1953; Ploebsch 1968, chapter 2; Carner 1975). In these publications the two recurring analytical issues, well known even to those who have read only the booklets accompanying recordings, are, first of all, the complex scheme of leitmotifs and, second, the relationship of the choice of small form and musical idea to the dramatic content and structure of each scene. As examples of his solution to the problem of continuity, both of these aspects of the opera were discussed in 1929 by Berg himself.

Let us examine Berg's own comments very carefully. Note that Berg defines the problem of unification with particular reference to the "*harmonic point of view*." Today the term "harmonic" (as opposed to "melodic") is understood to concern unordered (as opposed to ordered) pitch collections; "harmonies" are "chords," stated simultaneously, or "arpeggiated," in which case ordering is imposed. There is no reason to suspect that Berg used the term differently. As stressed above, Berg considered tonality to be a "form-generating means" (*formbildendes Mittel*; in Redlich 1957a, p. 317). His "new problem," then, was the problem of how unordered pitch collections could be organized to create cohesive small and large forms without the use of the triad, the functional diatonic harmonic progression, the tonal centers, and the linearizations of triadic structures that characterize tonality. Clearly Berg was not content to rely on motives and structural repetitions for the articulation of formal units without concern for the actual choice of pitch combinations and transformations with which the motives themselves would be projected. In fact he explicitly states that he sought an organizational method that would permit his atonal language to participate in the articulation of formal and dramatic units, just as tonal structures had participated earlier. The most outstanding example of that endeavor, and the first to be discussed by Berg in 1929, was his decision to use varied settings of the same eight-note structure at the close of each of the three acts of the opera. Whereas Redlich asserts that this structure functions "like a tonic" because it is "rooted in diatonic harmony" (Redlich 1957b, pp. 97–98), Berg simply says that "each act of the opera steers toward one and the same closing chord, quasi-cadential, and rests there, *as if on a tonic*" (in Redlich 1957a, p. 312; emphasis my own).[30] In my chapters 3 and 4 it will be shown that this eight-note chord plays a profound role within the specifically *atonal* pitch organization of the opera as a whole; as a "quasi-cadential" chord, this structure summarizes the atonal materials of the work *as if* it were the final cadential progression in a tonal composition.[31]

I propose, in short, that the relationship of pitch structures in *Wozzeck* to form and drama is just as decisive in the achievement of coherence and unification as the leitmotivic scheme or as the relationship of formal structure to dramatic design, if, indeed, it is not even more fundamental.

In "The Musical Language of *Wozzeck*" (1967a) George Perle made the first and only comprehensive attempt thus far "to describe certain means of integration and differentiation that are characteristic features" of the pitch organization of the opera as a whole. That essay, as well as others (Perle 1967b, 1971, 1980) in which Perle treats motivic and textual issues with great insight, has served as a stimulus to my own interest in the opera and furnished important background information without which a set-theoretic treatment would have been premature. Perle's concluding remarks in the 1967 article will be presented here because they have provided a strong incentive for my own undertaking:

> If I have not attempted to establish the coherence and unity of the work as a whole in terms of the interdependence and interaction of all the structural elements discussed in the foregoing survey, it is not because I am unaware of the importance and desirability of doing so. But the criteria upon which overall continuity depends cannot be determined apart from a fuller and more systematic presentation of such elements than can be offered here and now. Premature generalizations will not only fail to elucidate the larger relationships: they also ignore or distort the very details whose integration into the total work it is their chief business to explain. [Perle 1967a, p. 204; 1980, p. 185. In the present study all references to Perle 1967a will be references to material now also available in Perle 1980.]

The present project is an attempt to reach beyond the limits of Perle's examination toward a new understanding of the harmonic procedure with which Berg establishes contrast and cohesion in *Wozzeck*. Like Douglas Jarman, who also acknowledges Perle's strong influence, I offer my own view of "the way in which the most important melodic and harmonic features of the work are related to one another" (Jarman 1979, pp. 46–47)—a view that in certain respects challenges Perle's studies and Jarman's discussion (ibid., pp. 46–73) but in no way pretends to be the final word on this subject. Inasmuch as Forte's theory of unordered sets and set complexes provides the analytical procedure for a new "fuller and more systematic presentation" of pitch relations in *Wozzeck*, this theory will be uniformly applied here for the first time in the examination of a large and complete atonal work, a full-length opera. In my study, the question of the overriding importance of the drama in the large-scale pitch-organizational design of the work will be of foremost concern. Although the first task will be to elucidate relationships among pitch structures of both long-range and local significance, the fundamental goal of the study will be to show that three distinct and extraordinarily compact "families" of pitch structures interact on multiple levels with the dramatic as well as formal architecture of the work.

To the extent that this goal is accomplished, the reader will have an opportunity to assess the pitch-class set-analytic method on the basis of its power to illustrate the interdependence of pitch structures and formal as well as dramatic elements. It is hoped, moreover, that this study might project a new outlook on solutions to the problems of continuity and differentiation in the Viennese atonal repertory and contribute toward a refinement in our understanding of those compositional techniques and stylistic tendencies which distinguish Berg from other twentieth-century composers.

2 ACT I / SCENE 1:
FIRST APPLICATION OF THE
ANALYTICAL METHOD

My analysis of *Wozzeck* will begin with an introduction to certain basic analytical techniques as applied in the examination of pitch structures that originate in association with essential motivic components of the work. For the reader who has not studied the opera, this and the following two chapters may function as a survey of prominent themes and motives, one that distinguishes itself from other surveys and guides[1] by its emphasis upon pitch-structural properties and relationships.

Although some familiarity with the music and the drama will be assumed, special care has been taken to provide the reader with annotated musical examples for nearly every detailed reference to the score.[2] Each excerpt will be accompanied by a label that identifies its location by act, scene, and measure numbers; its formal as well as dramatic context will be clarified in the corresponding discussion. Just the same, the reader is encouraged to follow the discussion with reference to the complete score as well as a recording; and it cannot be urged too strongly that the reader require of himself the effort to hear pitch structures and relationships under observation. Although audibility of relationships has not been my only criterion for selection, it has been of paramount concern throughout this work. My position can be stated simply: we shall only know whether sometimes complex levels of construction can be aurally appreciated after we have seriously attempted to hear them.

Example 3 shows the opening six measures of *Wozzeck*—the three-measure Introduction and the first three measures of Scene 1. Using this passage as our first point of reference, we shall progress toward an overview of the first scene of the opera in which the following analytical procedures will be employed: (1) *segmentation*; (2) determination of pitch-class *set names*; (3) examination of sets that are equivalent under transposition or inversion; (4) specification of *invariant subsets* under transposition and inversion; (5) interpretation of the *complement relation*.

I

The terms *pitch combination* and *pitch collection* were used interchangeably in chapter 1 to refer to any collection of pitches sounded or represented in staff notation. By this definition the entire collection of pitches represented in Example 3, or any collection of two or more pitches—sounding simultaneously, stated in succession, or separated in time by other pitches—may be considered a pitch combination. Which pitch combinations, then, are to be regarded as analytical objects?

Answers to this question hinge upon a fundamental aspect of the analysis of pitch organization that must be clarified from the outset. There is a simple reason why the study of pitch structures cannot be a one-dimensional study, why it must implicitly—and, in this case, explicitly—be a study of the relationship of pitch structures to other dimensions of musical design: on the most basic level—the level of notation—symbols for pitch combinations share a complex interdependent relationship with symbols for rhythmic, metric, and durational values, articulation, tempo, dynamics, and instrumentation; by definition, pitch combinations are collections of pitches assigned to specific registers, and, in the case at hand, pitch combinations are coordinated with text, stage directions, and descriptions for dramatic action as well as characterization. Generally speaking, the process of deciding which pitch combinations should be considered in an analysis is a highly complex process involving the consideration of all musical dimensions. We shall refer to this process as the process of *segmentation*.

Even more generally, segmentation is the fundamental process undertaken by any analyst, regardless of his subject or his methodology: the analyst separates the whole into constituent parts for individual study; he does this in the hope of identifying relationships among constituents that clarify how they interact to form the whole. In our specific case, segmentation will be the process of determining which pitch combinations lend coherence, interest, and clarity to the immediate, intermediate, and long-range musical design. Toward that end, primary emphasis will be placed on pitch combinations that are made distinctive by means of association with fundamental formal, motivic, thematic, and dramatic ideas of the work; hence choices for consideration will depend at all times on the interaction of pitch combinations and other dimensions of their context. From the very beginning it must be understood that the context of any pitch combination under consideration will be multi-leveled: the immediate context—the passage at hand—will be regarded first as an entity but then as a sub-context in relationship to networks of recurring ideas as well as to the context of the work as a whole.

The time-honored notion of *musical unit* accommodates the notational interdependence of pitch combinations and other musical dimensions. As such, the musical unit can provide a point of departure for our examination of Example 3. By convention the term musical unit is used to describe configurations that are isolated by rests or distinguished contextually by other means—by notational features such as beams or articulation markings, by assignment to a single instrument or instrumental group, or by recurrence in the form of ostinato, sequence, contrapuntal imitation, or motive. Among the possibly many components of the musical unit, its pitch content may be presented as a simultaneity (i.e., the unit is a "chord"), stated as a succession of simultaneities (i.e., the unit is a "harmonic progression"), or projected as a series of tones (i.e., the unit is a "melodic figure"). For Allen Forte, segmentation is "the procedure of determining which musical units of a composition are to be regarded as analytical objects" (Forte 1973a, p. 83). It will be noted that Forte's definition leaves open the question of the relationship between "pitch combination" and "musical unit." By definition, a pitch combination may not necessarily form a musical unit. On the one hand, we shall see that the process of segmentation need not be limited to the selection of pitch combinations that form musical units. On the other hand, however, it will become evident as we proceed that the notion of musical unit provides an excellent first criterion with which to approach the problem of segmentation in *Wozzeck*.

In Example 3 the brackets with corresponding letters A through H delimit in the order of their appearance eight musical units that are heard at the opening of Act I. Each of these formations will be considered a *primary segment*, informally defined by Forte as "a configuration that is isolated as a unit by conventional means" (Forte 1973a, p. 83). At m. 6 the interaction of three components—the *subsegment* F♮-B♮ within the primary segment H (the Captain's first statement), the single repeated pitch D♭ in the English horn, and the vertical dyad G♮-D♮ in the 'cellos—produces what Forte calls a *composite segment*, "a segment formed by segments or subsegments that are contiguous or that are otherwise linked in some way" (p. 84). That composite segment, marked with the letter L, and all the primary segments A through H have been chosen for examination.

The examination procedure may be summarized as follows. First the pitch classes represented in each segment have been translated into integer notation. Next the best normal order and the prime form of each pitch-class set have been calculated as described in chapter 1. Finally, each prime form has been located on Forte's list of prime forms for the 220 distinct pitch-class sets of 3 to 9 elements. The list is reproduced as an appendix to this work; in

Example 3. Act I: mm. 1–6

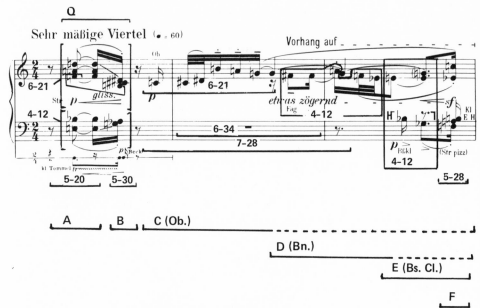

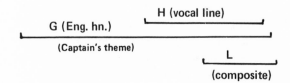

the list the reader will find the interval vector and a distinct *set name* for each prime form. The set name associated with the prime form for the pitch combination represented in each segment at Example 3 has been placed in the score.[3]

Note that each set name consists of numbers separated by a hyphen. The number to the left of the hyphen is the *cardinal number*, the number of elements in the set; the number to the right of the hyphen is the *ordinal number*, which is to say simply that it represents the position of the prime form on the list. Thus 5-20, the name of the pc set formed by segment A in Example 3, is the twentieth set on the list of 5-element sets.

By consulting appendix 1, the reader may ascertain that Forte's ordering of the prime forms is arbitrary but systematic. As explained in a footnote in his 1964 article, the ordering of the prime forms follows the pattern established in the interval vectors for the 2-element sets. The vector is treated as a number, so that proceeding from top to bottom of the list of vectors for sets of the same cardinality, if i, j, and k are three consecutive vectors, $i>j>k$.[4] In other words, for sets of the same cardinality, "the chords [sets] containing the most intervals of a semitone come first, and within these, the chords with the most intervals of two semitones, and so forth. In addition, if two chords share the same interval-content function, one of them is shifted to the end of the table, and inversions are simply omitted" (Regener 1974, pp. 194–95).

We are now prepared to make a number of observations about specific pitch combinations shown in Example 3, their relationship to certain formal aspects of Act I/Scene 1, and their importance in the motivic organization of the opera as a whole. Let us proceed by examining local and long-range relationships established by two segments whose pitch structures have the same set name.

Example 3 shows that the pc sets formed in segments F (m. 3) and L (m. 6) both have the set name 5-28. From this point forward, it will be understood that pitch-class sets with the same set name are equivalent in that they are reducible to the same prime form by transposition or by inversion. Hereafter referring to the pc sets formed in segments F and L as sets F and L respectively, let us determine whether it is by transposition or by inversion that set F is equivalent to set L. For comparison, it will be convenient to align the pc integers of each set in normal order as follows:

$$F: 9, 11, 0, 3, 5$$
$$L: 11, 1, 2, 5, 7$$

Now if set F is related to set L by transposition, then, as explained in chapter

1, there must be some integer t, representing some pc interval, that when added to each integer of set F will yield the corresponding integer (mod 12) of set L. Subtracting each integer (mod 12) of L from the corresponding integer of F, we find that the difference of each pair is 2; thus L is related to F by transposition, and the value of t, the pc interval of transposition, is 2.

Of what analytical interest is the fact that pc sets F and L are transpositionally equivalent? The answer to that question has everything to do with the formal function of each of the two segments. Segment F gives a final punctuation to the three-measure introductory phrase and coincides with the point where the curtain has fully risen and the action on stage begins. Segment L marks the end of the second phrase at the point where the Captain's theme, introduced by the English horn at m. 4, comes to rest with a notated ritard (♫♩♫♩♩ ♪) on the repeated D♭ while the Captain concludes his opening reproach—"Langsam, Wozzeck, langsam!" ("Slowly, Wozzeck, slowly!"). In short, segments F and L share not only the same pitch-class set-type but also the same formal function: both serve as cadential structures.

On the basis of information presented so far, the reader knows that whereas, on the one hand, some pc sets that have the same total interval content are not transpositionally or inversionally related (these are the Z-related sets), on the other hand, all sets that are transpositionally or inversionally related (i.e., equivalent sets) have the same total interval content as well as the same set name. It follows that when the composer chooses transpositionally or inversionally related pitch structures, he preserves a basic and general intervallic property shared by the pitch structures thus related, namely, total interval content. With non-identical pitch structures that nevertheless have identical total interval content, the composer can establish specific pitch-structural bonds between configurations that may or may not be widely separated in time and that may be dissimilar in every other respect. We shall see that that specific kind of bond can be established in coordination with motives and reiterations of larger units, or without dependence upon these recognizable features. In either case, the compositional purpose seems clear: bonds of this kind reinforce the cohesive overall formal and dramatic design.

Let us compare the two forms of pc set 5-28 in segments F and L with seven of the most prominent recurrences of that set within Act I/Scene 1. If the reader is not familiar with the musical design of this scene and its relationship to the dialogue between the Captain and Wozzeck, he may wish to consult chapter 3, "The Text and Formal Design," of Perle 1980; this essay includes an outline of each scene, showing parallel segments of the libretto and the formal plan. As summarized there, the first scene takes the shape of a dance suite, with principal sections cast in the following forms:

Each of the seven events shown in Examples 4 through 10 occurs at either the very beginning or the very end of one of those small dance-form sections.

The arrows in the outline shown above point to places where the transition from one section to the next may be described as a "ritornello" in that it consists of all or some of segments A through L from the opening of the opera. The ritornello that serves at mm. 24–29 as elided transition from Prelude to Pavane is a rhythmically compressed repetition of the opening six measures, with instrumental and registral exchanges but otherwise exact and complete. Example 4 shows the connecting point between first and second phrases of that ritornello. Here the vertical segment F reappears precisely as in m. 3, but this time the lower four voices are sustained while the oboe reintroduces the Captain's theme at its original pitch level. Several new composite segments are formed by the interaction of the oboe tune with the sustained tetrachord.

Example 4. Act I/Scene 1: mm. 25–28

Of foremost interest to us now is the fact that each of the first two pitches of the Captain's theme (F♯ and G♯) produces a new form of pc set 5-28 in coordination with the sustained tetrachord ⌊F♮-A♮-B♮-E♭⌋. The first of these sets (pcs 5, 9, 11, 3, 6),[5] labeled F^1, is transpositionally related to the original set 5-28 in segment F; the value of t is 6. [The symbolic notation for that relationship is: $F^1 = T(F,6)$.] The second of these pc sets, labeled F^2, is related to F by inversion followed by transposition with t = 8 [notated $F^2 = T(I(F),8)$]. This relationship can be illustrated in terms of a *double mapping* (see chapter 1) in which each element of F^2 is mapped first onto its inverse and then onto F by addition of the value of t:

$$
\begin{array}{ccl}
F^2 & t & F \\
3 \to 9 + 8 = & & 5 \,(\text{mod } 12) \\
5 \to 7 + 8 = & & 3 \,(\text{mod } 12) \\
8 \to 4 + 8 = & & 0 \,(\text{mod } 12) \\
9 \to 3 + 8 = & & 11 \\
11 \to 1 + 8 = & & 9
\end{array}
$$

It is granted that the analytical significance of the equivalent sets formed in segments F^1 and F^2 is limited by the short sixteenth-note durational value of each segment; however, in that segments F, F^1, and F^2 are contiguous, an entire metric unit is dominated by vertical statements of set 5-28, and thus the same total interval content is held constant among the verticals that serve to connect the end of one phrase unit with the beginning of the next. Homogeneity with respect to interval content is reinforced by homogeneity with respect to pitch content: the tetrachord ⌊F♮-A♮-B♮-E♭⌋ at m. 26—a subsegment of segment F, labeled *f*—is sustained throughout the next three measures, so that it becomes a subsegment of F^1 and F^2 as well. Or, in set-theoretic terms, the transpositional levels respectively for F^1 and for the inverted form F^2 are such that all three equivalent sets F, F^1, and F^2 hold those same four pitch classes ⌊F♮-A♮-B♮-E♭⌋ in common. The set represented in subsegment *f* is thus an *invariant subset*; this subset constitutes one of the three whole-tone tetrachords, and its set name is 4-25. Set *f* may be regarded as the *intersection* of F, F^1, and F^2, notated $f = \cdot(F, F^1, F^2)$. Were we to inspect the twelve forms of the set-type 5-28 produced by transposition and the twelve forms produced by inversion followed by transposition, we would find that there are only two other forms besides the forms represented in segments F^1 and F^2 that hold the pitch classes ⌊F♮-A♮-B♮-E♭⌋ invariant (as common tones). We shall return to the question of the long-range significance of two of those specific pitch classes (F♮ and B♮) after we have completed our survey of other appearances of pc set 5-28 in Act I/Scene 1.

Example 5. Act I/Scene 1: mm. 47–50

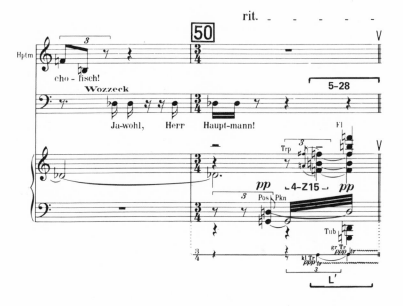

In the abbreviated ritornello that connects the Pavane with Cadenza I (Ex. 5), the Captain's theme from m. 4 is stated for the first time by the Captain himself ("oder ich werde melancholisch!" ["or I become melancholy!"]), now slightly slower (eighth-note triplets rather than sixteenths) to reflect the Captain's melancholy mood. The only response Wozzeck can muster is his recurring "Jawohl, Herr Hauptmann" ("Yes sir, Captain"), stated as in m. 25 (Ex. 4) on the repeated D♭ from mm. 5–6 (Ex. 3). With this second occurrence we come to understand that in Act I/Scene 1 the D♭, in coordination with the verbal motif "Jawohl . . . " and the rhythm ♪ ♫ ♪ ♪♫ , has been placed in association with Wozzeck's subservience to the Captain. That association will be reinforced by one further appearance of the "Jawohl . . . " motto on the same D♭ with an augmented version of the same rhythm (mm. 87–89). Finally, as shown at Example 5, just before the downbeat of Cadenza I, the form of pc set 5–28 first presented in segment L at m. 6 reappears pianissimo and untransposed. This vertical presentation of set 5-28 confirms the justness of our segmentation at m. 6 (Ex. 3): there we read the interaction of three distinct components—the tritone F♮-B♮, the pc D♭, and the dyad G♮-D♮—in terms of a composite segment; here the three components are combined at the same pitch-class levels to form a single vertical primary segment, L′, now scored for timpani, tuba, trombones, trumpets, horn, flutes, and harp. Notice, moreover, that despite the change of registration and orchestration, the registral distribution of pitches (i.e., the arrangement of pitches within the chord) and the instrumentation at segment L′ are such that the structural identity of each of the three components is preserved. These three components will be examined in greater detail shortly.

Example 6 shows the first measure of the Gigue. Observe that the set name for the vertical collection F′ (pcs 0,3,9,11,5) at the accented downbeat is again 5-28. As with L′ at Example 5 in relation to L in Example 3, set F′ is identical to set F (Ex. 3, m. 3) with respect to total pitch-class content; in addition, as vertical segments, F′ and F share similar articulation as well as dynamic markings, and their notated rhythmic values are the same.

Example 6. Act I/Scene 1: m. 65 (Gigue)

Only the registral distribution of pitches has been changed, with the result that now the tritone B♭-F♮ conspicuously forms the uppermost boundary of the chord just as it did in the form of set 5-28 shown in Example 5.

Like the Gigue, the Gavotte and both of its two Doubles begin with vertical pc collections represented by the set name 5-28. This time the initial figure in each of the three sections is even sequentially reiterated on the next two strong beats, with repetitions of the same vertical pitch structure successively transposed downward one semitone. Upon comparing the initial measures of Gavotte, Double I, and Double II, as shown respectively in Examples 7, 8, and 9, the reader will recognize that Doubles I and II present rhythmically and orchestratively varied repetitions of the basic harmonic and melodic material presented in the Gavotte. (The respective length of Gavotte, Double I, and Double II is progressively halved: 12 to 6 to 3 measures.) The reader may then notice that whereas the Gavotte and its second Double share the same pitch classes and combinations, the pitch content of the first Double is transposed "at the fifth" (i.e., at $t = 7$), with the result that Double I functions from the harmonic viewpoint as a middle section within an irregularly unbalanced ternary scheme. The transposition at Double I coincides with the point where Wozzeck is driven for the first time to interrupt the Captain and come to his own defense; the Captain's transpositional level is resumed when he regains control of the dialogue at the beginning of Double II.

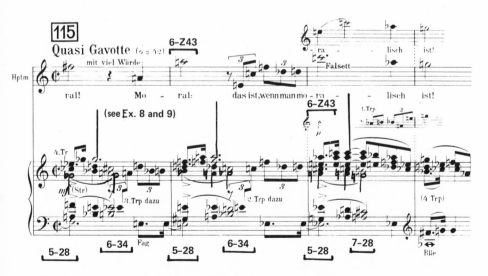

Example 7. Act I/Scene 1: mm. 115–18 (Gavotte)

Example 8. Act I/Scene 1: mm. 127–28 (Double I)

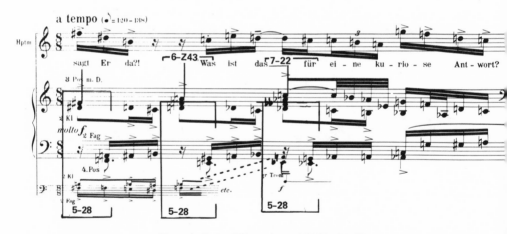

Example 9. Act I/Scene 1: m. 133 (Double II)

It can be shown that in comparison with the 5-element pc collections that mark the beginnings of Gavotte and Double II, the 6- and 7-element collections on strong beats of Double I not only participate in the making of a thicker texture but also reinforce the essential pitch-structural idea. As a member of the family of subsets that a given set contains, a set-type may be multiply represented—that is, represented at more than one transpositional or inversional level—within the larger set. This is the case with the vertical collections on the first and second strong beats of Double I (Ex. 8): their set names are 6-30 and 7-19, and each contains set 5-28 twice. For example, in pc set 6-30 (downbeat, m. 127) the two forms of 5-28 in normal order are 2, 4, 5, 8, 10 and 8, 10, 11, 2, 4; the second of these is the one that relates to the original set of the Gavotte (3, 5, 6, 9, 11) at t = 7. The vertical on the downbeat of m. 128—set 7-31—contains 5-28 three times (in normal order, 6, 8, 9, 0, 2, 0, 2, 3, 6, 8, and 0, 2, 5, 6, 8). In light of the fact that there is no other 7-element set in the twelve-pitch-class system which contains set 5-28 more than two times, the composer's choice of pitch combination here suggests that he made an extraordinary effort to control intervallic-structural relationships on the most local of compositional levels.

Observe that the transpositional level chosen for the accompaniment to Wozzeck's statement in Double I (Ex. 8) is such that once again the dyad B♮-F♮ is made prominent in the accented principal orchestral melody. The set name for the collection composed of the first six pitch classes of that melody—11, 2, 5, 3, 1, 9—is 6-21. Here our analysis reveals an important link between the Gavotte, with its two Doubles, and the Introduction to Act I: the set name for the very first melodic statement of the opera (Ex. 3, mm. 1-2: pcs 0, 1, 3, 11, 9, 7) is also 6-21, and four of the six pitch classes of each set-form—pcs 1, 3, 9, 11—are held invariant. The invariant subset is a form of the whole-tone tetrachord whose set name is 4-21. Significantly, this tetrachord figures elsewhere in the opera as a subset of several larger sets of utmost motivic importance; we shall also see shortly that set 4-21 is featured as the pitch-structural component of Wozzeck's "entrance" motive in Act II/ Scene 1 (Ex. 17d).

Finally, let us examine the appearance of pc set 5-28 in the closing mea-

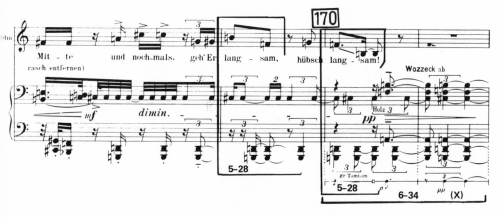

Example 10. Act I/Scene 1: mm. 168–71

sures of Act I/Scene 1 (Ex. 10). As in the ritornello at the end of the Pavane (Ex. 5), here the transpositional level and the arrangement of adjacencies within the vertical collection create a direct correspondence between this presentation of set 5-28 and the one heard in m. 6 (Ex. 3, segment L); despite the registral redistribution and the change of instrumentation, the identity of each of the three components—the perfect fifth G♮-D♮, the tritone B♮-F♮, and the single pitch D♭—is once again preserved. As the final event of Act I/Scene 1, this occurrence of set 5-28 provides a link with the beginning of the scene which underlines the fact that the Captain, now undone by Wozzeck's unexpected outburst (see the Aria, Ex. 24), is reduced to concluding his discourse by returning to the issue with which he began ("Langsam . . . !" ["Slowly . . . !"]).

II

In every setting of pc set 5-28 that we have examined above, this pitch structure has played a specific role with respect to the formal design: each statement of the set has served as a component of the last or the first event of a principal section. With the final appearance of set 5-28 (Ex. 10), at the point just before the curtain falls, the role of that set as a cadential structure in this scene is completed at the same time that the structure itself is absorbed within a larger, 6-element set that will now assume the cadential role over a much larger compositional span. As shown in Example 10, that hexachord emerges when the bass clarinet enters in m. 170, effecting the addition of pc9 (A♮) to the collection 7, 2, 1, 5, 11 (G♮-D♮-D♭-F♮-B♮) that forms set 5-28; the hexachord (normal order: 5, 7, 9, 11, 1, 2) is an inverted form of the set-type 6-34. George Perle (1967a, p. 208) appears to have been the first to note that the simultaneity formed specifically by the six pitch classes of this hexachord reappears untransposed as a component of the cadential figure that marks the close of each of the largest formal units of the opera, the three acts.

Example 11 shows the measures that accompany the descent of the curtain at the close of Act I. Here as well as at the end of Act III (Ex. 69), the perfect fifth G♮-D♮, first observed as a component of set 5-28 in m. 6 (Ex. 3), appears now in the role of pedal point beneath two oscillating tetrachords.[6] The entire pitch content from the middle of m. 715 to the end of the act forms pc set 8-24. The importance of this large pitch structure in relationship to the long-range organization of the opera will be discussed in chapters 3 and 4. The set name that represents one of the two tetrachords—4-24— indicates that this set is the 4-element *complement* of the large set 8-24, "embedded" within that 8-element structure but at the same time isolated as a discrete component. Complement relations of this kind will be discussed and examined in detail shortly.

Example 11. Act I/Scene 5: mm. 715–17

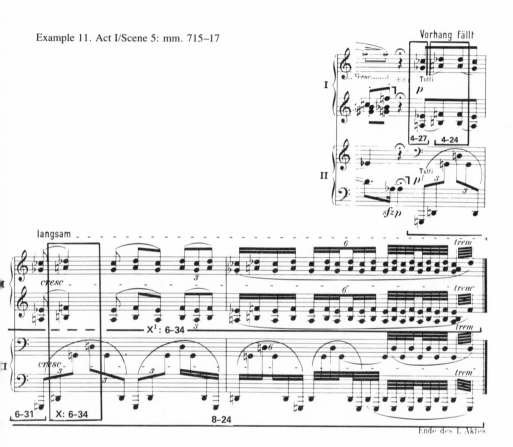

The other oscillating tetrachord, whose set name is 4-27, combines with the pedal point G♮–D♮ to produce a form of set 6-31. (The specific form of set 6-31 shown at Example 10 is Douglas Jarman's all-important "cadential chord A" at t = 0; see Jarman 1979, pp. 47–73.) This hexachord is not made motivically prominent in the long-range scheme, but its harmonic role as the container of many smaller sets associated with both Wozzeck and Marie will warrant further comment in chapter 5. Of special importance is the fact that the specific form of set 6-31 (pcs 7,2,9,3,6,11) featured vertically at Example 10 makes an earlier vertical appearance at mm. 317–23 of the Interlude connecting Scenes 2 and 3 of Act I. There, as shown at Example 60, a seventh pitch class (pc10) is added to the sustained fixed form of 6-31, and the complete seven-note collection is presented horizontally as well. (The seven-note collection [set 7-21] and the motivic-referential role of its horizontal presentation will be discussed in chapter 4.) As displayed by Jarman (ibid., p. 61), a transposed statement of the seven-note collection (Jarman's "cadential chord $A1$" at $t = 5$), with its subset 6-31, recurs in the Interlude between Scenes 3 and 4 of Act I (violins and violas, mm. 480–81), thus effecting a frame for Act I/Scene 3.

By comparing Example 10 with Example 11, the reader will see that the tetrachord 4-24 (B♮-F♮-A♮-D♭) in combination with the pedal point G♮-D♮, forms the segment (labeled X) that, as shown by Perle, is identical in respect to specific pitch-class content with the hexachord at the end of Act I/Scene 1. Now, further analysis reveals that the complete tremolo figure (normal order: 9, 11, 1, 3, 5, 6), that is, the unit formed by the two alternating tetrachords in combination with each other (labeled X^1), itself provides a transposed form of hexachord X, pc set 6-34 [$X^1 = T(X,4)$]—a fact that Perle overlooks. The independence of X^1 as a discrete unit is emphasized in the Prelude to Act II (Ex. 12), where continuity with the end of Act I is effected by means of recurring pitch structures as follows: (1) the opening 'cello statement, excluding the first pitch C♮, is an arpeggiation of segment X (compare Example 12 with Example 11);[7] (2) the 'cello statement is followed by a reiteration of the tremolo figure X^1, now rescored and also isolated from the pedal point G♮-D♮ with which it had sounded at the end of Act I.

Perle considers the specific collection of pitch classes G♮-D♮-A♮-D♭-

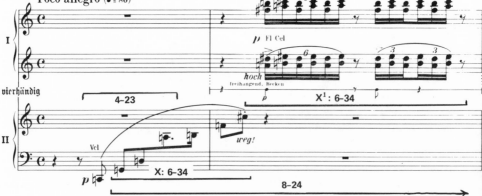

Example 12. Act II: mm. 1–2 (Prelude)

F♮-B♮, (7, 2, 9, 1, 5, 11) presented in our segment X to be "the principal referential chord of the work as a whole" (Perle 1967a, p. 208). He substantiates his claim only on the basis of the presence of that specific hexachord at the end of Act I/Scene 1, in the closing measures of each act, and in the Prelude to Act II. Whereas Perle is concerned here with "a chord that is stabilized at a specific pitch level" (p. 210), I wish to engage the reader's interest in pitch structures that can be regarded as significantly related by equivalence under transposition and inversion. (In this respect I follow Douglas Jarman, who refers to Perle's "principal referential chord" as "cadential chord B" at $t = 0$ and shows some of the thematically prominent appearances of transpositionally and inversionally related forms of this collection to be discussed below; see Jarman 1979, pp. 49–60.) On the basis of equivalence under transposition and inversion, it will become evident as we proceed that hexachord X is a "principal referential chord" not only because of its cadential role as a fixed pitch collection but also because inversionally and transpositionally related forms of hexachord X—that is, other forms of pc set 6-34—are given motivic prominence throughout the work. Let us now take a preliminary glance at several motives and figures whose pitch structures feature forms of set 6-34.

This set structure makes its first appearance at the very beginning of the opera (Ex. 3), where it takes the form of a composite segment consisting of the first six pitches of m. 2, that is, the first melodic statement in the oboe minus upbeat— 1, 3, 11, 9, 7, (C♯-D♯-B♮-A♮-G♮)—combined with the first attack in the bassoon, pc6 (F♯). A comparison of the pitch-class content of this form of set 6-34 with those forms discussed above reveals that whereas this form shares four pitch classes (the whole-tone subset 4-21 [1, 7, 9, 11], introduced earlier in this chapter) with Perle's "principal referential chord" (hexachord X), it shares five pitch classes (the subset 5-34 [1, 3, 6, 9, 11]) with the tremolo figure, segment X^1.

The next two examples (Examples 13 and 14) show figures of local significance within Act I/Scene 1 that feature pc set 6-34. At m. 154 (Ex. 13) a final, augmented ritornello statement of the initial three-bar Introduction (Ex. 3, segments A through F) signals a return to the opening Prelude—now to be restated in retrograde as the Captain's discourse turns back upon itself. In Example 13 we see the connecting link between ritornello and Prelude, where the fixed form of set 5-28 from the vertical segment F at m. 3 will be sustained this time by the original wind obbligato with parts exchanged. Meanwhile, the Captain, attempting to pacify Wozzeck and himself as well, falls back on an earlier motif (mm. 54–55, 110–11), his patronizing and limited observation that Wozzeck "ist ein guter Mensch" ("is a good man"). The Captain's sustained high G♮ (pc7) in mm. 155–56 provides the *only* pitch class that, when combined with the sustained pcs ‚5, 9, 11, 0, 3‚, forms set 6-34.

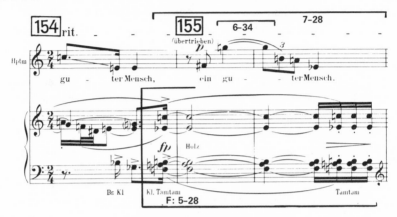

Example 13. Act I/Scene 1: mm. 154–56

To the reader who may still be doubtful, this example provides powerful evidence that pitch-class set-theoretic observations can offer explanations for compositional decisions. The five-note chord sustained by the wind obbligato has by now become a fixed point of reference in relation to which the composer will choose pitches for the Captain's statement. Note that, like many other vocal passages throughout the work, the pitches of the second part of the Captain's line are doublings of pitches sustained by the instrumentalists. All the more reason, perhaps, that the upbeat and climax pitches of the vocal line will be made more prominent by virtue of the fact that they are *not* doublings of the five-note sustained chord. Of the seven non-doubling pitch classes the composer might have chosen for the Captain's climax, the G♮ in combination with the sustained chord alone creates a pitch structure that is related (by t = 2) to "the principal referential chord of the work as a whole."[8] The high G♮ is by no means, then, an isolated and arbitrarily chosen melodic component; instead it plays a specific role in the harmonic design of the passage. (An explanation for the choice of upbeat pitch F♯ in combination with the climax pitch G♮ and the sustained chord is suggested by the indication in Example 13 that the total pitch-class content of mm. 155–56 forms the complement of set 5-28, set 7-28. The reader may wish to return to this example after the concept of complementation has been introduced later in this chapter.)

Only the first eleven bars of the Prelude—measures 4 through 14—reappear in retrograde in the final section of the scene, which commences immediately after the passage shown in Example 13. To observe how the retrograde statement is presented, begin by comparing its first measure (157) with m. 14. Notice that the vocal part does not participate whatsoever in the retrograde treatment; note also that successive horizontal and vertical pitch combinations at first reappear without their original rhythmic values. Thus everything but the vertical combinations will sound "new" until we reach the "neighbor-chord" figure in m. 161 (Ex. 14), marked *schwungvoll* ("animated"). Here the original rhythmic setting is resumed, and the figure, heard only twice in the corresponding m. 11, is now repeated nine times as the Captain reveals that Wozzeck's impassioned Aria has unnerved him. The alternating five- and six-note chords form sets 5-31 and 6-34 respectively. Observe that the only pitch classes shared by the two chords form the tritone B♮-F♮, whose importance as a motivic component we have witnessed growing throughout the scene with each recurrence of set 5-28. Thus not only by means of "obsessive" repetition but also by virtue of its association here with the B♮-F♮ motif, the pitch structure identified as set 6-34 is established as an important point of reference in Act I/Scene 1.

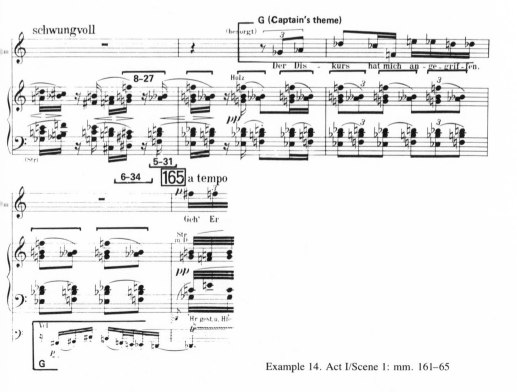

Example 14. Act I/Scene 1: mm. 161–65

III

The question of the long-range significance of pitch combinations represented by the set name 6-34 relates directly to the question of the importance
of whole-tone material in the large-scale pitch organization of the opera.
Among the fifty distinct hexachords, set 6-34 is one of the only four hexachords that contain the whole-tone pentachord (set 5-33: 0, 2, 4, 6, 8 [040402]).
Of the other three hexachords, 6-21, 6-22, and 6-35, the latter (0, 2, 4, 6, 8,
10 [060603]) is the whole-tone hexachord itself. The prime forms and the
interval vectors of sets 6-21, 6-22, and 6-34 are of course distinct from one
another, but when these sets are compared from the viewpoint of scale segments, their individual structural differences can be seen to result only from
a difference in the "location," or placement, of a semitone within the otherwise whole-tone series. Of interest here is the fact that all three of the sets
that I shall call the "almost whole-tone" hexachords appear in the form of
prominent melodic-thematic (horizontal) statements within the course of the
opera. This most striking feature of the work will be demonstrated with the
following series of examples accompanied by brief explanatory notes.[9]

Example 15a. Act I: mm. 1–3 (segment C)

6-21 (0,*1,3,11,9*,7)*
6-34 (*1,3,11,9,7*,6)*

(Cf. Examples 3 and 8; these appearances
of sets 6-21 and 6-34 have been discussed
earlier.)

Example 15b. Act I/Scene 1: mm. 29–31

6-21*   Introductory theme (segment C)
6-34*   transformed at the beginning of the Pavane.

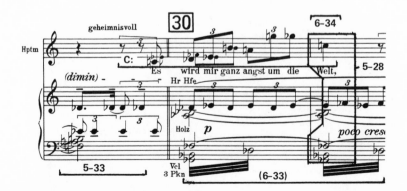

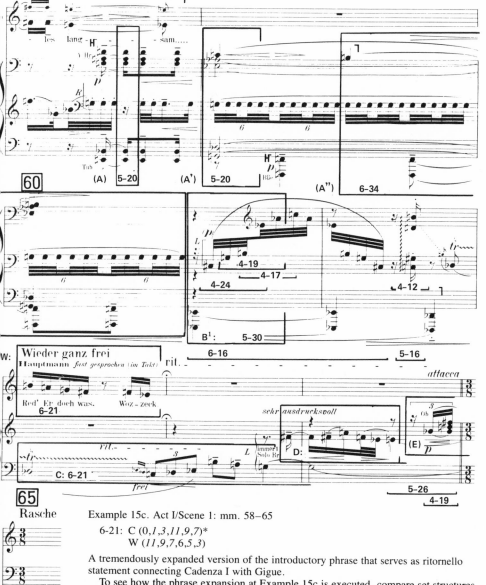

Example 15c. Act I/Scene 1: mm. 58–65

6-21: C (0,1,3,11,9,7)*
       W (11,9,7,6,5,3)

A tremendously expanded version of the introductory phrase that serves as ritornello statement connecting Cadenza I with Gigue.

To see how the phrase expansion at Example 15c is executed, compare set structures beginning at the third beat of m. 58 with those shown for segments A through F in Example 3. (The recurrence of set 5-28 at the beginning of the Gigue [segment F', m. 65] has been examined above; segment B¹ will be discussed in chapter 3.)

Note the vertical statement of set 6-34 (segment A″) sustained from the middle of m. 59 to the middle of m. 60. Observe also that this time the rhythmically transformed statement of the introductory theme (segment C) in the solo viola is preceded by another linear statement of set 6-21 in the Captain's part (segment W). The equivalence relation between segments C and W is "disguised" by virtue of the fact that the set structure at C is an inverted form of the set structure at W [C = T(I(W),6)].

For a startling motivic transformation of the Captain's statement (segment W), in which contour and register are preserved but the set structure is changed significantly in order to signify a change of speaker, see Example 17f below.

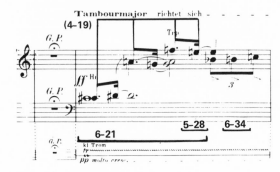

Example 15d. Act I/Scene 5: mm. 699–700

6-21 (*1,3,9,7,5,4*)

Beginning of the final climax of the seduction scene, closing section of Act I. Note that four pitch classes are held in common with the introductory theme (segment C) shown at Example 15a.

Example 15e. Act I/Scene 5: m. 712 (climax of the seduction scene)

6-34 (*1,3,11,9,7,6*)*

A final transformation: the contour is maintained, but the set structure of the linear statement is changed from 6-21 to 6-34. The pitch-class content is now exactly the same as that of the introductory theme shown at Example 15a.

Example 15f. Act I/Scene 4: mm. 620–23

6-21 (*3,1,11,9,7,0*)*

Variation 20: the Doctor ecstatically rhapsodizes about the fame his "scientific experimentation" with Wozzeck will bring him. The Doctor's motive here is the sequentially stated descending five-note "almost whole-tone" figure (set 5-9), first heard in his opening parlando recitative at mm. 491–92, here treated as the subject of a six-voice canon with entries at ascending thirds to create an appropriately bombastic increase in instrumental density and volume. Above this, the Doctor states an expanded and augmented version of the motive, whose "prefix" pitch (pc3) combines to yield 6-21. (See chapter 4 for a discussion of the diatonic "fourths chords" also featured in this passage.)

Example 15g. Act III/Scene 3: mm. 122–25

6-21 (*7,4,9,5,3,1*)

Opening of the scene, immediately preceded by the well-known tutti crescendo on B♮ that now represents Wozzeck's accomplished murder of Marie.

This linear statement of set 6-21 projects the rhythmic motive, introduced in the Interlude at the end of Scene 2, that will dominate Scene 3 as representative of Wozzeck's idée fixe— the murder.

Vorhang
rasch auf **3. Szene** Eine Schenke (Nacht, schwaches Licht)

51

Example 16a. Act I/Scene 2: mm. 212–16

6-22 (2,7,9,*11*,1,3)*

The first phrase of Andres's Song.

    As with the Polka theme shown above, the whole-tone aspect of the Song creates the impression of a rustic "wrong-note" or "out-of-tune" deviation from the "correct" diatonic norm (see the discussion in section IV below).

Example 16b. Act III: mm. 320–25

6-22 (2,*9*,4,8,10,0)

First phrase of the final Interlude.

    The appearance here of set 6-22 in a context that is, though briefly, nevertheless unequivocally tonal around D minor points in general to the "adaptability" of pitch combinations within the twelve-pitch-class system and to the inadequacy of ascriptions of such attributes as "tonal" or "atonal" to pitch-class sets in isolation from musical context.

    The total pc content of m. 322 (normal order: 8,10,0,2,4,5) and of m. 324 (normal order: 3,4,6,8,10,0) produces inversionally related forms of the set-type 6-34.

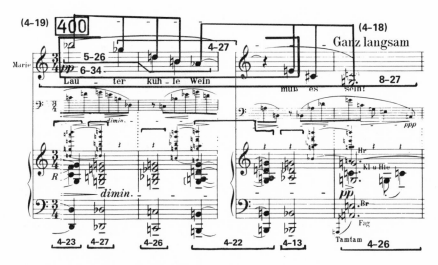

Example 17a. Act I/Scene 3: mm. 400–03

6-34 (10,6,2,*11*,8,4)

Closing phrase of Marie's Lullaby; the phrase recurs transposed (at t = 10) in the final scene at the moment when one of the children tells Marie's boy that his mother is dead (see Ex. 69, mm. 377–78).

The initial series of the descent—precisely that segment which projects a form of the set-type 6-34—is incorporated untransposed within the larger descending-thirds series that serves as the vocal setting for Wozzeck's reference to Marie's earrings in the drowning scene, Act III/Scene 4 (Ex. 61, mm. 244–46).

The overall importance of the initial and final tetrachords as well as the entire eight-note melodic unit will be discussed at length in chapter 4, where this passage will be placed within the larger context of a motivic chain that originates with the "Abgeblasen" tune from the Interlude connecting Scenes 2 and 3 of Act I (mm. 317–18).

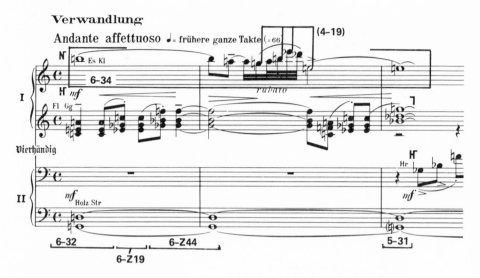

Example 17b. Act I: mm. 656–58

6-34 (*11,9,7,3,1,*4)*

Opening of the Interlude that serves as Prelude to Act I/Scene 5 (the seduction scene).

Scored for E♭ clarinets, the segment that features set 6-34 appears here in the context of Marie's agitated countermotive, juxtaposed with a variant of the Drum Major's rising "fanfare" motive in m. 656 (see Ex. 58). The association with Marie is established when the contour of the countermotive is developed at m. 686, where Marie admires the Drum Major, and at mm. 692–93 as well as at mm. 697–98, where she struggles to tear herself away from him. The entire passage shown in this example reappears in the final Interlude (Act III, mm. 352ff), more thickly orchestrated but at the same transpositional level, with pedal point on the same dyad G♮-D♮.

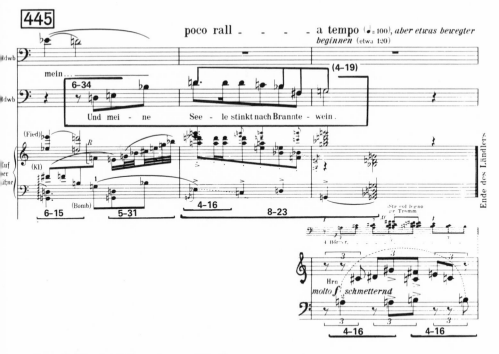

Example 17c. Act II/Scene 4: mm. 445–47

6-34 (2,4,10,0,6,7)

The "brandywine" refrain ("And my soul stinks of brandywine"), introduced by the first apprentice just after the curtain rises upon the first tavern scene (at the end of Scherzo I, the Ländler).

The complete melodic unit returns untransposed at mm. 633–34, where it again serves as the closing phrase of the repeated, varied Scherzo I. As with the melodic shape in which set 6–22 makes its appearance in Example 16b, the "almost whole-tone" set 6-34 is ordered here to accommodate and to reinforce a tonality—in this case the tonality of G minor, established straightforwardly by melody and bass, which just manage to prevail over the "raunchy" (dissonant) inner voices. The choice of tonal center here will be discussed shortly.

Two later occurrences of the "brandywine" refrain in Act II/Scene 5 place the tune—but not the set structure—in association with Wozzeck and the Drum Major. Wozzeck whistles a transposed (t = 5) and slightly altered variant of the tune (the set structure now becomes 6-Z28) at the point where the Drum Major, having finished bragging about his recent conquest of Marie, tries in vain to get Wozzeck to take a drink of schnapps (mm. 784–85). Toward the end of the scene, after the Drum Major has knocked all the wind out of Wozzeck, he rubs in the fact that Wozzeck can himself no longer whistle by mimicking Wozzeck's earlier version of the tune (mm. 802–04).

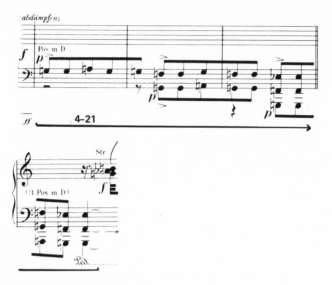

Example 17d. Act II/Scene 1: mm. 93–96

4-21 (7,9,5,3)

Of Wozzeck's three "entrance" themes (the first "entrance" theme [Ex. 28], from Act I/Scene 3, will be discussed in chapter 3), this is the second, coinciding with the beginning of the Development of the sonata-allegro movement that constitutes Act II/Scene 1 (see the detailed analysis of this scene in chapter 4).

The descending whole-tone tetrachord (set 4-21) reappears as a subset of the larger descending statement of set 6-34 that forms the third "entrance" theme in Act II/Scene 2, shown below (Ex. 17e). The pitch-structural connection between the second and the third "entrance" themes is strongly reinforced by means of additional similarities with respect to instrumentation (muted trombones), register, contour, and dramatic function.

Example 17e. Act II/Scene 2: mm. 313–14

6-34 (3,1,11,9,5,8)

This example shows the point at which the third "entrance" theme joins the Doctor's and the Captain's themes (review Examples 1 and 3 respectively) to serve as the third subject of a triple fugue. The fugal procedure will reflect the complex interplay between the Doctor and the Captain as together they administer psychological torture upon the cuckolded Wozzeck.[10]

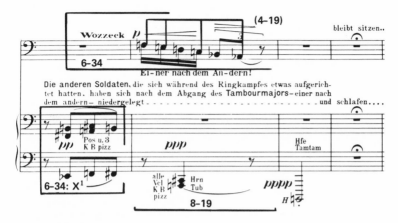

Example 17f. Act II/Scene 5: mm. 812–15

6-34 (5,4,2,0,10,8)

This excerpt is from the last moment of Act II, where, "one after another" ("Einer nach dem Andern"), the soldiers fall back to sleep, having indifferently watched the Drum Major humiliate Wozzeck, knock him to the ground, and then crash his way out the door.

Whereas the descending "almost whole-tone" feature of the preceding "entrance" themes becomes associated with the oppression of psychological abuse from the Doctor and the Captain, here it summarizes physical as well as emotional injury. With respect to the formal and dramatic design, this is—both literally and figuratively—an "exit" rather than an "entrance"; once again, however, equivalent set structures in coordination with similarities of register and contour establish a cohesive link between musical events separated in time but clearly connected by virtue of their relationship to the unfolding drama.

The excerpts presented above by no means exhaust the number of representations of the "almost whole-tone" hexachords that I have found in *Wozzeck*. From nearly six hundred examples, many of which take the form of vertical structures (e.g., see the vertical segments in m. 31 of Example 15b and in m. 59 of Example 15c above), the ones chosen for the present discussion have been *only* those melodic statements that become thematically associated with a specific character or other extramusical element, that dominate an entire scene or large section, and/or that occur in more than one scene of the opera. Of these, ten (excluding my Examples 15c, 15g, 17a, 17c, and 17f) have been discussed briefly by George Perle, who makes the following three outstanding observations: (1) a specific five-note whole-tone collection of pitch classes—G♮-A♮-B♮-C♯-D♯ (7, 9, 11, 1, 3)—is shared by six of Perle's ten examples (see the asterisks placed after pc integers in the examples above); (2) nine of Perle's examples together with his "principal referential chord" (the cadential component labeled X in my Examples 10 through 12 above) point to the fact that "of the two discrete whole-tone scales that together generate the twelve pitch classes [i.e., the hexachords ⌊C♮-D♮-E♮-F♯-G♯-A♯⌋ and ⌊D♭-E♭-F♮-G♮-A♮-B♮⌋], one . . . has distinct priority over the other throughout the work" (Perle 1967a, pp. 240–42; see also Perle 1962, 3d. ed. [1972], pp. 38–39); (3) that specific whole-tone "scale"—the hexachord ⌊D♭-E♭-F♮-G♮-A♮-B♮⌋—is represented in its entirety within the eight-note cadential figure that appears at the end of each act.

The reader may quickly examine these three points by comparing the integers and pitch classes displayed in Example 18 with those italicized and asterisked in Examples 15 through 17 above:

Example 18. Act I/Scene 5: m. 715

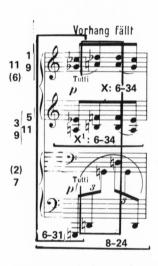

The fact that Perle does not acknowledge intervallic-structural differences among the three types of "almost whole-tone" hexachords is justified largely by his point (1) above and, to a lesser extent, by the apparent interchangeability of these distinct set-types, with the result that variety is achieved within the broader domain of the "almost whole-tone" group. Thus the first three excerpts included in Example 15 show an interlocking presentation of sets 6-21 and 6-34, and from Examples 15a through 15c to 15d and 15e we see the emergence of a "framing" element for the first and last scenes of Act I, accomplished by references to the opening theme of the opera (segment C) in the last scene, but disguised by a series of thematic transformations in which first the rhythm, then the contour, and finally the set structure itself is changed, with 6-34 taking the place of 6-21. On the other hand, once the extraordinary overall importance of the "odd-numbered" whole-tone series D♭-E♭-F♮-G♮-A♮-B♮ (1, 3, 5, 7, 9, 11) has been established, it is possible, with the aid of set-analytic procedures, to reach toward a more precise statement about certain crucial details of motivic construction. For instance, the reader will observe from the excerpts presented above that, generally speaking, whereas sets 6-21 and 6-22 are placed in association with subsidiary characters (Ex. 15c, the Captain; Ex. 15f, the Doctor; Ex. 15g, the tavern crowd and Margret with Wozzeck; Ex. 16a, Andres), set 6-34—the structure that gains special significance by virtue of its double presence in the 8-element cadential structure (Ex. 11)—is made prominent in motives especially associated with the central characters Wozzeck and Marie (Examples 17a through 17f). This observation will be much further substantiated as we proceed with our survey of pitch materials associated with Wozzeck and Marie (chapters 3 and 4) toward a statement in set-complex terms (chapter 5) about the role of set 6-34 in relationship to several "families" of pitch structures—"families" that help to characterize Marie and Wozzeck and distinguish these two from less important figures.

IV

Having now examined a wide range of material from *Wozzeck* in which set 6-34 distinguishes itself from the other "almost whole-tone" set-types as a prominent pitch structure, let us return briefly to examine the specific pitch-class content—G♮-D♮-F♮-B♮-D♭-A♮—of the cadential statement of set 6-34 designated as "the principal referential chord" (segment X in Examples 10–12). It was mentioned above that the 5-element whole-tone subset of "the principal referential chord" is the "odd-numbered" rather than the "even-numbered" series. We have seen, moreover, that the specific pitch-class content of "the principal referential chord" is the cumulative collection of pitch classes that results from a gradual verticalization, at prominent cadential points in Act I/Scene 1, of the three motivic components introduced in m. 6, at the very beginning of the opera (Ex. 3, segment L). These three components— (*a*) the singleton D♭/C♯, (*b*) the tritone B♮-F♮, and (*c*) the perfect fifth G♮-D♮, to which a sixth pitch, the A♮, is added at the end of the scene (Ex. 10)—gain motivic and referential significance as the opera progresses.

With foreknowledge of this aspect of the large-scale motivic design, we are alerted to the importance of examining the specific pitch-class content as well as the total interval content of pitch structures, especially whenever certain pitch classes are given priority as invariant subsets or by other means of reiteration in coordination with special orchestrative and/or registral treatment. The following preview of the long-range motivic significance of each of the three components that compose "the principal referential chord" is provided now in order to facilitate consideration of specific pc content throughout the rest of this study. Because the discussion below is meant to be a preview, the reader will frequently be sent ahead to examples that will be examined in greater detail later. Though many of the references I shall make to the score are represented by example elsewhere in this work, the obvious problem of space prevents me from reproducing every excerpt I cite below. Here, then, and only here, the reader who may wish to check each reference will need the complete score.

a) Wozzeck's association with the C♯/D♭ in Scene 1 is adumbrated at mm. 5–6, established at mm. 25–28, and confirmed at each repetition of the "Jawohl" motive. This pitch class dominates the Pavane by serving as its point of departure (Ex. 15b, m. 30), as pedal point (mm. 34–37), and as destination (mm. 47–50); it figures in the trill of the solo viola (Ex. 15c, mm. 61–62) when the opening theme (segment C) reappears at the end of Cadenza I; in the Gigue (mm. 76–79, 90–98) as well as in Wozzeck's Aria (Ex. 24, mm. 136–37; see also mm. 151–53), the C♯ returns as a pedal point, with the rhythmic figure from m. 3 now obstinately reiterated and then augmented. For other indications that C♯/D♭ is the single most important pitch class in Scene 1, the reader may examine the score at mm. 41, 123–24, and 147.[11] Although the motivic domain of the C♯/D♭ is in general restricted to Act I/Scene 1, its referential function is given a startling new dimension when this same pitch class reappears as the single recitative-note for Marie's outburst, "Lieber ein Messer in den Leib (als eine Hand auf mich)" (Act II/ Scene 3, mm. 395–96: "Better to have a knife in my body [than your hand on me]"), and for Wozzeck's ominous reply, "'Lieber ein Messer'. . . ."

b) In Act I/Scene 1 the descending tritone F♮-B♮ is a prominent figure in the vocal part of the Captain (see mm. 6, 40, 48–49, 56, 163, 167, 169–70); although that part is in general strongly characterized by descending tritones at all other pitch levels as well (mm. 18, 20, 24–25, 30–31, 39, 52, 110, 134, 156, 158–59, 160), the tritone F♮-B♮ is given preeminence by virtue of the fact that it originates as a motive in the Captain's theme itself (Ex. 3, m. 4) and is especially featured in reiterations of that theme (e.g., see Ex. 5, mm. 48–49) as well as in recurrences of segments that form set 5–28. Observe that this tritone is exposed as a discrete vertical unit in segment L′ (Ex. 5) by doublings and by the delayed entrance of the flutes in a registral area above that of the rest of the chord. See also mm. 32–33, 45, 59–60 (Ex. 15c), 91–96, 103, 123–24, 145, and 149, where pitch classes B♮ and F♮ mark the outer registral boundaries or, as in segment L′, form the uppermost or lowermost interval of prominent vertical structures.

In Act I/Scene 1 the tritone F♮-B♮ would appear to be associated with the Captain. Later, however, the referential domain of that tritone is tremendously expanded by its prominence (1) in the Drum Major's "fanfare" music (Ex. 58: Act I, m. 330); (2) in the motive for Marie's "waiting" (Ex. 28: Act I, m. 425); (3) at the point where the Drum Major first enters (Ex. 56: Act I, mm. 665–66); (4) in the Doctor's theme (Ex. 1: Act II, m. 171); (5) in Wozzeck's "entrance" theme of Act II/Scene 2 (Ex. 17e: mm. 313–14; see also mm. 273–74); (6) in the murder scene (Ex. 73: Act III, mm. 73–74; Ex. 74: Act III, mm. 97–102; Ex. 43: Act III, m. 103; see also Act III, mm. 80 and 87); (7) in the drowning scene (Act III, mm. 232–34); and (8) in the 8-element structure that serves as final chord for the three acts (Examples 11 and 69). Since the larger pitch structures referred to at (1), (2), (3), and (8) above all reappear as motives in more than one scene of the opera at fixed pitch-class levels that preserve the pitch-class invariants B♮ and F♮, the preeminence of that tritone can hardly pass unnoticed by the trained listener and the analyst.

In George Perle's view, "the priority of B-F is asserted . . . often as a means of reaffirming the dramatic, as well as the musical, 'keynote' of the opera" (Perle 1967a, p. 212).[12] For Werner König, the tritone B♮-F♮ is "the fate interval, the interval of the tormented creature," one whose "pitch relationship can recall a music-historical tradition (mi contra fa est diabolus in musica)" (König 1974, p. 103).[13] Perle's and König's positions gain strength in view of the fact that in the murder scene (Act III/Scene 2), described by Berg (1929) as an "Invention on a single pitch" (*Invention über einen Ton*), one member of the tritone—the pitch class B♮—sounds throughout every measure in fulfillment of its role as an ostinato that represents Wozzeck's obsession with killing Marie. For a premonition of the murder, Berg points to the end of Act II (Ex. 17f), where, one at a time, each of the eight pitches of the final chord is removed until only the B♮ is left just after the point at which Andres sees that Wozzeck is bleeding and Wozzeck mutters, "Einer nach dem Andern!" ("One after the other!").

If one member of the "fateful" tritone is exploited in special association with Wozzeck, who is fatally bound to Marie and must in the end destroy her, the other member of the tritone—the F♮—may be said to play a similar role in relation to Marie. In Marie's Bible-reading scene (Act III/Scene 1), just before the murder (see the discussion of Ex. 50 in chapter 4), Marie tells her boy a gruesome fairy tale about a poor child who "has no father and no mother" ("und hatt' kein Vater und keine Mutter"). The musical setting for the fairy tale (mm. 33–41) is one of only two sections of the opera in which a tonality is made unequivocal and reinforced by a key signature (for the other section, see Ex. 16b); the tonal center for Marie's fairy tale is F minor.[14]

Douglas Jarman has drawn attention to the fact that "the complementary note F is emphasized by both the vocal and the orchestral parts throughout the scene of Wozzeck's own death, Act III, sc. 4" (Jarman 1979, p. 48). Significantly, the fundamental event of the scene—Wozzeck's drowning—presents itself as the apparent outcome of Wozzeck's desperation to recover and then sink the murder weapon, the supporting evidence of his guilt (mm. 253–54: "Das Messer verrät mich!" ["The knife betrays me!"]). Before finding the knife, Wozzeck stumbles upon Marie's corpse itself. If the ostinato B♮ of Act III/Scene 2 represents Wozzeck's obsession with murdering Marie, the ostinato idea of Act III/Scene 4 now underlines Wozzeck's obsession that he has in fact committed that crime. I suggest that the all-pervasive hexachord of the drowning scene, whose fixed vertical arrangement and spacing at $t = 0$ is such that the complementary F♮ predominates as its highest pitch class (see Examples 22 and 23), reinforces the association of the F♮ with Marie by underscoring the inescapable evidence of her death, evidence that in turn exacerbates Wozzeck's need to drown out guilt (mm. 275–77: "Aber ich muss mich waschen. Ich bin blutig" ["But I must wash myself. I am bloody"]).

c) The reader will notice that in both segments L and L' (Examples 3 and 5) the third component—the perfect fifth G♮-D♮—defines the lowest register of the chord, with G♮ serving as bass foundation. This dyad appears as a pedal point in the same low register at the beginning of the *Andante affettuoso* (Ex. 17b) that serves as Prelude to Act I/Scene 5—the scene in which the Drum Major seduces Marie. There G♮ and D♮ are held by low strings and winds throughout six of the ten measures preceding the entrance of the Drum Major.[15] The same pedal point reappears at the end of the scene, where it functions as a framing device while providing a foundation for the 8-element structure with which Act I as well as Acts II and III will be concluded. Here, as at the beginning of Act I/Scene 5 and also at the end of the opera, the perfect fifth G♮-D♮ creates a semblance of tonal and dramatic stability despite the fact that the oscillating tetrachords in the upper register produce strong dissonances against the perfect fifth, while the only dramatic stability ultimately to be achieved is the stability accomplished in death.

Four more examples support evidence that the dyad G♮-D♮ not only refers to Marie-with-Drum Major but also in general plays a stabilizing role intentionally reminiscent of the role of the perfect fifth in tonal literature:

1. Andres's Song (Ex. 16a) pretends to be a folk song that begins in G

major but slides more and more "out-of-key" as Andres grows at first more rhapsodic, later more uneasy; the opening pitches of his song form the diatonic tetrachord set 4-22, and the initial upbeat and downbeat are D♮ and G♮.[16]

2. Marie's Lullaby in Act I/Scene 3 (Ex. 46) returns transposed and rhythmically altered to serve as her Gypsy Song in Act II/Scene 1 (Ex. 62); again, for one measure, the tonality promises to be G major and the opening pitches of the melody are G♮ and D♮.

3. The Ländler that functions as Interlude before the tavern scene of Act II is written to sound like the product of an amateur village orchestra whose members enjoy having a few drinks "on the job." The first two measures (Ex. 55: Act II, mm. 412–13) provide a hearty V-i harmonic progression in G minor, with 'cellos and bassoons supplying the fundamental bass pitches D♮ and G♮. As the dance continues, the high strings and winds slide into the key of E♭ major while the accompanying horns and lower strings remain in G minor. A middle section featuring strings, harp, and celesta is interrupted by bombardon and accordion, now heard from onstage as the curtain rises (these play the first two measures of the "onstage" Minuet from *Don Giovanni* as a warm-up); now the entire onstage orchestra accompanies two drunken apprentices toward a salutatory V-i cadence in G minor (Ex. 17c), with pitch classes D♮ and G♮ in the bombardon again controlling the progression.

4. At the opening of Act III (Ex. 50), where Marie struggles toward repentance as she associates her own situation with the story of Mary Magdalene from the Bible, the set structure of the first thematic component is not as important as the fact that all the pitches presented in the first two measures are diatonically related to the key of G minor; again, the initial pitches are G♮ and D♮. This time the composer turns to the tonal tradition in order to portray Marie's ingenuous, utterly sincere expression of traditional religious belief.

Like the final Interlude (see Ex. 16b), the four passages cited above are intended for dramatic reasons to bear a short-lived resemblance to tonal passages; at the same time the incorporation of pitch components that originate in nontonal contexts permits these passages to be linked with otherwise disparate and temporally remote events.

Finally, a promise will be made concerning that sixth pitch class—the A♮—which, when added at the end of Act I/Scene 1 to the three components discussed above, creates the fixed collection designated as "the principal referential chord." In chapter 4 we shall see that the A♮ becomes inextricably associated with Marie.

V

Our survey of the long-range motivic functions of three specific pitch components included in "the principal referential chord" has been provided as a supplement to the foregoing examination of prominent pitch structures and relationships introduced in Act I/Scene 1 that will have motivic significance throughout the opera. Of those analytical concepts that may be described as "pitch-class set-theoretic," only the most fundamental have been employed thus far: with the procedure of segmentation followed by determination of pitch-class set names, we have compared pitch structures that are identical with respect to total pitch-class content or equivalent under transposition or inversion, and we have examined invariant subsets shared by equivalent sets as well as by sets related in point of structural similarity and formal, motivic, or thematic function. In the closing section of this chapter, one final concept fundamental to the set-analytic method will be introduced—the notion of the complement relation.

The examples to follow are the first of many that will attest to the importance of the complement relation in the organization of pitch structures over both short and long time spans in *Wozzeck*. The excerpts shown in Example 19, from the orgiastic finale following the close of the curtain after the first tavern scene (Act II/Scene 4), illustrate the notion of complementation at its simplest. Segment J, the oboe line at m. 697, is a five-note ostinato figure that gives way at m. 705 to a seven-note figure, labeled K; the latter is introduced forte and *col legno* by violins in ostinato above an increasingly excited reprise of the waltz chain (see the first appearance of the waltz at mm. 481ff). The reader will note that segment K consists of all the pitch classes in the twelve-pitch-class system that were *not* heard in segment J. In pitch-class set-theoretic terms as presented by Allen Forte (1973a, pp. 73–74), when n pitch classes are selected from the universal set U of twelve pitch classes, the universal set is effectively divided into two sets, the set of n elements selected and the set of $12 - n$ elements not selected. If, as in this case, J represents a set of n elements selected and K represents the $12 - n$ elements that remain after J has been selected, then K is the *complement* of J with respect to U, and J is the complement of K with respect to U; or, with mathematical symbols:

$$J = \overline{K}$$
$$K = \overline{J}$$

(By convention, reference to U is understood.)[17]

Example 19a. Act II: mm. 697–98
(Interlude between Scenes 4 and 5)

J: 5-8 (4,10,8,6,7)

Example 19b. Act II: mm. 704–06 (Interlude between Scenes 4 and 5)

K: 7-8 (1,11,9,0,5,3,2)

For further illustration of the technique whereby complementary pitch structures are juxtaposed by a simple partitioning of the twelve-pitch-class universe, let us return to Act I/Scene 1, the focal point of this chapter. George Perle chooses the sixteen-note triplet figure shown in Example 20 as an instance of "overlapping 'white-note' and 'one-sharp' diatonic collections . . . equivalent in content to the following segment of the cycle of fifths: F-C-G-D-A-E-B-F#" (Perle 1967a, n. 21, p. 241). Since "white-note" collections play a prominent role elsewhere in the opera (the most notable examples are the descending and the ascending C-major scale passages with harp glissando that accompany respectively the descent and the ascent of the curtain at the close of Scene 1 and the opening of Scene 2 in Act II), Perle's observation has significance. Of equal interest, however, is the fact that the first four pitches of the *Hauptstimme* ("principal voice," marked H) in the double basses at mm. 14–15 constitute precisely those four pitch classes *not* included in the eight-pitch-class triplet figure that serves as accompaniment; in other words, the double bass figure in mm. 14–15 is the *literal pitch-class complement* of the triplet accompaniment figure, with the result that the entire set of twelve pitch classes is represented.[18]

Observe that the names of the complementary sets in Example 20 are 8-23 and 4-23; likewise in Example 19 the complement of set 5-8 is 7-8 and vice versa. Except with respect to the list of hexachords, Forte's arrangement of the list of prime forms (appendix 1) provides a direct correspondence be-

Example 20. Act I/Scene 1: mm. 14–17 (Prelude)
J: 8-23 (4,5,11,0,2,9,7,6)
K: 4-23 (3,10,1,8)

tween ordinal numbers of complementary set names, an arrangement that facilitates identification of and reference to complementary pairs. The set names for the fifty distinct hexachords reflect special treatment due to the fact that whereas hexachords which are not Z-related are self-complementary, the complement of a Z-hexachord is its Z-correspondent. For instance, in Example 21 the universal set is again represented, and this time that set results from the union of the two distinct six-note whole-tone scales juxtaposed in adjacent measures. Since both forms of the whole-tone hexachord reduce to the same prime form, these complementary sets have the same set name—6-35, which is to say that set 6-35 is self-complementary.

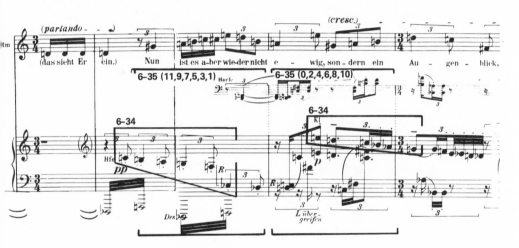

Example 21. Act I/Scene 1: mm. 35–39 (Pavane)

Example 22 shows yet another passage of very short time span where all twelve tones appear (this time not only within a single measure but also sounding simultaneously). The hexachord sustained at mm. 250–51 in the tremolando figure (segment M) has the same total interval content [233241] as that of its literal pc complement (segment $\overline{M}$), interjected by low trumpets and trombones in repeated sixteenths; in this case, however, the set represented at M does *not* reduce to the same prime form as that of the set represented at $\overline{M}$ (i.e., sets M and $\overline{M}$ are not related by equivalence under transposition or inversion). These complementary hexachords will therefore be Z-correspondents; their set names are 6-Z25 and 6-Z47.

Of a number of additional observations that might be made about Example 21, two pertinent to the preceding content of this chapter will be chosen here.

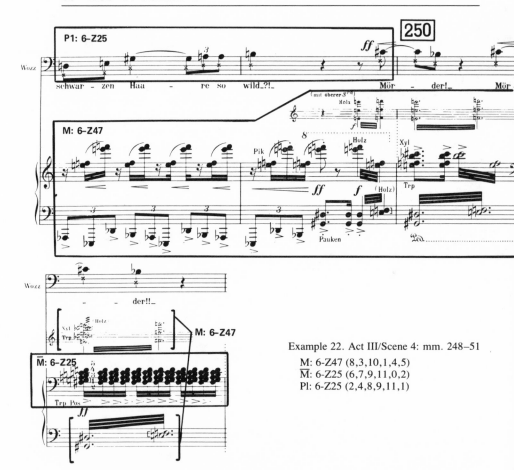

Example 22. Act III/Scene 4: mm. 248–51

M: 6-Z47 (8,3,10,1,4,5)
$\overline{M}$: 6-Z25 (6,7,9,11,0,2)
Pl: 6-Z25 (2,4,8,9,11,1)

First, the lowest-sounding pitch of the scene as a whole, introduced at m. 34 in harp and double basses *tremolando am Steg*, is the motivically pervasive D♭, the pedal point shown here and mentioned earlier. Second, although the juxtaposition of complementary ("even- and odd-numbered") whole-tone segments is a striking aspect of this passage, there is no reason why the "wrong" pitches included in the descending melodic statements by harp and clarinets need to be ignored: in fact the first six pitches of each descent, with a single semitone appearing at the beginning of the first otherwise whole-tone statement and at the end of the second, yield inversionally equivalent forms of set 6-34—the most important of the "almost whole-tone" hexachords discussed in the preceding section.[19]

Example 22 provides an excerpt from the drowning scene (Act III/Scene 4), whose musical form Berg (1929) describes as an "Invention on a hexachord" (*Invention über einen Sechsklang*). It is generally understood that the

matrix hexachord—the alleged source for the pitch materials of this scene—
is the collection whose fixed pitch content is G#-D#-Bb-C#-E♮-F♮ (8, 3, 10,
1, 4, 5) as presented in the tremolo figure labeled M at Example 22. With
one exception, however, writers about *Wozzeck* have evaded the questions of
how and to what extent throughout the scene the composer generated pitch
structures derived specifically from the basic hexachord. The exception is,
of course, George Perle, to whom the reader is referred for a summary of the
means by which changes of transpositional level help to effect a formal division of the scene into three large units (Perle 1967a, p. 220). Perle shows
that along with transposition, the means of derivation of pitch materials from
the single source set include permutation of the vertical disposition of pitch
elements, linearization, and registral displacement. It will be demonstrated
here that inversion and complementation also play a significant role.

With Example 22 we have seen what I continue to call the simplest of
complement relations. Here the composer presents an appropriately "murder-
ous" (see text) "tone cluster" in which the complete twelve-tone universe is
represented by the six pitch classes contained in the basic hexachord (set
6-Z47) juxtaposed with the six pitch classes not contained in that collection
(set 6-Z25). Telegraphically announcing the dynamic and dramatic climax of
the scene, the repeated sixteenth-note figure in the low brass recalls the very
opening of this scene, where the same sixteenth-note figure is used for the
introductory presentation of the basic hexachord M. As shown in Example
23, the repeated sixteenth-note figure in winds and horns at the opening of
the scene is immediately preceded by another rhythmically more complex
repeated-chord figure scored for brass (segment P)—a figure that serves as
link from the preceding Interlude and accompanies the ascent of the curtain.
Let us determine what, if any, relationship segment P has to the basic hexachord M.

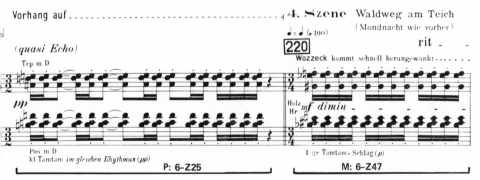

Example 23. Act III: mm. 219–20
P: 6-Z25 (11,0,5,9,2,4)
M: 6-Z47 (10,1,4,8,3,5)

First of all, the vertical "white-note" disposition of segment P prepares for a semitone "resolution" to M in all six voices; note that two pitch classes—E♮ and F♮—are held invariant through an exchange of voices.

Second, although only four out of six pitch classes (i.e., all pitch classes except the E♮ and the F♮) are shared between segment P and segment $\overline{M}$ in Example 22, sets P and $\overline{M}$ are inversionally equivalent [P = T(I($\overline{M}$,11))], so that the set name for both P and $\overline{M}$, the literal pitch-class complement of M, is 6-Z25.

The question is, since P is equivalent to $\overline{M}$, and $\overline{M}$ is the complement of the basic hexachord M, can we regard P also as a complement of M, even though P is not its literal pitch-class complement? From both logical and musical points of view, the answer appears to be affirmative. Admittedly, to accept as complement of a given set not only the literal pc complement of that set but also any transposed or inverted-and-transposed form of the literal complement is to extend the mathematical notion of complementation beyond its definitional boundaries; within the specific realm of pitch-class set theory, however, the extension is entirely consistent with the definition of equivalent sets. From a musical viewpoint, the complementary relationship between segments P and M in Example 23 and between segments M and $\overline{M}$ in Example 22 is highlighted by audible similarities between these two passages with respect to rhythmic-motivic setting and instrumentation. Note that both at the opening of the scene (Ex. 23) and later at the climax (Ex. 22) the pitch structure that is the complement of the basic hexachord is given to the brass; note also, however, that whereas at the beginning of the scene we hear the continuous sixteenth-note figure from the wind choir at mezzo forte, later we are bombarded by the same figure now scored for the more powerful low brass at fortissimo. Thus the first complementary pitch structure (P), presented as a "quasi Echo" at the ascent of the curtain, fulfills its role with the appearance of the second, literal pc, complement ($\overline{M}$), which enters at the climax with an explosion that seems dynamically and dramatically to mirror the goal of Wozzeck's mental journey: obsessed at the beginning of the scene predominantly with retrieving his murder weapon, Wozzeck grows ever more guilt-ridden and terrified until, stumbling upon Marie's body, he must now shout forth his crime in new and tragic realization of its magnitude.

On the basis of a detailed pitch-class set analysis of the drowning scene, it must be stressed that complementary forms of the basic hexachord do not appear with regularity throughout. Nevertheless, for one further illustration that the notion of complementation as defined above offers a convincing explanation for the choice of some pitch structures otherwise not accounted for as components of the basic hexachord, see the collection of pitches that forms Wozzeck's *Sprechstimme* ascent to the melodic climax in Example 22: this collection (2, 4, 8, 9, 11, 1) includes three pitch classes (2, 9, 11) not contained in the basic hexachord; however, the collection is a form of set 6-Z25, and thus its relationship to the basic hexachord set 6-Z47, is complementary.[20]

From the wealth of material in *Wozzeck* where complement relations play a vital role, the excerpts from the "Invention on a hexachord" have been chosen here because that basic hexachord itself shares an interesting structural relationship with fundamental material from Act I/Scene 1. Perhaps because Perle does not always examine sets that are related by inversion, he concurs with others who assume that the primary hexachord of Act III/Scene 4 is exploited *only* in that scene. On the one hand, to my knowledge it is true that the specific collection of pitch classes to which Perle refers—our hexachord M as shown in Examples 22 and 23—does not figure elsewhere in the opera but rather has been "saved" for its unique role in the drowning scene. It is also a fact, however, that transposed and inverted forms of the set-type of which that collection is representative—set 6-Z47—are featured throughout the opera. As with almost all of the pitch materials chosen for discussion in this chapter, a role of long-range significance is established for this set-type by virtue of its association with a prominent, often-recurring motive introduced at the very beginning of the work. Returning once again to the first example of this chapter (Ex. 3), the reader will discover that the first six pitch classes of the Captain's theme produce an inverted form of set 6-Z47. [The set-structural relationship of the Captain's theme (segment G) to the basic hexachord M is: $G = T(I(M),9)$.] Return also to Example 20, where, as mentioned by note, another form of set 6-Z47 suggests that the melodic statement in 'cellos and double basses represents an esoteric "development" of the Captain's theme. The set structure of the melodic statement in Example 20 is an elementary transposition of the Captain's set [T(G),2] that, notably, preserves the first three pitch classes (6, 8, 1) of the Captain's theme as common tones.

From the examples of complement relations examined thus far, we can observe that in short time spans complementary pitch structures tend to be juxtaposed as discrete musical units that are made recognizable one from the other (by such contrasts as those of instrumentation, articulation, register, and/or rhythm) but that also "complement" each other with respect to function (e.g., ostinato figures [Ex. 19], tune-and-accompaniment [Ex. 20]) and/ or rhythmic-motivic detail. In short, complementation tends to interact with other dimensions of musical construction. Presumably, then, the complement relation can reinforce other, more predictably audible relationships. How is this accomplished? One answer may be provided by reference to a special property of complement-related pc sets—a property that concerns interval class and is displayed accordingly by the interval vector.

The reader will recall that hexachords which are not Z-related are self-complementary, while sets of the same cardinality that are Z-correspondents have the same total interval content. It follows that any pair of complement-related hexachords (Z-related or otherwise) will share the same interval vector. This is to say, for instance, that the pitch structures represented by each member of the pair 6-Z25/6-Z47 in Examples 22 and 23 produce duplications of one and the same "package" of interval-class relationships, displayed by the single vector [233241]; likewise, the corresponding self-complementary occurrences of the whole-tone set 6-35 in Example 21 produce sequential statements of the same total number of each interval class, represented by the vector [060603]. Now let us compare interval vectors for complement-related sets that are *not* hexachords (i.e., that do not have the same cardinality):

(from Example 19:)   (from Example 20:)

5-8 [232201]   4-23 [021030]
7-8 [454422]   8-23 [465472]

Notice that every entry in the vector for 7-8 except the entry for ic6 is greater than the corresponding entry in the vector for 5-8 by precisely 2; likewise, every entry in the vector for 8-23, with the exception of the entry for ic6, is greater than the corresponding entry in the vector for 4-23 by precisely 4. This invariant correspondence, first documented by Lewin (1959, 1960) and then by Babbitt (1961), is formulated by Forte as follows: "The arithmetic difference of corresponding vector entries for complement-related sets is the same as the difference d of the cardinal numbers of the sets, with the exception of the entry for ic6, in which case d must be divided by 2 (since 6 is its own inverse mod 12)" (Forte 1973a, p. 77). Or, in simpler terms, the complement of a set can be regarded "as a reduced or enlarged replica of that set" (p. 78). Thus in Examples 19 and 20, where the juxtaposition of literal pc complements produces maximum variety with respect to pitch class, that same juxtaposition permits the larger of the complement-related pitch collections in each example to be maximally similar, though not identical, to the smaller collection with respect to distribution of total interval content; or, more simply, despite the fact that the larger collection in each example is comprised of an entirely different group of pitch classes from that of the smaller collection, the larger collection constitutes an enlarged replica of the smaller collection from an intervallic point of view. As a result, both audible contrast and a fundamental interval-class similarity between contiguous but discrete musical units is provided in support of the overall musical design.

When we proceed in chapters 3 and 4 to our examination of the "families" of pitch structures and their complements that are especially associated with Wozzeck and with Marie, we shall see that the large-scale motivic scheme is reinforced by complementary replications of temporally remote pitch structures over long time spans. For now, one final example will suffice to illustrate that on the foreground as well as on the long-range level complementation is a characteristic structuring device in *Wozzeck* that, like all other aspects of pitch organization discussed in this chapter, manifests itself at the very beginning of the work.

For one last time, then, the reader is asked to return to Example 3, where, with a glance at segments F and L in respectively the third and sixth measures of Act I/Scene 1, he will be reminded that our point of departure in this chapter concerned the role of set 5-28 as a cadential and initial structure that ultimately serves as foundation for the larger cadential figure at the close of each act. Our analysis of the role of set 5-28 led directly to a study of the larger set, 6-34, within which set 5-28 is absorbed at the final cadence of Act I/Scene 1. This in turn led to a survey of other prominent melodic statements that feature one or more of the "almost whole-tone" sets—6-34, 6-21, and 6-22; the first melodic statement of this kind to be presented was the opening linear statement of the opera—the oboe melody (segment C) that begins with the upbeat to m. 2. Having determined the structure formed by the first six pitch classes of that theme (set 6-21) and by the complete collection of m. 2

(set 6-34), let us now look at the entire seven-note series from the beginning of the oboe theme to the downbeat of m. 3. As indicated in Example 3, the set name for that larger collection (0, 1, 3, 11, 9, 7, 6) is 7-28, which the reader will recognize as the name for the complement of 5-28. We may observe, then, that the first linear statement of the opera shares an intimate intervallic relationship with that specific five-note collection (m. 6, segment L [set 5-28]) whose long-range importance has been firmly established. It may now be asserted, moreover, that the final chord of m. 3 (segment F) not only punctuates the end of the first phrase of the opera but also provides a tersely "compressed" (reduced) vertical intervallic replica of the oboe melody.

For the reader who may at this point be persuaded that Berg's choice of pitch collections exhibits a remarkable, perhaps even fanatic, control of interval-class and pitch-class relationships, a few closing observations about the Introduction to Act I/Scene 1 (Ex. 3, mm. 1–3) will be offered. First, all but two pitch classes—C♮ and F♯—participate as notated pitch components of the large musical unit Q formed by the union of segments A and B—the opening two chords with glissando, drum roll, and cymbal; immediately thereafter, the "missing" C♮ appears as the first note of the introductory theme, and the F♯ is "saved" to serve as first attack in the bassoon. The bracket beneath the upper staff of m. 1 calls attention to the fact that from the very outset of the opera the so-called "fate interval" B♮-F♮ makes an appearance as the linear statement in the second violin part. Next, vertical brackets in the first measure indicate that (a) the total pitch content (5, 9, 2, 11, 1, 3) in the upper staff (first and second violins) reduces to yet another form of set 6-21, the set that will be directly restated by the oboe, with four pitch classes (1, 3, 9, 11) held invariant; and (b) the total pitch content (4, 10, 7, 8) in the lower staff (violas and 'cellos) reduces to set 4-12, a set structure that reappears not only as a linear statement in the bassoon part beginning at m. 2 (the first four pitches of segment D (6, 9, 5, 3)—no pitch classes held invariant), but also as the composite segment (4, 10, 6, 7) shown by the box in m. 3. The appearance of sets 6-21 and 4-12 as consecutive linear statements, the first articulated as a discrete unit, the second as an initial sub-unit, and each stated by a single instrument, lends support to the segmentation into "upper" and "lower" sub-units at m. 1 and suggests an amazingly compact organization of pitch materials. But since this segmentation may be the most controversial one examined thus far, the doubtful reader is asked to reconsider Example 15c, from mm. 58 to 65 of Act I/Scene 1. In the expanded ritornello version of the opening phrase of the opera presented here, the set structure of the "lower" sub-unit from m. 1—4-12—is especially isolated and exposed at m. 61 as a pizzicato punctuation in the solo viola. From the set-structural viewpoint this whimsical vertical gesture is placed precisely where it "belongs" within the expanded introductory phrase—immediately after the horizontal expansion of segments A and B (the opening chord-pair) has been completed.

Should the reader wonder why those vertical segments A and B (sets 5-20 and 5-30) in m. 1 have been ignored thus far, he may rest assured that the outstanding long-range significance of these pitch structures will be made evident as we turn now to a study of materials associated with Wozzeck and Marie.

3 BERG'S CHARACTERIZATION OF WOZZECK: THE FAMILY OF SETS ASSO-CIATED WITH THE CENTRAL CHARACTER

With the modest but carefully chosen battery of analytical techniques presented in chapter 2, we are now prepared to survey in closer detail set structures that are clearly associated with specific characters of the opera. In a general sense it is hoped that this investigation will reinforce the argument that a study of set structures and relationships can shed new light on the richness of Berg's well-known leitmotivic scheme and his large formal plan. More specifically, the information presented in this and the next chapter constitutes a study of motivic functions assigned to certain sets and "families" of closely related sets. In chapter 5 the notion of the set complex will be introduced as a summary means of demonstrating that families of sets actively help to delineate character and thus play a remarkable role in the overall dramatic design.

Since the subject of motivic-thematic elements of the opera has been more than adequately covered by others (see my citations at the end of chapter 1 and in chapter 2, note 1), the reader is reminded that my emphasis continues to be placed upon relationships among pitch combinations—collections that appear as components of motives and themes but also exert an influence beyond those domains and thus create underlying harmonic and dramatic connections hitherto unexplored. A study of associations between set structures and characters nevertheless begins with an examination of motives and themes easily identifiable as representative of specific characters by virtue of repeated association. That task was begun in chapters 1 and 2, where we examined the pitch content of: the Doctor's theme (Ex. 1) and two figures also associated with that character (Examples 2 and 15f);[1] the Captain's theme (Ex. 3, segment G) and the aspect of the descending tritone that characterizes his melodic material in Act I/Scene 1; the opening phrase of Andres's Song from Act I/Scene 2 (Ex. 16a); material from the seduction scene associated with Marie and the Drum Major (Examples 15d, 15e, 17b); the closing phrase of Marie's Lullaby (Ex. 17a); Wozzeck's C#/Db-motive (Examples 3, 4, 5; Ex. 10) and two of his "entrance" themes (Examples 17d and 17e). Although in chapter 2 we were primarily concerned with recurring set structures that have cadential and melodic functions throughout the opera, we also saw the special role that set 6-34 plays in association with the main characters Marie and Wozzeck, a role that contrasts with the predominance of the other "almost whole-tone" hexachords 6-21 and 6-22 in melodic material relating to subsidiary characters. We shall be in a much stronger position to assess the importance of these distinctions in the long-range harmonic organization once we have given greater attention to the character Wozzeck, to his role in the dramatic design, to the configuration of subsidiary characters surrounding Wozzeck, and to the nature of the material directly associated with him.

I

No one who knows Alban Berg's opera *Wozzeck* or Georg Büchner's drama *Woyzeck* would question the appropriateness of either title as an indicator that the character Wozzeck/Woyzeck occupies the central dramatic position and represents the fundamental social and philosophical issues of the work. Büchner's choice of central character and the formal design he seems to have intended for establishing that centrality constitute a breakthrough in the history of German theatre. For circumstantial reasons the originality and "impropriety" of the unfinished *Woyzeck* (1837) passed unnoticed for more than half a century;[2] when the play was finally staged for the first time in Munich in 1913, it created a flurry of interest among the German Expressionists and has since been celebrated by all sectors of the avant-garde as a predecessor and kindred spirit. Today many assert "without hesitation or qualification that *Woyzeck* has had more influence on modern German drama than any other play of the nineteenth century" (Benn 1976, p. 262). In fact:

Büchner's finest, most original and most revolutionary play was so far in advance of its own time, so far out of phase with the modes of drama which commanded the stage throughout most of the nineteenth century, that the history of its reception and influence may be said to begin with the regeneration of the German drama in the last decade of the nineteenth century. [Richards 1977, p. 149.]

It is currently held that in 1837 Büchner was the first German dramatist to choose as his central tragic character a subject not only situated in the very lowest social class but also openly drawn from documented information about a real, contemporary person; that person was a soldier named Woyzeck, whose humble rank placed him on the lowest rung of Hessian society.[3] In this as well as in many other respects, and notably from the viewpoint of formal design, Büchner integrates innovations of the earlier *Sturm und Drang* playwright J. M. R. Lenz but moves beyond these toward a new and revolutionary break from the classical theatrical tradition.[4] In the great classical dramas of Schiller, about whose dramatic mode Büchner spoke deprecatingly,[5] formal focus is placed upon the act, and the plot develops linearly, with each scene dependent upon the preceding in a logical progression toward or away from a point of climax (see Schmidt 1969, p. 79). From Büchner's four unfinished drafts for *Woyzeck*, as many as twenty-seven short, unnumbered scenes have been reconstructed without indications for larger formal divisions. Many of these scene fragments seem at first to stand by themselves, begin and end abruptly, and give the impression of "going nowhere."

The absence of acts, the extraordinary number of scenes, their brevity, and their apparent disconnectedness together unquestionably point to an attitude toward form that sets *Woyzeck* apart from the mainstream of European drama in the nineteenth century; but efforts to evaluate Büchner's conception and find a category for *Woyzeck* in the history of theatre are complicated by the fact that at the time of his death the work remained unfinished, possibly to the extent that Büchner had not decided how the final scenes would be ordered or how the play would end:

> Why is it necessary to translate early drafts containing scenes which the author himself later rejected? It cannot be stressed enough that no editor may presume to construct a "final" version of *Woyzeck*. Büchner's second draft, besides being incomplete, contains contradictions which can only be resolved by resorting to his earlier plans. No one can say with authority how Büchner planned to end the play, or how he intended to unify the scene fragments of the second draft. . . . [Schmidt 1969, p. 81.]

Since a consensus cannot be reached concerning the "best" or "intended" arrangement of the scenes, various editors and directors have reordered a number of scenes in a number of different ways; of particular significance here is the fact that *within limits* reorderings can be made without damage to the structural whole.

The current debate among Germanists on the subject of Büchner's formal plan can lend perspective to the question of Berg's formal treatment of the play. For this reason it will be well to examine some recent responses to the view expressed in the above quotation, a view that represents and defends the editorial decisions of Werner Lehmann (see Büchner 1967, 1971), whose critical-historical edition of Büchner's complete works is at the moment admitted even by its critics to be authoritative.

David G. Richards holds that "Büchner had as little use for the classical, Aristotelian dramatic form with its linear, causal plot development . . . as he had sympathy for the idealistic, teleological, and hierarchical *Weltbild* which finds its proper medium in such a dramatic form" (Richards 1977, p. 190). For Richards, then, as for Henry Schmidt (1969), *Woyzeck* is an example par excellence of the "open or episodic form of drama," and it serves in this case as a reflection of Büchner's view that each moment is "important in its own right; life consists of a series of such individual moments, each of which is complete in itself and its own reason for being" (ibid., p. 191). But in light of the fact that Büchner's last draft of the play, containing seventeen scenes, is regarded by Lehmann to be a "preliminary fair copy" (*vorläufige Reinschrift*), Richards also holds that

> even if we were to assume that H4 [Büchner's last draft] was not intended as a final manuscript, it would still be indefensible from an editorial point of view to alter the sequence of the content of the scenes of the manuscript which represents Büchner's last word. An edition or construction [such as Lehmann's] which makes such alterations must be considered an adaptation. [P. 156.]

Richards's position is further based on the opinion that

> whether it be words in a sentence, sentences in a paragraph, or scenes in a play, the sequence of parts in a literary work is as much a determinant of meaning and effect as are the parts themselves. Thus, contrary to the claims of some critics and the practice of many directors, neither the position of the purely episodic scenes nor the sequence of scenes constituting the main action can be altered without changing the work's intended meaning and effect. . . . In *Woyzeck* the sequence of events which begin with Woyzeck's suspicion of Marie's disloyalty and culminate in the murder constitute a basic framework in relation to which the other scenes fall naturally into place. Given with this sequence is a continual and dramatically effective increase of intensity and tension. [P. 194.]

Now compare Richards's position with that of Maurice B. Benn. In respect to *Woyzeck* Benn traces the development of the concepts of "open" and "closed" form, "popularized by Wölfflin in his *Renaissance und Barock*" (Benn 1976, note 57 to chapter 8, p. 303), and stresses the limited usefulness of the term "open": " . . . one has to remember that within such categories there are infinite possibilities of variety and originality, and that this is true also of the 'closed' form of drama" (ibid., p. 304). Benn also objects to the suggestions of others that "the action of the play is circular, that the end is implicit in the beginning":

> The action has rather the form of a spiral ascending to an acme of tragic suffering. It is still legitimate, I think, to regard this as an 'open' form of drama in so far as each scene has its centre of interest within itself— in so far as Büchner presents only the high points of the action without the close continuity of classical drama. But there is nevertheless an architectonic principle shaping the work as a whole. [P. 254.]

Now, it strikes me that the non-contradictory yet distinctive viewpoints individually expressed above can be brought together toward a convincing overview if we clarify Benn's implicit concern for discrete but interdependent levels of formal structure. So far two levels have been probed simultaneously: an immediate level represented by the scenic design and a large-scale background level shaped by an "architectonic principle." On the one hand, no reordering of the twenty-seven fragments can be made without consideration for the fact that Woyzeck's murder of Marie constitutes a climax in the traditional classical sense—a climax that dictates the ordering of certain other events as "preceding" and "subsequent" and makes the overall dramatic effect cumulative. On the other hand, even had Büchner decided to group his scenes into acts, it seems very safe to guess that the scenes themselves would have retained their episodic rather than classical disposition, their "independent" and apparently non-linear rather than "panoramic" and goal-oriented design. Far from representing a lapse of organizational control, this deliberately fragmented *surface aspect* of the underlying architectonic design reflects not only Büchner's anti-teleological position, as expressed by Richards, but also his ultimately pessimistic, deterministic point of view:

> I studied the history of the Revolution. I felt annihilated by the dreadful fatalism of history. I find in human nature a terrible uniformity, in human relations an inevitable force given to all [collectively] and to none [individually]. The individual is only foam on the wave; greatness is simply chance; the rule of genius is a puppet play, a ridiculous struggle against a pitiless law: to recognize it is the ultimate; to control it is

impossible. [From Büchner's letter after 10 March 1834 to his fiancée, in Büchner 1971 (Lehmann edition), pp. 425–26; translation from Richards 1977, p. 12.]

In the near absence of an obviously linear cause-and-effect connection from one scene to the next, dramatic continuity is achieved by the following means. (1) A network of verbal motifs (recurring words and phrases) as well as images, ideas, and rhythms binds the scenes together to effect a unified whole; with each recurrence, motifs "extend the scope of their meaning and accumulate strength and intensity of expression" (Richards 1977, p. 196). (For instance, we have already noted the role in Act I/Scene 1 of the Captain's "Langsam . . . "; this verbal motif returns at the beginning of the Captain-Doctor-Wozzeck scene [Act II/Scene 2 in Berg's opera, Scene 9 in Lehmann's reconstruction of the play] as does the Captain's "guter Mensch" ["good man"] motif, which appears as many as twelve times in these two scenes, thus driving home the Captain's condescending, obsessive nature. Animal imagery plays an outstanding role in Büchner's delineation of Marie's partnership with the Drum Major and in his portrayal of Woyzeck's plight. We have touched upon the "knife" image, and we are about to examine Berg's idiosyncratic treatment of other verbal motifs, images, and ideas, each of which contributes toward continuity in both the play and the opera.) (2) The scenes themselves function as a series of "little actions" that repeat a basic pattern—a pattern of frustration. (3) A thematic bond at once connects each scene with all the others: the subject of the frustrated Woyzeck—the "common man," the "underdog," a tormented creature driven mad by his environment—provides a central unifying theme around which the individual events of the apparently, but not really autonomous scenes are "spaced" as if in a circular pattern.

Delineation of subsidiary characters in juxtaposition with the central figure reinforces the circular design. Three of these characters—the Captain, the Doctor, and the Drum Major—though distinctively drawn and disturbingly concrete, are at the same time portrayed as a group of stock social caricatures, grotesque carnival types whose "ancestors" may be traced back to the *commedia dell'arte* (see Schmidt 1969, p. 109), "elements pressing in on Woyzeck . . . characters from a fable about predatory animals" (Schechner 1969, p. 18); and each is given at least one scene in which to taunt Woyzeck and to play out his puppet-like role in Woyzeck's decline. Thus the Captain—a glib, self-satisfied philistine who chatters on and on but cannot formulate a single clear thought—exploits his rank by bombarding Woyzeck with pompous notions of "morality" ("Moral: das ist, wenn man moralisch ist!" ["Morality: that's when one is moral!"]). The Doctor (modelled after one of Büchner's eccentric professors during his student days at Giessen) reduces Woyzeck to the level of animal by making him the object of his contemptible "scientific experiments." The Drum Major, brainless but brawny, takes from Woyzeck what is his for the having—the woman who is the only good reason for Woyzeck's existence. And Andres, Woyzeck's one friend, hears but cannot comprehend what Woyzeck tries in vain to express.

The simple street language of Woyzeck, who "suffers like an animal, for he lacks the vocabulary to give his suffering expression" (Schmidt 1969, pp. 106–07), contrasts sharply with the elegant language of the classical hero, whom Büchner rejects. Unlike others, Woyzeck has visions, hears voices, and is by conventional standards "abnormal"; plagued by superstitions, he makes the great mistake of attempting to find reasons for things, to invest an incomprehensible universe with purpose. In Büchner's view, efforts of this kind are useless and self-destructive; in coordination with deprivations of the most fundamental nature, these tendencies give Woyzeck an insufferable handicap against the glibness of the really stupid people around him—the complacent middle-class fools who are in control. Just as the events of scenes effect the illusion of a circular pattern around a central theme, so the subsidiary characters behave like a menagerie that surrounds Woyzeck as the one caged animal in the center ring of a three-ring circus.[6] The circular design, sustained on both the formal and the characterizational level, gives exquisite justification to Berg's choice of final scene in the opera, where the townschildren are seen and heard playing the German equivalent of "Ring-around-a-Rosy" with Wozzeck's child now "at the center."[7] In keeping with the unspoken part of the game, which in some versions becomes "All fall down," Wozzeck's child is told that his mother is dead. When the oscillating *moto perpetuo* triplet figure is finally cut off, as if by arbitrary decision on the part of the conductor, we are left with the sense that, whether the dramatic structure is essentially "open" or "closed," whether the action is made circular or given an architectonic, even semi-classical design, we have been caught in an endless repetition of that structure; that is, we are almost convinced by the composer that the opera could very well begin over again and again, and we sense that "the cycle of inhumanity begins anew" (Brustein 1962, p. 236).[8]

Berg had no choice but to prepare his libretto from texts of the play that must now be regarded as first efforts in Büchner scholarship and have since been supplanted by more authoritative versions.[9] In view of the fact that Büchner's conception has grown all the more "contemporary" with historical perspective, it is especially impressive that Berg's opera continues to be regarded as an ideal musical setting of the play.

For reasons made evident in the preceding discussion, Berg's decision to connect Büchner's fragmentary scenes with musical interludes and to group scenes into acts constitutes the most critical divergence from the overall design Büchner apparently intended. Here are some of Berg's own comments on that decision:

> With the very necessity of making a selection from Büchner's 26 loose, in some cases fragmentary scenes for my libretto, hereby avoiding repetitions that did not lend themselves to musical variation, moreover where possible of bringing these scenes together, ordering them, and grouping them into acts, I was confronted with a problem that was more musical than literary—a problem that was only to be solved with the laws of musical architecture and not with those of dramaturgy. [Berg 1928, p. 286.][10]

> And even when I succeeded in finding a three-act plan, in which exposition, peripeteia, and catastrophe were clearly separated into three groups of five scenes, and with which unity of *action* and dramatic closure [completeness] were achieved by force, the *musical* unity and closure were by no means ensured. [From Berg's 1929 lecture, in Redlich 1957a, p. 312.][11]

It must be noted that Berg never questions the "rightness" of giving dramatic closure (*Geschlossenheit*) to his opera by grouping Büchner's fragments into the classical exposition-peripeteia-catastrophe mold. On the basis of our information concerning Büchner, some might question whether Berg fully grasped the non-traditional character of the dramatist's conception; but since we may never know conclusively how or even whether Büchner himself might have arranged his scene fragments within a more sharply defined larger plan, a definitive critical judgment on Berg's decision cannot be made. Berg himself testifies to his dedicated effort "to realize musically the intellectual content of Büchner's immortal drama; to translate his poetic language into a musical one" ("den geistigen Inhalt von Büchners unsterblichem Drama auch musikalisch zu erfüllen, seine dichterische Sprache in eine musikalische umzusetzen"); and "to give to the theatre what is the theatre's" ("dem Theater zu geben, was des Theaters ist") [Berg 1928, pp. 285–86]. Not only for the purpose of making his scenes "rich in variety" ("abwechslungreich"), giving them "musical clarity and memorability" ("musikalische Eindeutigkeit und

Einprägsamkeit"), and avoiding "boredom" ("Langweile"), but also perhaps in order to counteract the "necessary" imposition upon Büchner's fragments of the traditional three-act plan, Berg determines to conform with Büchner's fragmentary scenic design to the extent that each of the fifteen selected scenes must have "its own unmistakable profile as well as a rounded-off completeness" ("sowohl ihr eigenes, unverkennbares Gesicht als auch Abrundung und Geschlossenheit") [ibid., p. 286]. Or, in technical terms, Berg projects the apparent autonomy of each scene by conceiving each as a self-contained formal unit with a distinct set of themes and motives. As a point of departure for my study of Berg's characterization of Wozzeck, I shall briefly attempt to show that in this general formal respect, and in particular respect to Berg's choice and setting of the scenes for Act I, the opera *Wozzeck* demonstrates a remarkable faithfulness to the play *Woyzeck* as it is understood today.

Berg's plan for Act I strongly reinforces the centrality of the character Wozzeck and the formal illusion of a circular pattern around the central theme that Wozzeck represents. It is generally well known that each of the five scenes for Act I is a "character study" that exposes the idiosyncratic world of a single subsidiary character and his unique relationship to the central figure. As with all the other scenes of the opera, each scene of Act I is a self-contained formal unit articulated in part by the interaction of the components of a distinct collection of themes and motives; in Act I these help to underscore the individuality of each of the characters around Wozzeck—the Captain, Andres, Marie, the Doctor, and the Drum Major. As with the scenes of Acts II and III, each scene of Act I contains some motivic-thematic material that will not reappear elsewhere in the opera; and although as many as eight prominent motives from individual scenes of Act I do appear in more than one of the five scenes of this act, these are difficult to recognize on first or even second hearing, since in most cases the degree of transformational "disguise" is great (e.g., review the transformed reappearance of the opening theme of the opera [Examples 3, 15a] in the last scene of the act [Examples 15d, 15e]).

Act I/Scene 2—the scene with Andres and Wozzeck in the open field—is the only scene of the first act from which extended formal units are lifted for varied repetition in later scenes (Scenes 3 and 4) of the same act. Following Perle, who borrows the term from Hugo Weisgall, I shall refer to recurring segments of this kind as *Leitsektionen*—that is, "extended formal units whose referential function is comparable to that of the *Leitmotiv*" (Perle 1964, note 10, p. 183). Now it happens that in Act I/Scene 2, possibly intended by Büchner to be the first scene of his play,[12] the good-natured and ordinary

Andres serves as a foil to Wozzeck, whose extraordinary visions—apocalyptic, full of elemental mystery and terror—alert us for the first time to the fact that the central character is a uncommon man whose mental condition has grown unstable. It is especially significant that the only Leitsektionen of Act I originate in passages from Act I/Scene 2 directly associated with Wozzeck's hallucinations and that these Leitsektionen recur at places in the text where Wozzeck recaptures those fantasies. In an act whose primary dramatic function is to introduce the array of disparate, unrelated figures that surround Wozzeck and constitute the dominating elements of his world, these Leitsektionen fulfill their duty to the drama not only by focusing our attention upon the central character but also by making his unique mental and existential plight the one unifying dramatic theme. The prophetic nature of Wozzeck's hallucinations and the corresponding long-range role of musical materials from these Leitsektionen (see Examples 29, 54, 71, and 72) in relationship to the most prominent motives and pitch-structural features of the opera as a whole will be examined over the course of this and the next two chapters. First, however, we shall see how the unifying theme of Wozzeck's plight is projected by means of pitch structures associated with Wozzeck that permeate virtually every large segment of the opera.

II

Of all the material directly related to the central character, the single most important melodic statement, given utmost prominence by means of salient repetition at points of climax, is the figure with which Wozzeck's Aria begins in Act I/Scene 1 (Ex. 24).

Recalling our discussion of this first scene of the opera in chapter 2, the reader may be able to reconstruct the formal and dramatic situation. In the formal scheme, Wozzeck's Aria appears just after Double II (see Example 9) and just before the retrograde recapitulation of the Prelude; prior to the Aria, the Captain has berated Wozzeck about his "immorality" (Gavotte), Wozzeck has attempted to defend himself (Double I), and the Captain has cut him off, utterly confused (Double II). Now Wozzeck is pressed to express the one fact of his existence that he understands (Ex. 24): "We poor folks!" ("Wir arme Leut!") "You see, Captain—money, money! If you don't have money! Just try to put one of your own kind into this world 'in the moral way!'" ("Sehn Sie, Herr Hauptmann, Geld, Geld! Wer kein Geld hat! Da setz' einmal einer Seinesgleichen auf die moralische Art in die Welt!")

Example 24. Act I/Scene 1: mm. 136–42

The verbal keynote, or motto, of the Aria is Wozzeck's opening statement "Wir arme Leut!", an expression that is given only two literal repetitions among the extant scenes of the play but whose importance as a reminder of the underlying social issue is strengthened by other, more personal references to poverty: (Wozzeck:) "Aber ich bin ein armer Kerl!" ("But I'm just a poor guy!"); (Marie, to her child:) "Bist nur ein arm' Hurenkind . . . " ("You're only a poor whore's child . . . "); (Marie:) "Aber ich bin nur ein armes Weibsbild!" ("But I'm just a poor woman!"); (Wozzeck:) "Herr Hauptmann, ich bin ein armer Teufel!" ("Captain, I'm just a poor devil!"); (Captain, referring to Wozzeck:) "Nur ein Hundsfott hat Courage!" ("Only a son-of-a-bitch has courage!").

Like Manfred Gurlitt, the composer whose setting of *Wozzeck* appeared a few months after Berg's première (14 December 1925), Berg responded to Büchner's keynote "Wir arme Leut!" by treating his musical setting at its first literal appearance as a leitmotif throughout the rest of the opera. According to Schmidt (1969, pp. 115–16), Gurlitt inserts reiterations of the motto at the beginning and the end of his opera and has these intoned as a "universal commentary" by an offstage "Greek chorus." Berg exhibits greater fidelity to the Büchner text inasmuch as he inserts not one single additional statement of the motto within his libretto; instead, having at once established a direct association between the verbal motif and a specific musical setting, Berg reiterates with varying degrees of transformation *not only* the motivic-thematic components of that setting in isolation from the verbal motif *but also* the pitch-structural components of the original motive and theme in isolation from these as well as the verbal motif. He thus frees himself of the need for blatant verbal repetition and at the same time permits the message of the motto to speak throughout the opera: the message has been translated into his own harmonic language. We can begin to see how the process of translation and integration is accomplished by carefully examining the textural and orchestrative features of the first setting for Büchner's motto and comparing these with subsequent settings of the same theme.

The verbal keynote of the Aria, as shown in Example 24, is thrown into relief by an interruptive shift in orchestration from trombones to strings. Beneath the vocal line, low strings now sustain Wozzeck's C#-motive as a pedal point that also serves as the point of departure for an ascending arpeggiated presentation of the three discrete diminished-seventh chords; in this manner the entire pitch-class universe (1, 4, 7, 10; 2, 5, 8, 11; 3, 6, 9, 0) underscores the universality of Wozzeck's statement, and the ascending twelve-tone cycle is completed precisely at the apex (E♮) of Wozzeck's first phrase, where he repeates the word "Geld." The apex delimits that segment of the complete melodic phrase which is ensured thematic closure by means of full recapitulation at four climactic points later in the work: (1) at the central moment of the Aria (mm. 145–46); (2) in the following Interlude (mm. 191–95; 198–200); (3) in the middle (development) section of the sonata-allegro movement (Act II/Scene 1, mm. 114–15); and (4) in the final Interlude (mm. 362–64), just before the last scene of the opera.

At the first of these four climactic points, the central moment of the Aria (see Act I/Scene 1, mm. 145–46), the "Wir arme Leut!" theme is given canonic treatment. At point 2, in the subsequent Interlude, violins recapitulate Wozzeck's theme from mm. 136–37 at the original pitch-class level against the original C♯ pedal point, but now in counterpoint with other material, including the material of the vocal line from m. 141 of the Aria. The verbal keynote reappears along with the melodic theme *only* at point (3), that is, in Act II/Scene 1, where Wozzeck sees drops of sweat on the brow of his sleeping child and remembers that there is nothing in life but work for poor people of his kind; there the canonic setting from point (1), the midpoint of the Aria, is combined with a rescored and compressed but otherwise complete recapitulation of the twelve-tone diminished-seventh-chord series, with the pedal point now on E♭. The restatement of the theme at point (4), in the final Interlude, is a textless recapitulation (rescored) of point (3); here the E♭ pedal point in the bass is interpreted as an upper neighbor that prepares the climactic return to the D-minor tonality with which the final Interlude began (review Ex. 16b). To summarize, the composer avoids not only unnecessary repetitions of the verbal keynote but also exact repetitions of its original musical setting; however, at each of the four varied restatements of the theme, at least one other feature of the original Aria setting—the twelve-tone accompaniment, the canonic texture from mm. 145–46, and/or the text itself—returns to strengthen the association of theme with dramatic message.

For the listener who is at all attuned to thematic development in nineteenth-century operatic literature, the four restatements of the opening melodic theme from the Aria will not be missed. As we move now from the thematic to the motivic and set-structural means by which the verbal "Wir arme Leut!" motif is extended, we approach new levels of structure that are less easily perceived. Let us begin by examining Wozzeck's initial four-note figure in the Aria (Ex. 24), the syllabic setting for "Wir arme Leut!" Apparently in order to maintain a distinction between "*Leitmotiv*" and larger "recurring theme," George Perle (1971, p. 284) includes this figure in his list of twenty Leitmotive even though he finds only one instance in a later scene (Act II/Scene

5, mm. 776–77) where the figure reappears in isolation from its larger melodic context. In the discussion that follows, I intend to show that from a set-structural point of view, the "Wir arme Leut!" figure assumes a motivic function whose domain extends from the first to the last scene of the opera and whose preeminence corresponds to the all-pervasive nature of the dramatic theme it represents.[13]

As shown in Example 24, the set name for the "Wir arme Leut!" motive is 4-19. For easy identification hereafter, the reader may find it useful to remember that this set, with the vector [101310], is one of the only two 4-element sets (the other is set 4-24) that contain the maximum number of ic4 (major thirds, minor sixths). The total interval content of set 4-19 yields a structure sometimes called the "minor triad with added major seventh":

or, literally inverted around an axis pitch, sometimes called the "augmented triad with added major seventh":[14]

Note that the inverted form chosen for display holds three pitch classes—those yielding the augmented triad ⎣3, 7, 11⎦—in common with the form of the set as it first appears with the "Wir arme Leut!" text in Example 24. That inverted form is prominently featured in the closing half of Wozzeck's melodic statement shown in Example 25.

The complete vocal line in this example represents the second of the two melodic ideas that are introduced in the Gavotte and then reiterated, with modifications of rhythm and transpositional level, in both Double I and Double II—the sections of Act I/Scene 1 immediately preceding the Aria. (For the first of these ideas, see Examples 7, 8, and 9 in chapter 2.) Appearing thus melodically five times in the course of the Gavotte, Double I, and Double II, the inverted form of set 4-19 shown in Example 25 underlines the textual relationship that this passage has with the opening statement of the Aria in Example 24. In the Gavotte the Captain, quoting "our Reverend Chaplain" as his authority, has charged Wozzeck with immorality on the grounds that Wozzeck has an illegitimate child. At Example 25 (end of Double I) Wozzeck tries to defend the child by quoting Christ's words in the New Testament: "Suffer the little children to come unto me." Although the child's destiny as an orphan, a victim of tragic circumstances, does not make its impact until the final scene of the opera, the importance of his silent existence—the only bond between Wozzeck and Marie—is already suggested here. In defending him, Wozzeck at first attempts to place the issue of the child's "morality" on a spiritual plane. This enrages the Captain, who dares not question his own "safe" understanding of right and wrong. The Captain's outrage (Double II) provides the link between Wozzeck's spiritual defense at Example 25 and his subsequent Aria statement, shown at Example 24, where Wozzeck is now impelled to try again, this time defending the child from the viewpoint provided by cold, hard material exigency—a viewpoint that only poor people can understand: it's not easy to be moral if you don't have money.[15] The "Wir arme Leut!" set structure in Example 24 now appears as representative of a desperate modification in Wozzeck's position: the inverse relation of this figure to the figure at Example 25 corresponds with the inversion from spiritual to material values that Wozzeck's argument has been forced to undergo.[16]

Example 25. Act I/Scene 1: m. 132

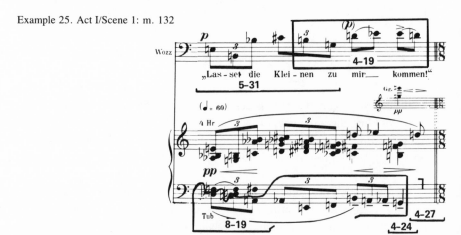

By featuring an inverted form of set 4-19 in the material immediately preceding the Aria statement, the composer subtly prepares the entrance of this statement in a manner that parallels the logical progression of the dramatist toward the utterance that summarizes the social plight of his central character. In coordination with Example 15c from chapter 2, the next example will show that an even earlier preparation for the Aria statement has been made on the part of both dramatist and composer.

With Example 26 we move backwards from the Aria even farther toward the opening of the scene. This example comes from the first of the two Cadenzas, the section that provides the musical setting for the first occurrence of the Captain's above-mentioned verbal motif "Ein guter Mensch . . . " ("A good man . . . "). (Here the reader might wish to review Example 13 and examine the libretto for Act I/Scene 1 and Act II/Scene 1, the two scenes in which the Captain is featured.) Büchner's Captain is drawn as a garrulous, repetitive type whose complacent self-righteousness gives him only illusory control over a more fundamental insecurity; here is a character who needs constantly to reinforce his belief that he is "a good man" by comparing himself favorably with the less fortunate, "immoral" Wozzeck. With each repetition of the "guter Mensch" motif, Büchner further establishes that the Captain's uneasy preoccupation with "morality" has an obsessive quality. Wozzeck poses a threat to the Captain's shaky sense of well-being because Wozzeck does not try to hide his anxiety under the cloak of conventional "good behavior." Just prior to the excerpt in Example 26, the Captain has grown disturbed by Wozzeck's "harassed look" ("Er sieht immer so verhetzt aus!")—unbecoming to "a good man." Curious and uneasy about this "phenomenon" Wozzeck (see the end of Act II/Scene 1, mm. 349–50), the Captain tries to engage him in a ridiculous conversation about the weather (Gigue), which the Captain stages in order to conclude that Wozzeck is "dumb" (m. 97). Then the "guter Mensch" motif returns, highlighted by a modified return (mm. 109–14) of the Cadenza material shown in Example 26. This time the Cadenza serves as preparatory link to the Gavotte, and the function of the "guter Mensch" motif as a preparation for the Captain's harangue about Wozzeck's "immorality" is made explicit: "Wozzeck, Er ist ein guter Mensch,—aber . . . Er hat keine Moral!" ("Wozzeck, you are a good man, but . . . you have no morality!").

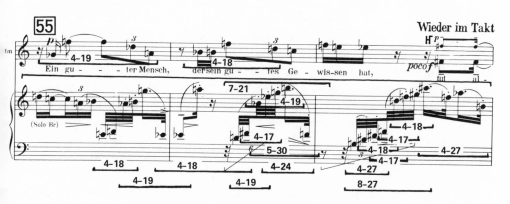

Example 26. Act I/Scene 1: mm. 55–57

A careful examination of the solo viola Cadenza shown in Example 26 reveals that the tetrachordal structure consists of interlocking forms of sets 4-19 and 4-24 in company with 4-18, 4-17, and 4-27—sets whose importance in association with Marie will be discussed in the next chapter. Note that, like the form of set 4-19 shown in Example 25, two of the four forms of this set in mm. 55–56 hold the same three pitch classes—3, 7, 11—in common with the "Wir arme Leut!" motive from Example 24. Finally, and most especially, note that the syllabic setting for the Captain's reference to Wozzeck as "ein guter Mensch" itself features the tetrachord 4-19.

The material immediately following the passage at Example 26 has been shown at Example 15c in chapter 2. In mm. 60–61 of Example 15c the reader will see one additional statement of set 4-19, reiterated at the point where the viola resumes its arpeggiated cadenza figure; again the invariant augmented triad ⌐3, 7, 11⌐ is made prominent. Now compare m. 56 in Example 26 with the segment of m. 60 in Example 15c labeled B[1]: you will see that in both cases set 4-19 appears within the larger context of set 5-30, which is to say that 4-19 is included within this pentachord. Set 5-30 is the set that is formed by the first five pitches (3, 11, 4, 7, 8) of the "Wir arme Leut!" theme, as shown in Example 24. It is also the set that, for those who anticipate purposeful rather than arbitrary compositional choices, promised to be of long-range significance when it appeared as the second of the two chords with which the opera began (Ex. 3, segment B).

Lest the reader doubt the justness of a segmentation in Example 24 that seems to ignore the declamation, two instances within the "Wir arme Leut!" domain where set 5-30 is treated as a discrete unit should suffice. First, at the only other moment in the opera when Wozzeck himself reiterates the "Wir arme Leut!" motive, the original syllabic setting is altered to produce a five- rather than four-note melodic figure, whose set structure, as shown in Example 27, is 5-30. Second, the reader will see from Example 24 that at the beginning of the second large melodic phrase unit of the Aria (mm. 139–40), the homophonic chordal accompaniment (scored for strings) features a consecutive quarter-note series of no fewer than nine vertical statements of set 5-30. (Inverted forms of the set are presented in five-part parallel motion until the last beat of m. 139, where an uninverted form breaks the pattern.) Note that the inverted form of set 5-30 (3, 5, 9, 1, 8) that initiates the harmonic progression at m. 139 is resumed at the downbeats of the next two measures, serving as point of departure for an extension of the large phrase unit at m. 141; meanwhile, double basses and contrabassoon provide a counterpoint against Wozzeck's vocal line in which the opening segment is a restatement of the first part of Wozzeck's "Wir arme Leut!" theme at its original pitch level.

We can effectively conclude that the composer has responded to the importance of the verbal motif "ein guter Mensch" as a preparation for Wozzeck's Aria statement by permitting the pitch material of the "guter Mensch" Cadenzas to foreshadow the salient presentation of the inclusion-related sets 4-19 and 5-30 in the Aria itself. The set-structural relationship between the Aria statement in Example 24 and the Cadenza at Examples 26 and 15c, once recognized, serves to intensify the dramatic situation in a way that the text alone cannot accomplish. In Example 26, while the Captain is busy asking Wozzeck why it is that he looks so harassed and cannot "slow down," the violist provides the answer: Wozzeck's membership in the *arme Leut* class gives him no time to slow down, since he is driven from one menial task to the next in a frenzied effort to make enough money to survive.

Example 27. Act II/Scene 1: m. 114

By the remarkable fact that the very second chord of the opera may be regarded as a compressed promise of the "Wir arme Leut!" motive (complete with the subset 3, 7, 11 !), we are alerted to the possibility that the specific association of sets 4-19 and 5-30 with the character Wozzeck and the plight of the poor people whom he represents will be extended throughout the opera to encompass even more fundamental issues with which the drama is concerned. The next examples will provide evidence that the referential bond established between these sets and Wozzeck himself in Act I/Scene 1 is reinforced elsewhere; from these examples, understood not only in relation to their immediate context but also as part of a network of associations that extends from the first scene, a broader interpretation of the function of sets 4-19 and 5-30 will emerge.

III

The crucial role that Marie plays in the configuration of characters surrounding Wozzeck (Wozzeck [Act II/Scene 2, mm. 332–33]: "Hab' sonst nichts auf dieser Welt!" ["I have nothing else in this world!"]) is underlined by the fact that Marie's scene in the series of "character studies" of Act I is given the central position. From this central scene, Act I/Scene 3, the first of several passages to be discussed (Ex. 28) is itself a central moment, the moment when Wozzeck and Marie are seen together for the first time.

Example 28. Act I/Scene 3: mm. 425–33

Just prior to the excerpt shown in Example 28, Marie, alone with her child (Lullaby), is silent and "lost in her thoughts" (Ex. 48, m. 415: "in Gedanken versunken"). With snatches of the Military March from the opening of the scene, where we watched Marie catching her first glance at the Drum Major as he marched by her window, the orchestra informs us that Marie has begun to daydream about a new man. All the more reason that she is visibly startled when, as shown in Example 28, Wozzeck suddenly raps at her window. The knock is accompanied by a loud, rapid thirty-second-note figure (m. 427) in low winds, marked *hastig* ("hasty," "hurried") in the vocal score, *gehetzt* ("agitated," "pursued") in the full score. The first of Wozzeck's three "entrance" themes, associated specifically with Wozzeck entering or leaving the presence of Marie, this figure—like the knock itself—cuts into the sustained fifth A♮-E♮ and overpowers the oscillating bass tritone (the "fateful" B♮-F♮), severing these quiet fifths (mm. 425–28) from the larger context of Marie's "waiting" motive (see the discussion of Marie's material in chapter 4) and destroying one of the few moments of repose in the entire opera. Note that the complete thirty-second-note figure (normal order: 2, 3, 6, 8, 10) is a form of set 5-30, transpositionally related by semitone to the Aria figure (normal order: 3, 4, 7, 9, 11) in Example 24. The all-important "Wir arme Leut!" subset 4-19, though tremendously "disguised" by means of contour, rhythm, register, scoring, and even pitch content, is given some prominence by virtue of the fact that it is formed by the last four notes of the figure, where the contour is made memorable by the disruptive changes of direction. The complete figure is followed in m. 427 by an augmented restatement of its first four notes in muted trombones, herewith promising the ever larger and slower muted-trombone statements that will constitute Wozzeck's second and third "entrance" themes in Act II (see Examples 17d and 17e). Finally, note that the entire pitch content of the thirty-second-note figure is reiterated vertically at m. 428.

As when he was with the Captain in Act I/Scene 1, Wozzeck is troubled and pressed for time. From the exchange between Wozzeck and Marie that ensues (mm. 428–33), we learn that Wozzeck is rushing as usual from one job to the next: having finished cutting firewood for his army Major (Act I/Scene 2), he cannot even stop in to see his mistress because he must now report back at the barracks.[17] Like the Captain, but with affection, Marie tries to get Wozzeck to "slow down"; like the Captain, Marie also notices that Wozzeck is harassed (m. 433: "Du siehst so verstört?" ["You look so distraught?"]). The dramatic parallel between this passage and the Captain's first "guter Mensch" Cadenza (Ex. 26) is highlighted in mm. 429–30 by both the scoring and the choice of pitch structures: the plodding, "expressionless" (*ohne Ausdruck*) eighth-note passage hardly bears resemblance here to the whimsical cadenza material in Act I/Scene 1; but once again interlocking forms of sets 4-19, 4-18, 4-17, and 4-27, this time clearly embedded within the larger complements 8-19 and 8-18, characterize the tetrachordal structure of the unison linear statement, and once again that statement is scored for the viola(s).

At m. 431 the violas are reinforced by muted trombones in note-by-note alternation with oboes and English horn, and each of these instruments sustains one of the last six notes of the viola passage, permitting that final arpeggiation to congeal just before the next downbeat. As shown in Example 28, the resulting vertical structure (0, 4, 7, 1, 3, 8), is a form of set 6-Z19, a hexachord that appears many times throughout the opera and is eminently featured along with its Z-related complement 6-Z44 in the very next scene that concerns Wozzeck and Marie together—Act II/Scene 1 (see Examples 65 and 66). The large-scale importance of set 6-Z19 in *Wozzeck* may be best expressed in terms of its inclusion relations. First of all, 6-Z19 contains Wozzeck's set 4-19 as many as *three times*. (In the form of the hexachord shown at m. 431, set 4-19 appears in these three forms: $\underline{0, 1, 4, 8}$; $\underline{0, 3, 4, 8}$; $\underline{0, 4, 7, 8}$.) Second, set 6-Z19 contains Marie's most prominent tetrachord—set 4-18—*twice* (represented here as $\underline{0, 1, 4, 7}$; $\underline{1, 4, 7, 8}$; see chapter 4). Finally, by comparing m. 431 of Example 28 with the first of the three "hallucination" chords shown in Example 29—the chords that supply the "harmonic skeleton" for the preceding scene in the open fields (see Berg's 1929 lecture, in Redlich 1957a, p. 316), the reader will quickly see that the form of set 6-Z19 presented in Example 28 not just theoretically but also *audibly* contains the first 5-element set (5-Z17) of the "hallucination" progression, with transpositional level, register, vertical arrangement, and the muted-trombone instrumentation held invariant.

Why this explicit musical reference to the open field scene? At the very moment in Example 28 when Marie feels compelled to ask Wozzeck what is wrong with him, the composer prepares a complex explanation whose ambiguity accords with the dramatic undercurrent. As mentioned before, it is in the open fields of Act I/Scene 2 where we first learn that Wozzeck has become haunted by terrifying visions, to the extent that his "normal" friend Andres has already begun to suspect that Wozzeck is mad (m. 279: "He, bist Du toll?" ["Hey, are you crazy?"]). Natural, circumstantial reasons for Wozzeck's mental decline have been carefully planted by the dramatist from the moment the play begins. We know at the outset that Wozzeck is a poor man—

2. Szene Freies Feld, die Stadt in der Ferne (Spätnachmittag)

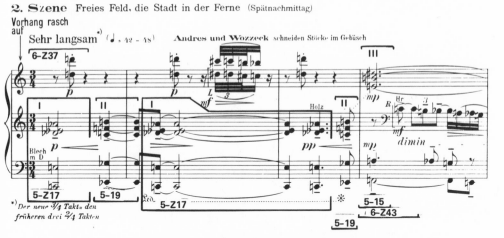

Example 29. Act I/Scene 2: mm. 201–04

overworked, pressed for time, whose regimented army life affords him neither the social prestige of the Captain, the sexual freedom of the Drum Major, nor the "theoretical knowledge" that "stabilizes" the Doctor. In the fourth
scene of the opera we learn, moreover, that Wozzeck makes a few extra
pennies by serving as the dietary guinea pig for the Doctor's grotesquely
inhuman progressivist-determinist "scientific" experiments. A perfectly convincing explanation for Wozzeck's hallucinations now emerges: Wozzeck has
been eating nothing but *beans* for the last three months! (In an act of self-
identification with Wozzeck based on his dietary experiences in the Austrian
army, Berg substitutes "beans" for Büchner's "peas"; see Blaukopf 1954, pp.
156–57). So far the inclusion of the "Wir arme Leut!" set structure (4-19),
tucked three times within the vertical presentation of set 6-Z19 in Example
28, provides an adequate economic-sociological answer to Marie's question,
"What's wrong with you, Franz?" However, the presence of the fundamental
"hallucination" chord from the open field scene (set 5-Z17) suggests that the
horrible visions plaguing Wozzeck have become a much more immediate
preoccupation to him than the potential causes of those visions—the drudg-
eries of his daily existence. It is one thing to hallucinate. It is quite another
to begin to invest the color and sound of each vision with apocalyptic significance; and this, as we learn from Wozzeck's response to Marie in the passage
immediately following Example 28, is what Wozzeck has begun to do. In his
effort to explain what is bothering him, Wozzeck *almost relives* his experi-
ence in the open fields (mm. 433–37: "Pst, Still! Ich hab's heraus! Es war
ein Gebild am Himmel, und Alles in Glut!" ["Sh! Quiet! I've got it! There

was a figure in the sky, and everything glowing!"]). And then, groping for a
larger meaning (mm. 437–38: "Ich bin Vielem auf der Spur!" ["I'm on the
track of many things!"]), Wozzeck is struck by the darkness now, and this
reminds him (mm. 444–46) of a passage from the Old Testament that concerns the judgment of God on Sodom and Gomorrah (Genesis 19:28)—"'Und
sieh, es ging der Rauch auf vom land, wie ein Rauch vom Ofen'" ("'. . .
and beheld, the smoke went up from the land as the smoke from a furnace'")—a passage that reappears in the New Testament Book of Revelation
(the Apocalypse) 9:2: " . . . and there arose a smoke out of the great furnace;
and the sun and the air were darkened by reason of the smoke of the pit."
The musical setting for Wozzeck's narrative (mm. 435–50) consists of material that originated in the open field scene and coincided there with the
images Wozzeck is now recapturing. From a strictly musical point of view,
then, the appearance of the first "hallucination" chord included within set
6-Z19 at m. 431 prepares that recapitulation of material from the preceding
scene. In dramatic terms, a statement by Leo Treitler that concerns the relationship of Marie's "Komm, mein Bub!" motive (see chapter 4) to the three
"hallucination" chords of Act I/Scene 2 might have been made with equal
appropriateness about the vertical structure 6-Z19 in Example 28:

> The dramatic significance of the association seems clear. The motives
> of lamentation ["Komm, mein Bub!"; "Ach, Marie"; "Wir arme Leut!"]
> refer again and again to the hard circumstances of Wozzeck's and Ma-
> rie's life—there is no getting away from that—but they have their mu-
> sical source in the mystery and terror of the imagined supernatural [rep-
> resented by the fundamental chords of Act I/Scene 2]. These are then
> two different manifestations—we might say material and spiritual, or
> external and psychological—of the forces that press in on Wozzeck and
> his family. For Wozzeck the two blend into one in his perceptions of
> a threatening world. [Treitler 1976, p. 264; bracketed clarifications
> my own.]

The "blending" in the vertical structure 6-Z19 of the "Wir arme Leut!" set
4-19 with the "hallucination" chord 5-Z17 (which itself includes 4-19 twice)
suggests an expansion of the motivic function of Wozzeck's 4-19 that is further reinforced in the remaining part of the passage shown in Example 28.
Notice that when the "hallucination" chord begins to dissolve at m. 432,
linear statements of set 4-19 emerge in parallel-fifth motion (xylophone with
oboe and English horn) above the sustained C-major triad in the bass; the
pitch content of the complete eighth-note passage here yields a form of the

complement of 4-19, set 8-19. Even more striking is the prominent display of set 4-19 included in Marie's line at the very point where she notes how troubled Wozzeck seems (m. 433: "Du siehst so verstört?"). Here the pitch-class content of 4-19 (4, 7, 11, 3) is *exactly the same* as that of the original "Wir arme Leut!" figure in the Aria of the first scene (Ex. 24). The implicit reference to the Aria is further substantiated in the violins by a juxtaposition of two discrete arpeggiated diminished-seventh chords (10, 7, 4, 1 ; 6, 3, 0, 9) moving in parallel-sixth motion over the sustained pitch classes 11, 3, 8; and, as in the original "Wir arme Leut!" setting, the complete twelve-tone universe is represented in m. 433 if we dare to include Wozzeck's Sprech-stimme indication for "Pst," which theoretically supplies the otherwise missing pc2. Finally, as if by command at the moment Wozzeck utters his "Pst," the sixteenth-note diminished-seventh-chord motion stops, and the vertical structure left suspended into the next bar is none other than set 4-19.

From this moment, ever after throughout the opera, appearances of Woz-zeck's set 4-19 may serve to remind the listener not only of Wozzeck's social plight—his "Wir arme Leut!" status—but also of his peculiarly troubled mental condition, which was first exposed in the "hallucination" material of Act I/Scene 2 and which will inexorably grow more severe as we see him driven nearer the murder of Marie and his own demise. Wozzeck's revelation to Marie in Act I/Scene 3 clearly leaves her frightened for his welfare, not to mention her own and their child's. When the "entrance" motive from Ex-ample 28 returns to become an "exit" motive (Ex. 30) at the point where Wozzeck rushes offstage, Marie's reaction intensifies the association with "distractedness" that that motive and its set structures have gained in the course of this scene: "Der Mann! So vergeistert! Er hat sein Kind nicht an-gesehn! Er schnappt noch über mit den Gedanken!" ("That man! So haunted! He didn't even look at his child! He'll go crazy with those thoughts of his!"). As shown in Example 30, the contour of the "entrance" motive has been inverted to "describe" Wozzeck's change in stage direction, but a literal in-version of adjacent intervals has not been strictly maintained throughout; as a result, the last four pitches of the motive retain the "minor triad with added major seventh" disposition of set 4-19 as it appeared in Example 28 and in the original "Wir arme Leut!" figure (Ex. 24):

The noticeable but only partial transformation corresponds with the fact that we, like Marie, must now see the same Wozzeck in a new light.

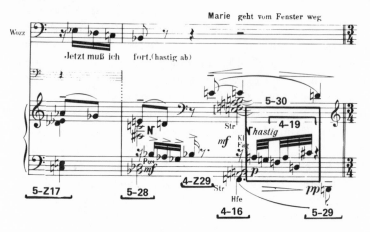

Example 30. Act I/Scene 3: mm. 453–54

IV

From among the eleven later appearances of Wozzeck's first "entrance" motive from Example 28 (two of these announce actual entrances into Marie's presence [Act II/Scene 3, m. 373; Act II/Scene 4, m. 495]; one corresponds with an exit [Act III/Scene 2, m. 107]; one forecasts Wozzeck's "entry," with knife, into Marie [Act III/Scene 2, m. 101]), one further example will be presented—an example that does not announce an entrance but rather reminds the alert listener of the additional, more fundamental issues with which the figure has become linked.

The modified form of the "entrance" motive shown in Example 31 is the first of five presentations of this motive in variation 5 of Act I/Scene 4 (the passacaglia-variation movement that constitutes the Doctor's scene); in this variation the Doctor has been chastising Wozzeck for having "coughed" ("pissed" [see note 6]) in the street. Although Marie is not present here, the association of the motive with Wozzeck's entering or leaving the presence of Marie is sustained: several motives identified with Marie (to be discussed) "occur in the same context, and her presence in Wozzeck's thoughts is expressly indicated when he suddenly cries out her name in the midst of his relation of his neurotic fantasies to the doctor" (Perle 1971, p. 290). Of added significance is the fact that the "entrance" motive recurs as many as three times in the last measure of variation 5, just before the point where

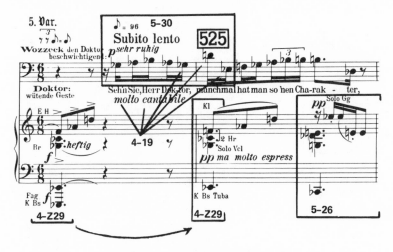

Example 31. Act I/Scene 4: mm. 524–25

Wozzeck begins trying to relate the problem of "losing control over Nature" (m. 495: " . . . wenn einem die Natur kommt!" [" . . . when Nature calls!"]) to his own frightening notion of "when Nature runs out" (m. 531: " . . . wenn die Natur aus ist")—that is, "when the world gets so dark that you have to grope around it with your hands, and you think it will run away, like spider webs! That's when something is and yet isn't!" (mm. 532–36: " . . . wenn die Welt so finster wird, dass man mit den Händen an ihr herumtappen muss, dass man meint, sie verrinnt, wie Spinnengewebe! Ach,—wenn was is und doch nicht is!"). The "entrance" motive now signals that once again Wozzeck will "enter into" his unique relationship with the Nature of the open fields; once again his revelation will be accompanied by material that originates in the open-field scene, and in fact, this material will be an exact restatement of the open-field material that appeared during Wozzeck's disclosure to Marie in Act I/Scene 3 (mm. 440–43). Example 32 shows the closing segment of that Leitsektion as it appears in Act I/Scene 4, at the point where the oscillating augmented second ␣A♭-B♮␣, which originated in the soprano line connecting the first "hallucination" chord to the second (see Ex. 29), now dies away in 'cello and celesta.

At this point (m. 537) a unique presentation of the Doctor's twelve-tone passacaglia theme reveals that this theme shares a remarkable albeit esoteric relationship with Wozzeck's set 4-19 and his "hallucination" chord 5-Z17. The sixteenth-note triplet figure for two muted violas at m. 537 (Ex. 32) is a

Example 32. Act I/Scene 4: mm. 536–40

Example 33. Act I: mm. 486–87 (Interlude connecting Scenes 3 and 4)

dyadic verticalization of the passacaglia theme shown in Example 33, with one dyad (pcs 5, 9) removed from the row to serve as pedal point in muted trombones. Note that the upper voice of the triplet figure (pcs 11, 1, 6, 10, 2) presents a form of the "hallucination" chord—set 5-Z17, with the last four pitches spelling the "augmented triad with added major seventh" inverted form of the all-important 4-19. Meanwhile, the melodic setting for the last four words of the text quoted above (" . . . und doch nicht is!") features interlocking forms (11, 2, 10, 6 ; 2, 10, 6, 3) of set 4-19 within the larger pentachord 5-21. An augmented version of this presentation of the passacaglia row, rescored for muted horns with the pedal point in the 'cellos, directs the one-measure variation 7 into variation 8, where, as shown at mm. 539–40, Wozzeck's "Ach, Marie!" now contiguously features one additional form of the "Wir arme Leut!" set (pcs 3, 11, 8, 7), again within the larger 5-21. This form once again holds the augmented triad 3, 11, 7 in common with the original setting and presents itself in a melodic shape that emphasizes the containment within set 4-19 of Marie's "Komm, mein Bub!" set 3-3 (see the discussion of Examples 45 and 46 in chapter 4).

Should it come as a surprise that the Doctor's passacaglia row would be manipulated to produce pitch combinations that have grown more and more clearly linked with Wozzeck's "unnatural" mental state, consider that fact that the Doctor has his own peculiar, probably sadistic, certainly obsessive, clinical fascination with "mental aberrations" (a fact that might, incidentally, explain the overriding predominance in the passacaglia theme of those "diabolical," "anti-natural" tritones). Like Marie and, before her, Andres, the Doctor is astonished at Wozzeck's unbalanced behavior; but far from being alarmed, the Doctor exhibits blatant ecstasy upon discovering that his "patient" is fast becoming a new kind of "specimen" for "analysis." In the next two examples, from the beginnings of variations 13 and 14, we hear the Doctor first raving with glee that Wozzeck is "on his way to the insane asylum" (mm. 562–64: "Wozzeck, Er kommt in's Narrenhaus") and then enthusiastically describing Wozzeck's "condition": "Aberatio mentalis partialis, second species!" In these examples the association of Wozzeck's set 4-19 with his "aberatio" becomes unequivocal.

At m. 562 of Example 34, the brilliant E-minor triad throbs jubilantly in flutes and clarinets against a sustained D♯ that announces the beginning of a statement of the passacaglia row in the bass. Together within the larger context of set 5-26, these components—pcs 4, 7, 11, and 3—pronounce a form of set 4-19 whose pitch content is exactly the same as that of the original "Wir arme Leut!" figure. Now the Doctor's theme for Act II/Scene 2 (review

Ex. 1 and note 21 to chapter 1) makes its very first appearance, while the winds present three more vertical statements of set 4-19 in descending arpeggiation. In Example 35 Wozzeck's "aberatio mentalis" is prognosticated in counterpoint with a "cold-blooded," "academic" presentation of set 4-19, in which the descending arpeggiated figure (11, 8, 3, 11, 7) is "monotonously" iterated four times by four solo horns, while each of four clarinets reinforces

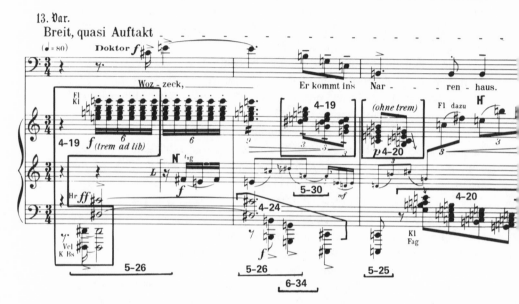

Example 34. Act I/Scene 4: mm. 562–64

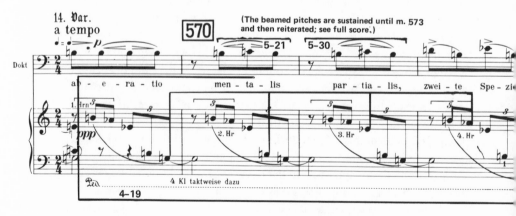

Example 35. Act I/Scene 4: mm. 569–72

and sustains one of the pitches of the set, creating a slower, longer-range arpeggiation in contrary motion (see the extended, beamed stems in the score). As with most of the recurring forms of set 4-19 in Act I/Scene 1 that were discussed earlier, the two forms of this set presented in Examples 34 and 35 hold pcs 3, 11, and 7 invariant. This observation points to a much more convincing relationship between the "Wir arme Leut!" set *in its original setting* and the Doctor's passacaglia theme: the first three notes of the passacaglia theme (see Ex. 33) are none other than pcs 3, 11, and 7.

Even this author hesitates to suggest that Berg chose every other note of his ordered passacaglia theme with the intention of featuring the "Wir arme Leut!" set 4-19 within a transposed form of the first "hallucination" chord as shown in Example 32. It might be added, nevertheless, that the compound melodic aspect of the passacaglia theme as it first appears (Ex. 33) clearly prepares the way for a dyadic presentation of the row and gives rhythmic stress at the outset to the crucial upper voice; and this observation in no way conflicts with the equally remarkable fact that the first two pitches and the rhythmic disposition of the passacaglia theme more immediately derive from a disguised reference in the preceding measures (mm. 483–85) to the "fanfare" opening of the Drum Major's Military March from the beginning of Act I/Scene 3 (mm. 328–31; see Ex. 58). Immediate and long-range relationships among motives first associated with apparently disparate characters and events abound throughout the opera, as noted by many who have attempted to penetrate Berg's uniquely complex leitmotivic scheme (see especially Perle 1971 and Treitler 1976). Recognition of this aspect of the composer's language may lend credibility to the forthcoming information, which provides further evidence that Wozzeck's "Wir arme Leut!" set 4-19 permeates a vast and disparate array of the pitch materials of the opera, in much the same way that the progress of Wozzeck's psychic disintegration serves as the all-pervading dramatic force.

V

We have seen that set 4-19 is displayed as a component of Wozzeck's protrusive first "entrance"(-"exit") motive and is carefully preserved at subsequent reappearances of the same. Like these entrances and exits, several beginnings and endings of major sections of the opera straightforwardly feature set 4-19 in a reiterative context that ensures memorability.

Examples 36 and 37 show the beginnings of the Interludes respectively preceding and following Act II/Scene 3—the Largo movement that appears at the absolute center of the act as well as of the opera, and whose dramatic import not only as midpoint but also as turning point cannot be overstated. About these passages, the composer himself has offered the following:

> To return once more to that Largo: The manner in which it is introduced and dies away could be yet another example of how a closure, formerly possible only through a return to the tonic, was achieved by other means. The clarinet figurations, as if running away from the fugal subject-matter of the preceding scene, form a transition to the entry of the Largo, where, as if coming to a standstill, these figurations compose the first harmonic basis of the Largo theme.
>
> The ending of this Largo flows into the same harmony, which, again set into motion, takes in retrograde the shape of those clarinet figurations out of which this chord had grown. [From the 1929 lecture, in Redlich 1957a, pp. 321–22.][18]

As indicated in each of the two examples, the "harmony" upon which Berg focuses our attention is the fixed form

of set 4-19 that begins to be reiterated in an eighth-note oscillating pattern at the end of m. 365, comes to rest at m. 368, reappears as a vertical structure at m. 405, and resumes its eighth-note motion again at m. 406. The reader may wish to verify the composer's claim that the eighth-note passage in violins at m. 409 (Ex. 37) constitutes a retrograde statement of the clarinet figurations that precede the entry of set 4-19 in m. 365 (Ex. 36). (The retrograde procedure featured in the Interludes that frame the Largo should, incidentally, remind the reader of the retrograde recapitulation of the Prelude at the end of Act I/Scene 1 and provide an additional example of Berg's fondness for cyclical design [see note 8]). The parentheses added to the score at mm. 408 and 409 indicate deviations from an exact retrograde statement of the lower voice in mm. 364 and 365. Since it is the bassoon, rather than the clarinet, that plays this lower voice from mm. 365 to 368, Berg possibly did not have the lower voice in mind when describing the retrograde procedure. Of interest, however, is the fact that except at the points indicated with parentheses in Example 37, the lower voice from m. 408 to m. 411 is indeed a retrograde version of the lower voice from m. 363 to m. 365. Note that at the point in m. 409 where the second deviation occurs, the composite segment, given weight within the eighth-note passage by virtue of the staggered quarter notes in the two voices, produces a form of 4-19 (0, 3, 7, 11) that acts as a sequential reiteration of the now no longer fixed form of the set in m. 408. Likewise, when a deviation from the otherwise strict retrograde statement again appears at m. 411, as indicated by the parentheses in the lower part, the compositional "reason" seems clearly to present itself in the form of one final statement of set 4-19—produced by the composite segment (10, 7, 6, 2) that occupies the complete first half of the measure.

Example 36. Act II: mm. 364–70 (Interlude connecting Scenes 2 and 3)

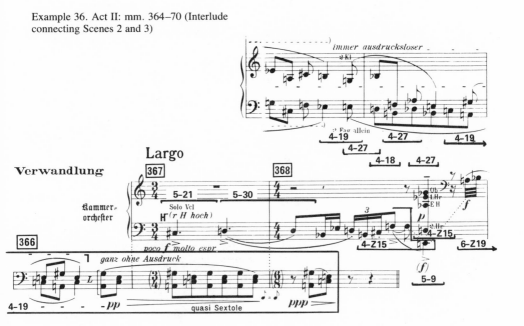

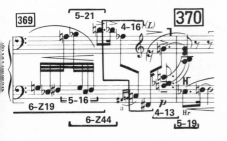

Example 37. Act II: mm. 405–11 (Interlude connecting Scenes 3 and 4)

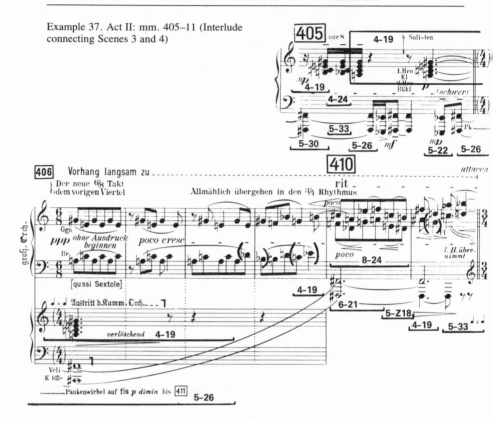

Of all the excerpts from the opera that Berg discussed and played in his lecture of 1929, the only two examples that Redlich chose to include in musical notation within the first publication of the lecture (in Redlich 1957a) are the "Wir arme Leut!" motive (Ex. 24) and the fixed harmony (9, 0, 4, 8) discussed above. In light of this, it comes as a surprise that neither Redlich nor any of the other *Wozzeck* specialists save Douglas Jarman (1979, p. 56) has made note of the extremely clear fact that one of these two pitch structures is simply an ordered transposition of the other (Ex. 38).

Example 38. Reduction of the two musical examples shown in Berg's published lecture (Redlich 1957a, pp. 320–21).

Whereas the relationship shown at Example 38 can most certainly be recognized without reference to set structures, the set-analytical procedure brings to light a certain less obvious way in which set 4-19 not only provides a fixed "harmonic basis for the Largo theme" but also pervades the linear design of the theme itself.

The Largo theme has a four-part structure, of which the first and second parts, dominated by a rhapsodic solo 'cello, are shown in Example 36. The second part of the theme (beginning with the thirty-second-note upbeat to m. 369 and delimited from the first part by the vertical punctuation and the rest in m. 368) features interlocking statements of set 6-Z19 and its Z-related complement 6-Z44 as follows:

$$6\text{-}Z19:\ 9,\ 10,\ 7,\ 3,\ 6,\ 2$$
$$\underline{10,\ 7,\ 3,\ 6,\ 2},\ 1\ :6\text{-}Z44$$
$$5\text{-}21$$

It can be seen in Example 36 that set 5-21—the pentachord formed by the melodic segment (10, 7, 3, 6, 2) within which sets 6-Z19 and 6-Z44 intersect—has already appeared as the very first composite segment of the Largo (m. 367); there the functional distinction between "melody" and "harmonic basis" clearly exposes the inclusion relation between sets 5-21 and 4-19. In fact set 4-19 is the only four-note set that 5-21 contains not just once but twice (review Ex. 32). The reader will recall, furthermore, that 6-Z19, featured in Example 28 from Act I/Scene 3, contains Wozzeck's set 4-19 three times as well as Marie's set 4-18 twice, and the same is true of the complementary 6-Z44. A straightforward dramatic reason for the prominence of the 6-Z19/6-Z44 pair in the Largo theme can be offered now and will be examined more carefully later: like Act I/Scene 3 and like the first scene of Act II, where the 6-Z19/6-Z44 hexachords play an outstanding role in the long-range organization of the sonata design (see the discussion of Ex. 65 in chapter 4), the Largo scene presents Wozzeck and Marie alone together. And, as with the other two preceding Wozzeck-Marie scenes, in the Largo movement of Act II/Scene 3 Marie is found "waiting" onstage while Wozzeck makes both an entrance and an exit. Here, then, the introductory appearance of the fixed form of set 4-19 effectively forecasts the now predictable entrance of Wozzeck by serving as a long-range harmonic preparation for the "entrance" motive from Act I/Scene 3, which features the same 4-element set and in fact reappears in the Largo at the point where Wozzeck actually enters (m. 373). This interpretation of the fixed 4-19 harmony is strengthened by the fact that set 5-30—the important 5-element structure that characterizes the "entrance" motive in toto and that was heard at the very beginning of the opera—can be heard at m. 367 in Example 36 as the second composite segment of the Largo; like the fixed form of set 4-19, set 5-30 also reappears fleetingly at the end of the scene, as shown at m. 405 in Example 37. An invariant subset consisting of pcs 0, 4, and 8 is shared not only by these two forms of set 5-30 but also by the form of the set in which the "entrance" motive itself appears at m. 373 (4, 6, 8, 1, 0). It need hardly be pointed out that these three pitch classes find their origin in the fixed form of set 4-19 around which our discussion of the beginning and the ending of the Largo movement has centered.[19]

The same three pitch classes determine our choice of the next example—an excerpt in which once again these pitches appear as a prominent subset within a form of set 4-19 that is used reiteratively to announce the beginning of a major section. This time the major section in question is not an Interlude but rather a scene itself—Act III/Scene 3, the second of the two big Tavern scenes. Readers will find the frenzied fast-Polka beginning of this scene at Example 15g, in chapter 2, where the "almost-whole-tone" linear aspect of the Polka theme was presented within a series of examples showing melodic structures that feature set 6-21. There it will also be seen that 4-19 is the set name of the vertical composite structure $\underline{0, 4, 7, 8}$, hammered out through the first two bars of the Polka by an onstage player at an out-of-tune upright piano. Note in Example 15g that at the third bar of the Polka (m. 124), set 4-19 is "sustained" by virtue of its inclusion within the larger set 5-26, the set that appeared at the end of the Largo (Ex. 37, mm. 405–08) with the same pitch content:

$$\overset{\displaystyle 4\text{-}19}{\overline{0,\ 4,\ 6,\ 8,\ 9}}$$

A third form of set 4-19 (0, 4, 8, 1) punctuates the end of the phrase at m. 125, where the ruthlessly persistent accompaniment figure—featuring the subset $\underline{0, 4, 8}$—combines with the last note of the tune. As with the beginning of the Largo in Act II/ Scene 3, vertical and horizontal dimensions interact to unfold a single pitch-structural idea: as will be stressed in greater detail at the end of this chapter, the set structure of the tune (7, 4, 9, 5, 3, 1)—set 6-21—itself contains set 4-19 in the form of pcs $\underline{4, 9, 5, 1}$; although that tetrachord is not a prominent substructure of the tune, the subset 4-24, the only other 4-element set having the maximum number of major thirds (of ic4), appears contiguously at mm. 124–25 and supplies the distinctive descending whole-tone segment of the line.

The appearance of set 4-19 at the beginning of Act III/Scene 3 does not coincide with a Wozzeck-entrance; when the curtain quickly rises, Wozzeck is in full view onstage, about to gulp down a glass of wine in an effort to repress the irrepressible memory that he has just murdered Marie. Here the appropriateness of the recurring set 4-19 extends far beyond surface similitudes (i.e., opening of major section, presence of central character). We shall see that from the beginning of Act II, the motivic-referential function of set 4-19 has undergone a further expansion to the extent that it will now be associated not only with Wozzeck's unstable psychic condition but also with the direct consequence of that condition—the act of violence that will haunt Wozzeck to the point of his own death. In the next series of examples, key moments from among the literally hundreds of occurrences of set 4-19 in Acts II and III have been chosen in order to trace the progress of this referential expansion.

VI

From the loosely connected scenes of Act I, we receive a kaleidoscopic view of Wozzeck's wretched social and economic situation, his tendency toward instability, the restlessness and growing dissatisfaction of his mistress, and, finally, her seduction by the Drum Major—an exposition, in short, of all the seemingly disparate but fundamentally related elements that motivate the conflict between Wozzeck and Marie. The conflict itself materializes only at the beginning of Act II, where Wozzeck sees the earrings Marie has accepted from the Drum Major and begins to grow suspicious. The large, tightly unified symphonic design of Act II effects a formal contrast with the shorter, apparently autonomous scenes of Acts I and III; but more important, the choice of symphonic structure for Act II parallels a change from the circular, static organization of the dramatic elements of Act I to the closely linked forward-moving series of confrontations in Act II that lead to Marie's death in Act III.

Examples 39 and 40 show crucial moments within the first of these confrontations, from the development section of the sonata-allegro movement that forms the first scene of Act II. For a preview of the extent to which the large formal divisions of the sonata movement correspond with the textual-dramatic organization of the scene, the reader is referred to the composer's lecture of 1929 (Redlich 1957a) and to George Perle (1967a, pp. 223–39), whose "basic cell" analysis of this movement will be examined in chapter 4. For now it will suffice to recall that the development section of the sonata parallels the portion of the scene during which Wozzeck and Marie "come to

blows" ("aneinandergeraten" [see Berg in Redlich 1957a, p. 320]) over the
subject of the earrings. Prior to the excerpt at Example 39, Wozzeck's entrance has again startled Marie, who thereupon inadvertently calls attention
to her new earrings in a frantic effort to hide them. A smart man despite his
distractedness, Wozzeck is not at all convinced that Marie could have "found"
the earrings, since it is quite unusual to find a *pair* of earrings, "two at once"
(mm. 104–05: "zwei auf einmal"). Challenged and guilty, Marie knows full
well what Wozzeck is thinking, and again she inadvertently spells out his and
her own worst fear by blurting forth a defensive retort that betrays her: "Bin
ich ein schlecht Mensch?" ("Am I a bad person?"). Wozzeck, however, has
not yet "seen" Marie's infidelity; in fact he will still be looking for visible
proof at the beginning of Act II/Scene 3 (mm. 375–76: "Ich seh' nichts, ich
seh' nichts. O man müsst's seh'n, man müsst's greifen können mit den Fäus-
ten!" ["I don't see anything, I don't see anything. Oh, I must see it; I should
be able to grab it with my fists!"]). Distracted instead by the sight of his
perspiring child, which reminds him of the plight of the "arme Leut," Wozzeck drops the issue of the earrings, gives Marie some money, and leaves.
Marie, left alone with her guilt, whose magnitude has grown in the light of
Wozzeck's loyalty, now provides her own indictment with an answer to the
question Wozzeck himself had pretended to ignore: (Ex. 40) "Ich bin doch
ein schlecht Mensch" ("I really am a bad person").

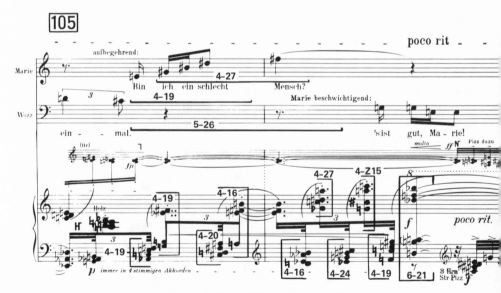

Example 39. Act II/Scene 1: mm. 105–06

Example 40. Act II/Scene 1: mm. 126–28

For self-evident textual-dramatic reasons, Marie's "answer," shown at Example 40, is presented as a descending retrograde (transpositionally related by semitone) of the five-note figure that serves as the setting for the "question" in Example 39. Less obvious here are the reasons for the choice of set structures. Thus far in this survey, the inclusion-related sets 4-19 and 5-26, heard together at both the ending of the Largo and the beginning of the Polka, have appeared in association with Wozzeck rather than Marie. An explanation for the display of set 5-26 in Marie's melodic figure at Example 39 is suggested by the accompanying orchestral material, which features a developmental variation of Marie's "earrings" theme (Ex. 41)—the principal subject of the sonata Exposition; that theme announces the beginning of the scene, where the curtain rises to reveal Marie admiring her gift from the Drum Major. The reader will see in Example 41 that the very first soprano melodic unit of the "earrings" theme (11, 7, 3, 1, 10) produces a form of set 5-26, transpositionally related (t = 5) to Marie's figure (4, 8, 0, 3, 6) at Example 39. The outstanding tetrachord in the opening soprano melody of the "earrings" theme, featured vertically as well at the downbeats of mm. 8 and 11 (Ex. 41), is not 4-19, but rather 4-24, the other four-note set that maximizes the interval of the major third (ic4); however, the inclusion relation between sets 4-19 and 5-26 permits the change of vertical structures from 4-24 to 4-19 at mm. 11–12 to unfold just as logically from the opening melodic idea. And this close pitch-structural relationship between the principal melodic idea of the Exposition and Wozzeck's set 4-19 could suffice to "explain" the appearance of set 4-19 at Example 39, not only in Marie's "Bin ich ein schlecht Mensch?" figure but also as a recurring accented vertical structure in the accompanying orchestral material itself.

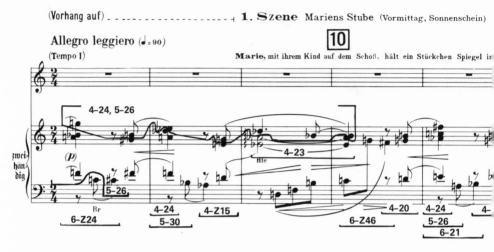

Example 41. Act II: mm. 7–12

However, as a crucial link in a network of associations that extends throughout the opera, the appearance of set 4-19 in this passage and in the corresponding passage at Example 40 invites a much broader interpretation. Consider, first of all, the import of these moments as the first in a series of painful confrontations and disclosures that lead to the murder scene. Second, notice the extreme harshness of Marie's verbal expression at the parallel points where set 4-19 occurs: Marie does not simply suggest that she has been unfaithful; instead, in her effort to jolt Wozzeck away from that truth, she brazenly dares him to regard her as "bad," "wicked" (*schlecht*). Marie's choice of language has the effect of creating a direct connection for Wozzeck between the possibility of her infidelity and the terrifying visions he has experienced in the open fields—visions that, as indicated in Act I/Scene 3 (see my comments in section III above), remind him of references in the Scriptures to the signs of wickedness and impending doom in Sodom and in the days before the Last Judgment.

For Leo Treitler (1976, pp. 256–58), who reads Büchner's *Woyzeck* as a forceful statement of opposition to the Enlightenment doctrine of progress as expressed in the writings of Kant and Hegel, Büchner's Woyzeck is at once a product and a victim of the teleological viewpoint that individual events must always be understood to signify something larger, that the individual can be known "only as something that is to fulfill a purpose outside of itself" ("Sie kennt das Individuum nur als etwas, das einen Zweck ausser sich erreichen soll") [Büchner 1971, p. 291]. Wozzeck is haunted not only by his visions but by the compulsion to interpret them as prophetic; more specifically, Wozzeck's hallucinations warn him of imminent disaster with earthshattering consequences. In light of the fact that set 4-19 has been carefully planted in association not only with Wozzeck's social plight but also with the "aberatio" that manifests itself in visions and compels him to sense doom, the occurrence of this set at the moment when Marie first hints that she is "ein schlecht Mensch" suggests that Wozzeck has already begun to draw a link between Marie's unfaithfulness and the universal demise about which the visions had warned him. This is to say that Marie's words at Example 39 are taken by Wozzeck as the first indication that what in Act I/Scene 2 was only a vision is about to become a reality. In Act II/Scene 1 Marie's adultery is at first only suggested by the earrings; in the subsequent scene it is ruthlessly insinuated to Wozzeck by the Captain and the Doctor. As Wozzeck's suspicions grow stronger, Wozzeck, like most people who are about to lose the only thing that has given meaning to their lives, becomes increasingly unable to accept Marie's infidelity as an ordinary act, a natural consequence of her "natural" needs; rather, he must see this fact as a symbol of universal depravity, "a sin so fat and so wide—it stinks enough to smoke the angels out of Heaven" (Act II/Scene 3 [the Largo movement], mm. 378–81: "Eine Sünde, so dick und breit—das müsst' stinken, dass man die Engel zum Himmel hinausräuchern könnt'"). On that basis, his need to kill Marie becomes a need to punish sin, an act that the visions themselves have called upon him to execute.

VII

The notion that he must kill Marie begins to take shape in Wozzeck's mind at the end of the Largo movement (Act II/Scene 3), where Marie, now violently angry and frightened by his accusations, again inadvertently predisposes Wozzeck to consider a thought that would otherwise possibly not have entered his mind. This time she suggests the murder weapon itself: (mm. 395–96) "Lieber ein Messer in den Leib, als eine Hand auf mich" ("Better to have a knife in my body than your hand on me" [see comments in chapter 2, section IV]). The impression that Wozzeck is being led toward Marie's murder by forces "outside of himself" is further enhanced in the very next scene at the tavern (Act II/Scene 4). There, as if in a mysteriously direct response to the fact that the *sight* of Marie dancing with the Drum Major has just confirmed Wozzeck's every suspicion by providing him with the necessary "visible proof," the Idiot now presses close to Wozzeck and, with the prophetic insight of the Shakespearian fool, announces that he "smells blood" (mm. 665–68: "aber es riecht—Ich riech, ich riech Blut!"). The word "blood" has the immediate, catalytic effect of inciting Wozzeck and putting him into a trancelike state, in much the same way that Marie's mention of the word "knife" had made him dizzy (mm. 400–01: "Es schwindelt Einem . . . "). As if receiving a new message from a supernatural agent, Wozzeck takes the word from the Idiot and repeats it, each time more loudly as its meaning for him grows clearer in his mind (see Ex. 42), until at last he shouts: "Mir wird rot vor den Augen. Mir ist, als wälzten sie sich alle übereinander . . . " ("I'm beginning to see red. It's as if they are rolling all over each other"). The second part of this text recalls in an abbreviated version Wozzeck's words shortly after he enters the tavern and first sees Marie and the Drum Major dancing together; there his need to understand Marie's infidelity as a sign of universal depravity was made even more explicit: (mm. 522–28) "Alles wälzt sich in Unzucht übereinander: Mann und Weib, Mensch und Vieh!" ("They're all lewdly rolling over each other: male and female, man and beast!").

At the point (Ex. 42) where Wozzeck's reiteration of the word "Blut" reaches its highest, most intense pitch, the entire brass section bursts forth with a throbbing, blood-curdling figure that will be reiterated in ostinato throughout Wozzeck's bloody vision against the ever more frenzied waltz in the strings. As shown in Example 42, the first of the two tetrachords in the dotted ostinato figure is a fixed form (3, 6, 10, 2) of Wozzeck's set 4-19, the same form featured in the initial statement and in as many as six subsequent statements of Wozzeck's first "entrance" motive (review Examples 28 and 31), now accented fortissimo fifteen times in the course of this passage; the second of the two chords is the half-diminished-seventh chord (4, 7, 11, 1)—set 4-27—a structure associated with Marie but whose pitch content here contains three of the four pitch classes (4, 7, 11) heard in the very first statement of Wozzeck's "Wir arme Leut!" figure (Ex. 24). In sum, like many other passages to be examined in the next chapter, the ostinato figure combines

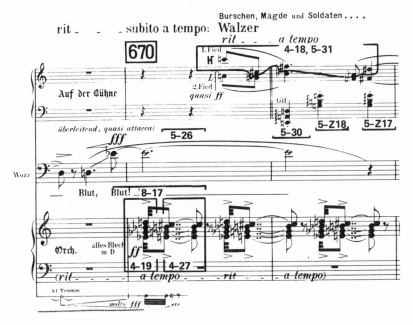

Example 42. Act II/Scene 4: mm. 669–71

pitch classes and pitch structures whose association with *both* Marie and Wozzeck provides a musical correspondence for the crucial fact that the lives of these two characters interlock to the point where each must bring about the other's destruction. Obsessively reiterated in inseparable company with Marie's set 4-27, the fixed form of set 4-19 in this passage, coinciding with the last and bloodiest vision before the murder itself, establishes once and for all the expanded referential domain of the set: unquestionably associated with the external conditions of Wozzeck's world conveyed by the "Wir arme Leut!" figure, and—as a component of both the first of the "entrance" motives and the first of the "hallucination" chords—fundamentally connected with Wozzeck's internal distractedness and his unstable visionary nature, set 4-19 now appears at the point where the consequential outcome of these aspects of his character, in conflict with Marie's needs, is made explicit by the vision of blood.[20]

The appearance of set 4-19 in this passage provides exquisite preparation for the moment of murder itself (Act III/Scene 2, m. 103), where, as shown in Example 43, the set returns at the precise point where the vision of blood becomes an actuality.[21] Finally, as the magnitude of this event penetrates Wozzeck's mind to the extent that he is now driven back to the tavern in the hope of expiating his guilt (Ex. 44), set 4-19, having reached its last stage in the process of motivic-dramatic expansion, appears to confirm the answer to Wozzeck's question, "Bin ich ein Mörder?" ("Am I a murderer?").[22]

VIII

As we near the close of our examination of Wozzeck's set 4-19, the reader must be reminded that the all-pervasive nature of this set precludes a systematic presentation of its countless other appearances throughout the opera. Some of the most striking of these appearances will be seen in the context of their juxtaposition with sets related to Marie, sets to which the reader's attention will be drawn in chapter 4. But before this, one final indication of the

Example 43. Act III/Scene 2: m. 103

Example 44. Act III/Scene 3: mm. 206–11

extent to which set 4-19 permeates the pitch materials of the opera may be expressed in terms of an important relationship that exists between this set and the "almost whole-tone" hexachords 6-21, 6-22, and 6-34, discussed in chapter 2: *set 4-19 is contained one time in each of these hexachords* (4-19 ⊂ 6-21, 6-22, 6-34).

Let us briefly review several occurrences of these hexachords to see where the presence of the subset 4-19 is made compositionally clear. First, the reader may turn again to Example 24, which shows the first appearance of the "Wir arme Leut!" motive. There, at m. 142, Wozzeck's vocal line displays a statement of set 6-34 in counterpoint with a presentation of set 4-19 in the form of a transposed repetition of the "Wir arme Leut!" motive by the solo horn. The extended, beamed stems added to the score reveal that Wozzeck's vocal line features an arpeggiation of the subset 4-19, one that, when reduced to a vertical structure, can be viewed as an ordered inversion ($t = 2$) of the "Wir arme Leut!" collection itself, with pcs 9, 5, and 1 held invariant:

(reduction from m. 142, Ex. 24)

(vocal part)   (hn. part)

Note, moreover, that the total pitch content of the horn solo (pcs 9, 5, 10, 1) in combination with the accompanying triad sustained by trombones (pcs 3, 10, 7) in m. 142 expresses yet another form of set 6-34. Second, long beamed stems demonstrating the presence of set 4-19 have been added to the excerpts shown in Examples 15–17 (chapter 2) where linear-thematic statements of the "almost whole-tone" hexachords occur. There the reader's attention is called especially to Examples 15a, 16a, and 17a, where the presence of the subset 4-19 is made prominent in the following ways:

Example 15a (first melodic configuration of the opera): The interlocking statements of sets 6-21 and 6-34 produce two forms of set 4-19 (0, 3, 11, 7, and 3, 11, 7, 6), the first of which includes the first-and-lowest note (pc0), the apex (pc11), and the last-and-longest note (pc7) of the opening melodic idea.

Example 16a (opening of Andres's Song): Here three of the four pitch classes comprising the subset 4-19 also supply the arpeggiated G-major triad (2, 7, 11) that gives this first phrase of the Song its quasi-tonal quality; the apex and pitch goal of the line (pc3) provides the fourth pitch class of the subset.

Example 17a (closing phrase of Marie's Lullaby): As will be discussed in chapter 4, the first four notes (10, 6, 2, 11) of the complete eight-note descending line display Wozzeck's set 4-19 as a subset within set 6-34, while the last four notes (8, 4, 1, 7) project Marie's set 4-18.

If the reader has the patience to examine the remaining examples of the "almost whole-tone" hexachords in chapter 2, he may discover that in seven of those excerpts (Examples 15a, 15b, 15c, 15e, 15f, 16a, 17b) the subset 4-19 appears in a form that itself includes the all-important augmented triad ⌊3, 7, 11⌋; this is simply another manifestation of the long-range priority given throughout the opera to pitch classes included in the "odd-numbered" whole-tone series (see chapter 2, section III).

It may come as a surprise that Wozzeck's set 4-19 is given prominence in statements of sets 6-21 and 6-22 that establish links between these hexachords and the subsidiary characters. I propose that whereas, for instance, in the case of Example 16a, the hexachord 6-22 relates to Andres, the prominence of the subset 4-19 parallels the remarkable degree to which we see Andres (as well as the Captain, the Doctor, the Drum Major, the tavern crowd, and Margret) fundamentally in terms of his relationship to Wozzeck, whose particular fate is the central dramatic theme that influences every structural level of the work.

The reader will remember that of the three "almost whole-tone" hexachords under discussion, set 6-34 has been shown in direct association with Wozzeck by virtue of its appearances at his third "entrance" theme (Ex. 17e) and at his words "Einer nach dem Andern!" ("One after the other!") in the last moment of Act II (Ex. 17f). The same hexachord had served as the cadential structure at the end of Act I/Scene 1 (Ex. 10), then to be absorbed within the larger 8-element configuration—set 8-24—that appears at the close of each of the three acts. A chain of inclusion-related sets now emerges, the importance of each of which has been discussed in this and the preceding chapter:

$$4\text{-}19 \subset \begin{matrix} 5\text{-}26 \\ 5\text{-}30 \end{matrix} \qquad 6\text{-}34 \subset 8\text{-}24$$

The symbolic presentation expresses the fact that each set in the ordered series contains all of the smaller sets that precede it; the fundamental "building block," from which each of the larger sets can be constructed by adding respectively one, two, and four carefully chosen pitch classes, is none other than Wozzeck's set 4-19.

Two additional properties of the largest set in the series—the cadential structure 8-24—intensify the interlocking nature of the chain and make the network of inclusion relationships too astoundingly complex for a concise notational display: *set 8-24 contains each of the other sets of the series not just one time but four times; set 8-24 also contains the other "almost whole-tone" hexachords 6-21 and 6-22 four times each.* Berg's own reference to this closing eight-note structure as "quasi-cadential" (see chapter 1) may now strike the reader as, to say the least, something of an understatement. The closing pitch structure of *Wozzeck* has the capacity to assume the role of a "cadence"—a term borrowed from tonal theory—because it summarizes by containment the fundamental pitch materials of this atonal opera; in that respect, but only in that respect, the closing structure has a function analogous to that of the final cadential progression in a tonal composition, the progression that serves not only as goal but also as matrix of the tonal work.

From this point forward, the chain of sets presented above will be regarded as the "family of origin" of sets that "belong" directly to Wozzeck and, by virtue of his centrality in the dramatic structure, provide the fundamental pitch-structural matrix of the opera. I use the word *matrix* here and in chapter 4 not in its mathematical sense but rather in the sense of the binding substance within which something originates, develops, or is contained. Both the extent to which Wozzeck's chain of sets constitutes a "family of origin" and the degree to which that family serves as a matrix will become more evident when an even stronger relationship shared by the members of the family can be revealed in terms of the theory of set complexes to be presented in chapter 5. For now, the notion of the "family of origin" brings together five of the most outstanding pitch structures of the opera, provides a summary statement about pitch materials associated with the central character, and looks forward to my conclusion that the large-scale harmonic organization of *Wozzeck* may be characterized as most amazingly cohesive.

4 MARIE'S PITCH-STRUCTURAL MATRIX

It may be noted that I have been careful to avoid including Marie in the roster of subsidiary characters who surround Wozzeck in the circular dramatic design and stand in a primarily functional relationship to him. The roles of the Captain, the Doctor, the Drum Major, Andres, the tavern crowd, and Margret, though carefully drawn, serve largely as foils that underscore Wozzeck's misery. In sharp contrast to these characters, the first three of whom also function in varying degrees as inhumane stereotypes, Marie provides an all too human counterpart to Wozzeck; tied down to him in an unhappy bond personified by the child, Marie's life moves parallel with Wozzeck's toward catastrophe.

Quite apart from the intensity and the outcome of the conflict between this man and this woman, statistics concerning the large-scale dramatic and musical structure suggest that the conflict itself constitutes a dramatic issue that is secondary only to the plight of the central character himself. In five of the twelve scenes where Wozzeck is present, Marie is there too; furthermore, two of the three scenes in which Wozzeck does not appear feature Marie instead. As mentioned earlier, the decisive confrontation between Marie and Wozzeck is placed at the absolute center of the opera (Act II/Scene 3); and whereas the Interlude before the final scene of the opera recapitulates themes associated with all of the characters except Marie, achieving its climax with material directly related to Wozzeck, the last scene features pitch structures and motives that (as will be shown in this chapter) are indisputably linked with Marie and with her role as the mother of Wozzeck's child.

Set-theoretical analysis provides further evidence that the composer favors Marie by placing her role very near to the center of his large-scale dramatic and musical design. First of all, whereas Wozzeck has a "family of origin" of sets, consisting of a tightly unified small-to-large series made structurally homogeneous by its expansion from a single tetrachord, Marie is likewise given a "family" of set structures—an equally distinctive *group of tetra-chords*; Marie's group is characterized by greater diversity with respect to structural properties and relationships, perhaps reflecting the multiple nature of her role—Marie as mother, Marie as sensual woman, Marie as Wozzeck's unfaithful mistress, Marie in the end as repentant but incorrigible "sinner." Second, we are about to see that all of the tetrachords that become firmly associated with Marie when she first appears subsequently recur throughout the opera in a manner comparable to the all-pervasive nature of Wozzeck's set 4-19. Juxtapositions of Marie's sets with material related to Wozzeck (instances of which have already been observed [see Examples 26, 28, and 42, with others to follow]) portray in pitch-structural terms the conflict be-tween complementary partners of nearly equal dramatic importance. And, finally, it will be shown that the notion of the inclusion relation and the theory of set complexes (chapter 5) provide relationships that bind together certain members from each of the two "families" of sets that distinguish Wozzeck from Marie; these relationships supply a long-range pitch-structural correla-tive for the fact that, though in conflict, Wozzeck, Marie, and their child themselves constitute a "nuclear family" whose interdependence, in the face of cruel circumstances and an indifferent world, is such that the individual actions of Wozzeck and Marie must lead to family disaster.

The tetrachordal aspect of the group of set structures associated with Marie is strikingly exhibited in the very first passage where she is seen alone on-stage with her child—the passage from Act I/Scene 3 shown in Example 45. At the instant Marie slams her window shut, cutting off the sound of the behind-the-scenes military band, the violins and violas effect a rapid shift from the thick, raucous five- and six-voice harmonies of the Military March to a tetrachordal tune-and-accompaniment "chamber" texture, with triplet sixteenth-note arpeggiated doublings in lower strings. Jolting the listener's attention from the distant military band to the much closer pit orchestra, this sudden instrumental and textural change spatially underscores Marie's vio-lent effort to close out the external world and, with it, thoughts of the Drum Major, whom she has just seen for the first time. With the material that fol-lows, the listener is drawn into Marie's chamber, which in turn represents her impoverished internal life with the child.

A comparative examination of the passage shown in Example 45 and pas-sages in the examples to follow will reveal that the moment of entry into Marie's private world coincides with an exposition of virtually all the pitch-structural ideas that will be important in relation to Marie not only in this scene but throughout the rest of the opera. More specifically, the passage at Example 45 from m. 363 to m. 364, to which we will hereafter refer as the "Komm, mein Bub!" ("Come, my boy!") passage, contains the set structures that will constitute Marie's pitch-structural matrix—a matrix comparable in scope and significance to the fundamental matrix established in chapter 3, the chain of sets designated as Wozzeck's "family of origin." Our survey of Marie's pitch structural matrix begins, then, with an examination of the pitch

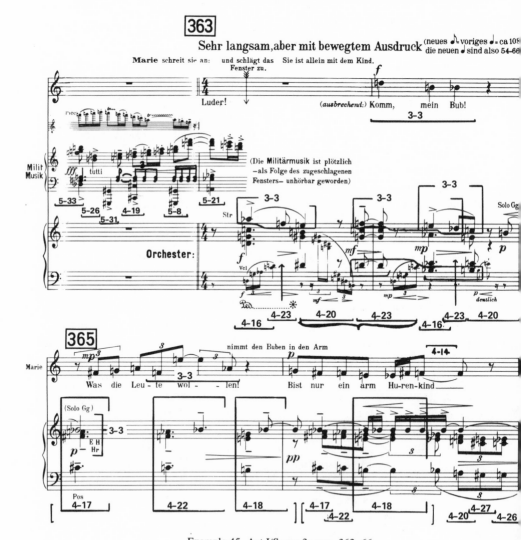

Example 45. Act I/Scene 3: mm. 362–66

structures that will assume local and long-range significance as components of the "Komm, mein Bub!" passage.

I

Decisions concerning segmentation at Example 45 are facilitated by the recognition of a straightforward melodic and harmonic relationship between the introductory "Komm, mein Bub!" passage and the opening of Marie's Lullaby—the section that begins ten measures later and whose opening is shown at Example 46. The "Komm, mein Bub!" melody is the three-note setting (pcs 2, 11, 10) given to those words at m. 364 (Ex. 45); in fact this figure is anticipated a tritone higher by the first violins one measure earlier and then repeated sequentially as part of the larger descending violin line (mm. 363–65: 8, 5, 4, 5, 4, 1, 0) against which Marie's setting is counterpointed. An inverted form of the three-note motive (pcs 5, 4, 1) connects the first and

Example 46. Act I/Scene 3: mm. 370–75

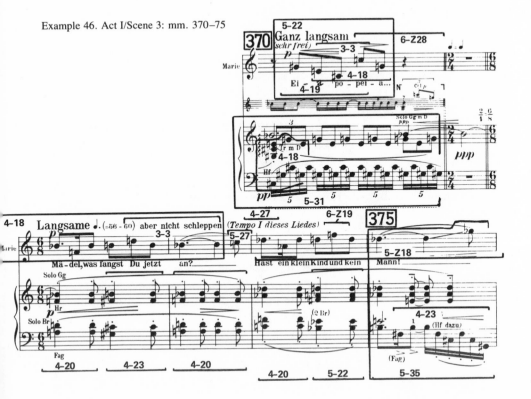

second statements of the sequence. One further iteration of the motive, whose set name is 3-3, may be heard in the fundamental bass line of the harmonic progression at m. 364: that bass line begins as a doubling of Marie's statement of the motive but effects a voice exchange with her figure as follows:

$$\text{(Marie:)} \quad 2 \;\; 11 \;\; \diagdown\!\!\!\diagup \;\; 10$$
$$\text{(bass line:)} \; 2 \;\; 10 \;\; \diagup\!\!\!\diagdown \;\; 11$$

Note, first of all, that Marie's version of the three-note motive reappears rhythmically altered but otherwise intact as a prominent segment of her statement at the beginning of the Lullaby (Ex. 46, m. 372). Now consider the sequential pattern that constitutes the harmonic component of the "Komm, mein Bub!" passage (Ex. 45), and compare the chord pair indicated by a brace at m. 363 with the chord pair that is featured at the beginning of the Lullaby (Ex. 46):

all vertical segments
(primary and composite)
excluding vocal part,
mm. 363–64: |̲ 4-16 4-23 4-20 ̲| 4-23 |̲ 4-16 4-23 4-20 ̲|

Clearly two of the three tetrachords that provide the harmonic basis of the "Komm, mein Bub!" passage have been transposed (at the tritone) and transplanted from their setting at the point indicated in Example 45 to serve as the fundamental vertical components of the Lullaby. Note that in both settings the disposition and spacing of set 4-20 [101220] and set 4-23 [021030] throw into relief the maximized perfect-fourth interval, prepared as a motivic feature of this scene by the oscillating fourth-motion in the "wrong" basses of the preceding Military March. Berg's own comments about the folksong function of these fourths will be considered later.

As George Perle's work demonstrates (1971, p. 287), it is entirely possible to observe, even hear, the melodic and harmonic relationship between the "Komm, mein Bub!" passage and the Lullaby without recourse to set analysis. The same is true with regard to subsequent appearances of each of these ideas in which both the harmonic and melodic components described above are preserved (see Perle's lists in Perle 1971, pp. 287, 289). Of the eight passages in which the "Komm, mein Bub!" idea reappears intact, two coincide with Wozzeck's utterance "Ach, Marie!" (Act I/Scene 4, mm. 539–41 [Ex. 32] and mm. 606–10), decisively confirming the association of this motive with her, or, more especially, with her as Wozzeck's mistress and the mother of his child. A third recurrence, at the single moment when Marie utters the verbal keynote "Wir arme Leut!" (Act I/Scene 3, m. 467), has been eloquently interpreted by Perle, whose statement warrants full quotation here on the grounds that it may give further substance to the notion of the expansion of motivic domains, a fundamental issue of this and the preceding chapter:

> Here we have a superb example of the complexity and subtlety of Berg's use of *Leitmotive*, and of the concrete, rather than abstract, connotations that he assigns to them. Had Marie's exclamation at this point recapitulated the figure to which these words are set in Wozzeck's aria in the opening scene, and that is the principal thematic element of that aria, it would have emphasized her tie to Wozzeck rather than the desperate need for release that is expressed in her very next words, "I can't bear it!", and her sudden rush to the door to escape from the house as the curtain falls, and that is expressed again, when we next see her, in her readiness to accept the attentions of the Drum Major. The climactic development of [the "Komm, mein Bub!" motive] in the Change of Scene music that follows Marie's despairing cry re-echoes that cry. The sense of "Wir arme Leut!" remains implicitly identified with this *Leitmotiv* at the moment of Marie's death (III/2, mm. 105f), according to Berg's own interpretation. In his list of the *Leitmotive* that, at the moment of her death, "pass through her consciousness with lightning speed and in a macabre grimace, like the real characters which had permeated her life," the composer describes this *Leitmotiv* as "the motif of Marie bemoaning her wretched life" [see Berg's 1929 lecture (Redlich 1957a, pp. 323– 24)]. And, indeed, though Marie's "Come, my child!" indelibly stamps the basic melodic cell of the *Leitmotiv*, there is a reference to her poverty within the context dominated by the *Leitmotiv* at its first appearance ("Bist nur ein arm Hurenkind") and again at its return in II/1 ("Ich bin nur ein armes Weibsbild!"). [Perle 1971, pp. 288–89; bracketed information my own.]

The set-analytical method further verifies that the domain of the "Komm, mein Bub!" motive, initially presented in straightforward association with Marie as mother, extends far beyond this aspect of her role and beyond her bond with Wozzeck to embrace in a much larger sense her personal misery and the impoverished life of the child. As with pitch structures examined in relationship to Wozzeck, pitch structures that originate as components of motives associated with Marie provide a means of expanding the connotative domain of these motives by recurring in contexts that free the pitch structures from dependence upon motives yet also reinforce the association of both with Marie; by this process the relationship of her role to the all-pervasive central issues of the drama is strengthened. Recurrences within Act I/Scene 3 and elsewhere in the opera of the three vertical components from the "Komm, mein Bub!" motive—sets 4-16, 4-23, and 4-20—will provide our first case in point.

II

To my knowledge no writer about *Wozzeck* has yet called attention to the fact that the pitch structure that constitutes the opening vertical sonority of the "Komm, mein Bub!" motive (normal order: 7, 8, 0, 2) is related by simple transposition (t = 9) to the pitch structure of Marie's well-known motive of "waiting for the indefinite" ("das ins Unbestimmte hinzielende Warten"; see Berg's 1929 lecture in Redlich 1957a, p. 318). I refer here to the sonority that effects the single ominous moment of repose at the end of the first large section of Act I/Scene 3, just before Wozzeck enters (see Ex. 28, mm. 425–27; the normal order of the "waiting" motive set is 4, 5, 9, 11). As shown in Examples 28 and 45, the set name for these transpositionally equivalent sonorities is 4-16. The importance of this set structure as a component of the two most frequently recurring and utterly memorable motives associated with Marie may be clinched with a survey of the outstanding moments in the opera where the "waiting" motive itself returns: Act I/Scene 3, m. 455: Wozzeck's exit (Marie is left alone and "waiting" again); Act I/Scene 4, m. 528: Wozzeck with the Doctor, thinking of Marie; Act II/Scene 3, mm. 372–74: the precise moment when the curtain rises upon the central scene of the opera; Act III/Scene 2, m. 106: the exact moment of Marie's death; Act III/Scene 3, mm. 152–53: Wozzeck fails to dispel the memory of having murdered Marie; Act III/Scene 5, m. 379: the children tell Marie's boy that his mother is dead. Of incidental interest is the fact that Berg chose the same pitch structure for the first vertical sonority of his first published work—the Sonata Op. 1 (Ex. 47).[1]

Whereas the recurrence in the Lullaby of the three-note melodic cell from the "Komm, mein Bub!" motive effects a logical link between Marie's first reference to the child and the song that she subsequently sings to him, the recurrence of set 4-16 at the "waiting" motive strongly substantiates Perle's observation that the aspect of Marie's impoverished existence—now enlarged to include her solitude and her undefined attitude of waiting—is already suggested at the first appearance of "Komm, mein Bub!" Even further

Example 47. Berg, Sonata Op. 1 (1908): mm. 1–3.

Example 48. Act I/Scene 3: mm. 410–18

evidence to this effect may be found in the passage that prepares the entrance of the "waiting" motive shown in Example 28. We have seen that two of the three tetrachords of the "Komm, mein Bub!" motive—sets 4-20 and 4-23—have been transplanted and paired to serve as the neighbor-chord harmonic component of the sequentially related first two phrases of the Lullaby. The same pairing procedure may be observed at the end of the first section of this scene: this time set 4-20, in the form (4, 5, 9, 0) and disposition shown at Example 48, is chosen from the "Komm, mein Bub!" motive not only to prepare but also to adumbrate that form of set 4-16 which will become the fixed collection (4, 5, 9, 11) of the "waiting" motive (Ex. 28).

If the reader has not already noticed that the pitch structure known in tonal theory as "the major-seventh chord" produces set 4-20, that fact ought to become apparent at Example 48. Observe that the form of this set that serves as the adumbration of the "waiting" motive emerges from a closing reference to the Lullaby, which had also featured set 4-20 as its opening vertical structure (cf. Ex. 46). Now the characteristic fourths-motive from the tune of the Lullaby

moves sequentially in harp and contrabassoon to the following pitch level at m. 412,

there to become the quarter-note oscillating bass motion of the "waiting" motive, while strings complete the set structure with an ascending four-octave presentation of the verticalized open-fifth dyad ‿A♮-E♮‿, hereafter to be associated with the waiting Marie, "lost in her thoughts." At this point the reader may wish to turn to the full score in order to examine in toto the passage that connects the adumbration of the "waiting" motive at m. 415 (Ex. 48) with the ultimately fixed form of the "waiting" motive at m. 425 (Ex. 28). The utterly simple voice-leading motion that controls the passage (mm. 413–25) is only somewhat obscured by snatches of the Drum Major's Military March in the brass, superimposed upon the eleven-measure prolongation of the "major-seventh chord" set 4-20 in winds, celesta, and harp; the Military March betrays Marie's thoughts while waiting. As shown in the following reduction, a single pitch class requires alteration for the adumbration of the "waiting" motive to become the "waiting" motive itself:

That alteration first appears in the celesta-harp arpeggiations at m. 422; descending in sixteenth-note motion through the four octaves originally spanned by the strings, these arpeggiations carry the new set structure into the lower register, where now the quarter-note oscillating figure is resumed, the fourths-motive from the Lullaby having been replaced by the "fateful" tritone B♮-F♯. Note that the set structure formed by the complete harmonic progression shown in reduction—the progression from "adumbration"-chord to "waiting"-chord proper—is none other than the structure that is presented vertically as the first chord of the opera (Ex. 3)—5-20. This fact will be given further attention in chapter 5, after our broad survey of pitch structures associated specifically with Marie has been completed.

The passage just described is the one that immediately precedes Wozzeck's entrance into Act I/Scene 3. A parallel set-structural situation prevails in the passage just prior to Wozzeck's exit from the same scene twenty-seven measures later (i.e., the passage that precedes the excerpt showing Wozzeck's "exit" motive at Ex. 30). We shall see that as a formal and harmonic response to the parallel dramatic situation, this passage brilliantly exemplifies the manner in which the musical design of this scene gains both cohesion and variety by means of new juxtapositions and recombinations of Marie's tetrachords; these collections have been established from the outset in association with Marie, but their intrinsic structural properties permit extensions of their motivic domain in contexts that underscore Marie's relation to Wozzeck.

The sixteenth-note triplet arpeggiated figure appearing in strings *col legno* at m. 450 (Ex. 49) and continuing until one bar before Wozzeck's exit at m. 454 may or may not remind the listener of the earlier arpeggiations that began at m. 417 (Ex. 48), just prior to Wozzeck's entrance. Although from a rhythmic and dynamic viewpoint the four-part arpeggiated pattern and the spasmodic repeated-chord figure at Example 49 bear little resemblance to their predecessors at Example 48, the texture that these components together create supports a comparison further warranted by the choice and disposition of set structures. In the earlier passage a single tetrachord—the fixed form 4, 5, 9, 0 of set 4-20—was prolonged by the sixteenth-note arpeggiated pattern and reinforced by a much quieter, more restrained repeated-chord figure; that single arpeggiated-verticalized form of set 4-20 served as a long-range preparation for the single arpeggiated-verticalized form of set 4-16 that becomes the "waiting" motive. In the later passage, as shown at Example 49, the new repeated-chord figure in winds, brass, and harp once again yields a form of set 4-20—this time the very form (6, 7, 11, 2) that will be heard in Act II/Scene 1 (Ex. 62) when Marie's Lullaby reappears transformed to serve as her Gypsy Song (see the comments concerning the G♮-D♮ motive in chapter 2).

Meanwhile, rather than reinforcing that same pitch structure, the four-part arpeggiated figure in the strings now simultaneously projects on both the horizontal and the vertical plane a new form (3, 4, 8, 10) of set 4-16, clearly a transposed (t = 11) and intensified reference to the arpeggiations of this set that had earlier led to the entrance of the "waiting" motive. In sum, the long-range twofold harmonic progression that had accompanied Marie's waiting just before Wozzeck's entrance has now been compressed into a single gesture to match her intense frustration at the moment just before he will leave.

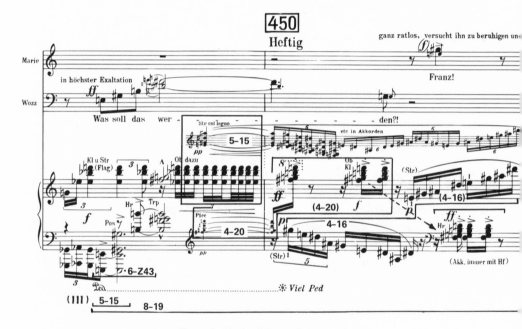

Example 49. Act I/Scene 3: mm. 449–50

Marie is frustrated ("ganz ratlos" ["extremely perplexed"]) because Wozzeck has just revealed his agitation over the visions from the field that remind him of the Apocalypse. The Leitsektion from Act I/Scene 2 that accompanied this disclosure—the immediate cause for Marie's alarm—culminates at m. 449 (Ex. 49) in a transposed, reiterated statement of the third of the three "hallucination" chords that had formed the harmonic basis of that preceding scene. Up to this point only the first of these three pentachords—set 5-Z17—has been discussed; the reader may examine the third "hallucination" chord in its original setting at the beginning of the open-field scene by turning once again to Example 29. Appearing there at the downbeat of m. 204, this third pentachord takes the form (normal order: 3, 4, 5, 9, 11) of set 5-15 but is quickly subsumed at the entrance of the solo horn (pc0) within a hexachord of equal importance in Act I/Scene 2 and of more far-reaching significance in the opera as a whole—set 6-Z43.[2] That complete six-note structure, with its pentachord subset 5-15, reappears transposed at the semitone (2, 3, 4, 8, 10, 11; t = 11) on the second beat of m. 449. Two earlier appearances in the open-field scene (mm. 231f, 283f) of the same pentachord (2, 3, 4, 8, 10) with the same spacing at the same transpositional level scored for the same string harmonics facilitate identification of this structure as the third "hallucination" chord here. In at least one respect, however, the source for the setting of the third "hallucination" chord shown in Example 49 may be found at the point that marks the climactic boundary between first and second large sections of the open-field scene (m. 270). There, as in Example 49, the third "halluci-nation" chord appears not only as a subset of the hexachord 6-Z43 but also in the larger context of an 8-element structure that is none other than the complement of Wozzeck's 4-19—set 8-19. A single series of set-theoretical properties peculiar to the large set 8-19 more than justifies the notion that this complement-related set may be regarded as an outstanding member of Wozzeck's pitch-structural "family of origin": whereas it is true, as presented at the close of chapter 3, that

$$4\text{-}19 \subset \begin{matrix} 5\text{-}26 \\ 5\text{-}30 \end{matrix} \subset 6\text{-}34 \subset 8\text{-}24,$$

it is also true that

$$4\text{-}19 \subset \begin{matrix} 5\text{-}26 \\ 5\text{-}30 \end{matrix} \subset 6\text{-}34 \subset 8\text{-}19.$$

Let us carefully inspect the manner in which set 8-19 is first amassed and then dispersed as shown in Example 49. It has been noted thus far that the "hallucination" chord becomes stabilized on the second beat of m. 449 with the congealing of pcs 2, 3, 4, 8, 10. This pentachord will be sustained throughout the measure: trombones and contrabass tuba provide the pedal point on pcs 4 and 8, while strings with clarinets, reinforced on the third beat by oboes, reiterate the trichord 2, 10, 3. Meanwhile, the horn entrance on the second half of the second beat effects the addition to the collection of pc11 and, with this, the formation of the hexachord 6-Z43; next, the trumpets enter on the third beat with the semitone 6, 7 and, like the low brass and horns, sustain these pitches until the end of the measure, completing the 8-

element configuration 2, 3, 4, 8, 10, 11, 6, 7. Finally, and quite remarkably, on the fourth beat of m. 449, the entire same 8-element collection is reinforced but also redistributed as follows: piccolos project the collection 6, 7, 11, 2—Marie's set 4-20—while strings *col legno* enter with the vertical tetrachord 3, 4, 8, 10, which on the downbeat of m. 450 will become the arpeggiation of Marie's set 4-16 discussed above. Here we have a musically cogent display of the theoretical fact that the large structure 8-19—the complement of Wozzeck's set 4-19—contains not only Wozzeck's third "hallucination" structure 5-15, 6-Z43 but also Marie's tetrachords 4-16 and 4-20. These inclusion relationships are not in themselves so remarkable when we consider that the subset families of the 29 discrete 8-element sets are all large. (Set 8-19 itself contains 16 of the 50 hexachords, 23 of the 38 pentachords, and 22 of the 29 tetrachords.) What is striking here is the segmentally (orchestratively) vivid manner in which the composer utilizes the inclusion properties of the Wozzeck-set 8-19 in order precisely to represent the dramatic situation: the pitch organization of this passage underlines the fact that Marie's alarm arises from and is precipitated by Wozzeck's display of instability, the direct result of his hallucinations in the open field. As Marie now tries to direct Wozzeck's attention toward the child (mm. 450f: "Franz! Franz! Dein Bub . . . " ["Franz! Your boy . . . "]), the new simultaneous juxtaposition of sets 4-16 and 4-20, prolonging the form of set 8-19 shown in Example 49 up to the measure before Wozzeck leaves, yields a pitch-structural representative for each of the three members of the Wozzeck family—8-19 for Wozzeck himself, 4-16 for Marie, and the set-pair 4-16, 4-20 that originated with Marie's first reference to the child. The Marie/child sets are moreover now united within the context of one large Wozzeck-structure, and thus underscored is the fatal family bond that Marie implores Wozzeck to remember but privately longs to escape.

III

For the moment we will now leave Act I/Scene 3 to examine four excerpts from later scenes that feature the first of the three harmonic structures from the "Komm, mein Bub!" motive, the set that becomes the pitch-structural component of Marie's "waiting" motive—4-16. From among the myriad occurrences of this set throughout the opera, these four excerpts have been chosen on the basis that each includes a texted and easily identifiable melodic presentation of the set. Of potentially peculiar interest is the fact that only one of the four excerpts (Ex. 50) is from a passage where Marie herself is present. The other three examples, though indirectly related to Marie, point more especially to the unrestricted harmonic importance of this pitch combination, a characteristic sonority of the composer's language; moreover, these excerpts suggest further extensions of the motivic domain that set 4-16 undergoes in the course of the work.

1. We turn first to the opening of the one scene that is solely Marie's from beginning to end—Act III/Scene 1. It is nighttime. Marie sits in her room throughout the scene at a table in candlelight, alone with her child and with a Bible from which she seeks hope for mercy in the face of unbearable guilt. The juxtaposition of this scene with the immediately subsequent murder scene casts an ironic light on Marie's efforts: little does she know that this is her only chance to repent, that she is in fact "preparing" for death, the only form of mercy she will receive. (In the 1929 lecture [Redlich 1957a, p. 318], Berg interprets Marie's attitude of "waiting" as "a waiting that finds its end only in her death" ["ein Warten, welches erst in ihrem Tod den Abschluss findet"].) Twelve words from Büchner's setting of the scene that are crucial to an understanding of Marie's character unfortunately do not appear in Berg's libretto: (Lehmann edition [1967, p. 424]) "Ich kann nicht! Herrgott gieb mir nur soviel, dass ich beten kann" ("I can't ['go and sin no more']! Lord God, just give me enough [strength] to pray"). In Henry Schmidt's terms, "the final tragedy of Marie is not her death for a sin but her despairing recognition that, given another chance, she would again succumb" (Schmidt 1969, p. 109).

From Marie's "Ich bin doch ein schlecht Mensch—Ich könnt mich erstechen" (Act II/Scene 1, mm. 126–30: "I really am a bad person—I could stab myself"), we have already learned that Marie is remorseful for her infidelity. At the beginning of Act III/Scene 1 the curtain rises to reveal that Marie's remorse is the dictate of a conscience that, like Wozzeck's, is activated by an unquestioning religious belief in the Christian concepts of good and evil. The first biblical text Marie chooses to read aloud provides her with a painful contrast to her own "fallen" state. Shown in Example 50, the immediate juxtaposition of that text as objective statement—(mm. 5–7, from the New Testament, I Peter 2:2) "And neither was guile found in his mouth"— with Marie's personal, subjective response—(mm. 7–10) "Lord God, Lord God! Don't look upon me!"—establishes a textual pattern to be repeated in the course of the scene. This pattern clearly provides the inspiration for Berg's choice of variation form, with dual *Thema* consisting of intensely contrasting antecedent and consequent phrases. Readers may turn to Berg's lecture (Redlich 1957b [English translation]), and to Ploebsch (1968, pp. 65ff), Perle

(1971a, p. 307), or Carner (1975, pp. 185ff) for further background on the unfolding of the variations in the scene at large and for details about the esoteric role of the number 7 in this 70-bar scene. (The scene features a 7-bar *Thema* (4 + 3) and 7 variations followed by a double fugue of 7 × 3 measures whose dual fugal sections are each based upon a 7-pitch subject; the number of beats per variation as well as all the metronome markings are multiples of 7.)

Four distinctive melodic components of the *Thema* have been identified and traced throughout the scene by Perle (1967a, pp. 245–46, 252–56). A fifth and a sixth component, indicated numerically in Example 50, reappear in varied guises within all the variations save variation 4, components #3 and #4 having been omitted in variation 3. This is to say that components #5 and #6 play a joint role in this scene that is secondary *only* to the diatonic "G-minor" antecedent component #1, introduced in stretto at mm. 3–4 (see earlier comments about this theme in chapter 2), and the contrasting chromatic twelve-tone component #2, first heard in 'cellos and basses at mm. 7–9.

Component #5 (m. 7, trumpets) is characterized in the *Thema* and in all but three variations by verticalized major seconds in chromatic descent. (The seconds are expanded to become major ninths in variation 1 [m. 14, solo violin and solo 'cello]; the motive appears as a series of chromatically descending minor thirds in the F-minor variation 5 [m. 38, horns and violas]; and the original seconds return ascending and inverted as minor sevenths in variation 7 [mm. 48–51, violins and violas].) Although in a general descriptive sense this component may have been included to "depict" Marie's "fallen" state, as held by Gerd Ploebsch (1968, p. 66–67), its similarity to the descending component of Perle's "knife" motive (see Perle 1971, pp. 296–97) also suggests that from the beginning of his setting for this scene, Berg looked forward to the point where Marie pushes the child away because the child gives her "a stab in the heart" (variation 3, mm. 21–23: "Der Bub gibt mir einen Stich in's Herz"). In two of its eight appearances in the opera—in Act II/Scene 4 (m. 752; see below), where Wozzeck imagines a knife flashing before his eyes, and in the murder scene itself (see Ex. 74), where Wozzeck's "Wie ein blutig Eisen!" ("Like a bloody blade!") serves as his own cue for drawing the knife—the chromatically descending component of the "knife" motive, like component #5 here, features major ninths (seconds) in outer voices. As always, Berg's orchestrative subtleties warrant comment. In sharp contrast to its piercing introductory presentation by trumpets (accented and forte) in the *Thema*, the "knife" motive at variation 3 appears delicately

Example 50. Act III/Scene 1: mm. 1–9.

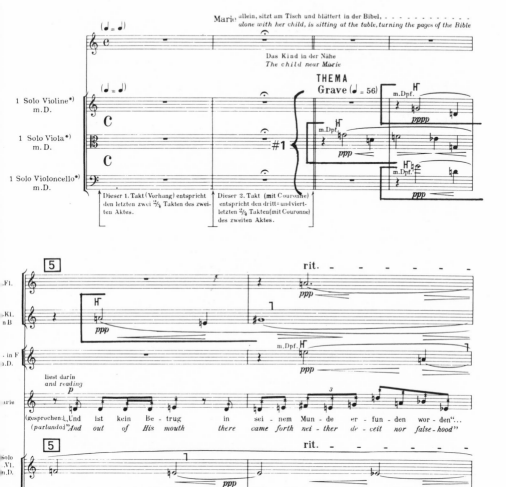

*) Diese 4 ersten Solisten (Viol., Viola und Vlc.) und der 2. Solo Violinspieler und 1. Kontrabassist behalten während der ganzen Szene den Dämpfer auf. Alle übrigen Streicher durchwegs ohne Dämpfer.

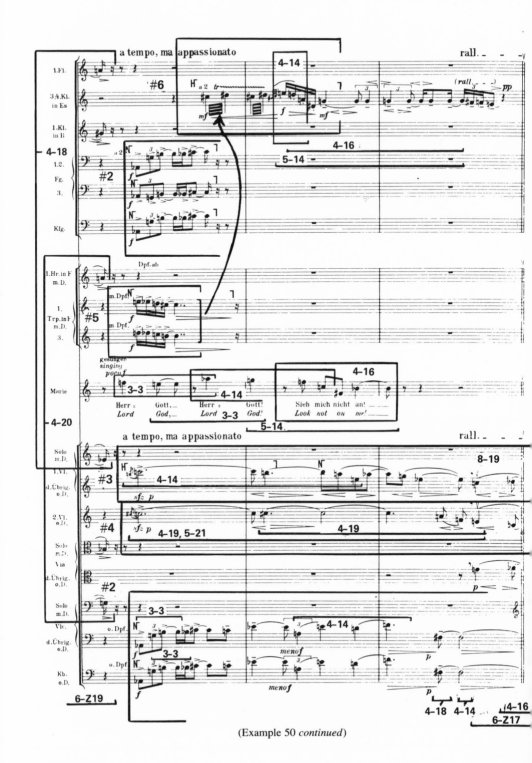

(Example 50 *continued*)

scored for flutter-tonguing flutes—an unpenetrating sound that corresponds with the fact that Marie's very small child can only "stab" Marie to the extent that his silent presence is a constant reminder of her breach of responsibility toward Wozzeck.

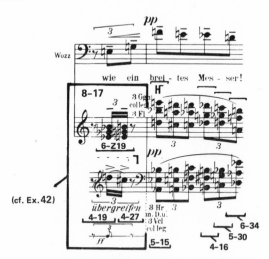

(the "knive" motive: Act II/Scene 4, m. 752.)

The preceding remarks have been offered to provide a context for the discussion of component #6, marked as a principal voice (H⁻ for *Hauptstimme*) in all but the second variation. In the *Thema* as in variations 1, 2, and 6 (see full score), component #6 appears as an outgrowth of component #5. The arrow at m. 7 in Example 50 points to the pitch-structural connection between the two ideas: the last major second of component #5 in trumpets (pcs 4, 6) becomes the trill figure that announces the beginning of component #6 in E♭-clarinets. As indicated in the score and below, the set structure formed by the last four pitches of component #6 is 4-16, the set structure of Marie's "waiting" motive:

$$
\begin{array}{c}
\text{5-14} \\
\text{(pcs, E}^\flat\text{-clarinets, mm. 7–8:)} \ \underbrace{4\ 6\ (3)\ 4}_{\text{Tr.}}\ \overbrace{7\ 5\ 0\ 6\ 10} \\
\underbrace{\text{4-14}} \\
\underbrace{\text{4-16}}
\end{array}
$$

The fleeting sixteenth-note disposition of component #6 may certainly call into question the audibility of its set-structural composition; the reader may be more willing, however, to acknowledge the importance of component #6 in the overall contrapuntal design of the *Thema* when he recognizes that Marie's vocal line at m. 8 is an augmented statement (at $t = 0$) of the very same component. Of special interest is the fact that the "waiting"-motive set 4-16 appears as an isolated and clearly discernible setting for Marie's "Sieh mich nicht an!" ("Don't look upon me!") Now consider carefully the melodic contour and rhythmic disposition of this statement; its resemblance in these respects to Wozzeck's "Wir arme Leut!" motive (Ex. 24) should become readily apparent. It will be remembered that even though Marie shares Wozzeck's status as a member of the "arme Leut" class, her personal plight as impoverished woman rather than her tie to Wozzeck is emphasized at the one point where she pronounces the words "Wir arme Leut!" (Act I/Scene 3, m. 467); there her vocal line is a statement of the melodic component—set 3-3—from her own "Komm, mein Bub!" motive rather than a repetition of Wozzeck's "Wir arme Leut!" set 4-19. Here in Act III/Scene 1, Marie's appeal for mercy contains within its melodic design a reminder of her relationship to Wozzeck, a relationship based to a large extent upon her economic helplessness; once again, however, the predominant set structure is *Marie's* set structure, whose association with Marie is further strengthened by its appearance in this her utterly private hour of despair. As such the passage may be added to the increasing number of examples offered to support the thesis that Berg's choice of pitch structures plays a role just as fundamental to his tremendously complex leitmotivic scheme as his manipulation of melodic contour, rhythmic organization, spacing, register, orchestration—in short, musical dimensions that have traditionally served as variables and constants in the nineteenth-century operatic leitmotivic design.

Before leaving this excerpt, the reader may wish to observe a few additional set-structural features of the remarkable network of components that constitutes the *Thema* for this scene. First of all, it must be mentioned that Marie's vocal line in the consequent phrase of the *Thema* provides a wonderful display of the essential melodic and even harmonic ideas of the scene, not the least important of which is her concluding segment—the statement of set 4–16. Note that the initial four-note segment of her line at mm. 7–8 (pcs 5, 4, 8, 7)—the setting for her "Herr Gott, Herr Gott!"—represents a transposed version of the first four-note segment (pcs 8, 7, 11, 10) in the faster-moving twelve-tone bass line—component #2; the equivalent set structures for these segments consist of interlocking inversionally related statements of set 3-3, itself the melodic component from Marie's "Komm, mein Bub!" motive (see Ex. 45). The descent from the apex of Marie's line (the A♭, m. 7) moreover displays a form of set 4-14 (pcs 8, 7, 5, 0)—the set structure that is unfolded within a slower descent by the first four pitches of component #3 in the violins (pcs 0, 11, 9, 4) and that also makes an appearance in component #6 as shown in the score and in the diagram above. The "F-minor triad" subset clearly outlined by Marie's form of this set promises the F-minor tonal center with its corresponding key signature in variations 5 and 6.

Three final details from Example 50 warrant our attention. (1) The so-called "bitonal chord (D Major and the Neapolitan E flat Major)" (Carner 1975, p. 185; see also Reich and Ploebsch) that marks the end of the antecedent phrase (mm. 6–7) and returns at the end of the Interlude subsequent to this scene (see Ex. 68) happens to be a representation of set 6-Z19, the set whose outstanding importance in the opera has been discussed in terms of its special inclusion relations (see the comments concerning Examples 28, 36, and 43). I venture to suggest that the vertical juxtaposition of triads within this 6-element chord is not as significant here as the juxtaposition of interlocking forms of two tetrachords that are both strongly associated with Marie—set 4-20 (see earlier comments) and set 4-18 (see forthcoming discussion). (2) Components #3 and #4 in the violins (mm. 7–9) are not only welded to each other by virtue of their scoring and their initial rhythmic similarities but also complement each other in set-theoretical terms: whereas the complete 8-element component #3 features the by now well-known large Wozzeck-set 8-19, component #4 displays two interlocking inversion-related forms of the complement 4-19 within a single statement of the larger set 5-21. (3) Last of all, note that the final vertical sonority to be heard in the *Thema* (pcs 6, 8, 0, 1) is none other than an inverted form of the "waiting"-motive set 4-16.

2. Our next example comes from the development section of the sonata-allegro movement that constitutes Act II/Scene 1. The passage shown at Example 51 immediately precedes the full orchestral recapitulation of the original "Wir arme Leut!" theme from Act I/Scene 1; that is, this passage precedes the only other moment in the opera when Wozzeck himself restates that verbal motif, complete with its original melodic setting (see Ex. 27 and the corresponding comments). As mentioned in chapter 3, Wozzeck has just noticed drops of perspiration on the brow of his sleeping child; this provokes him to observe that there is "nothing but work under the sun; sweat, even in sleep" ("Nichts als Arbeit unter der Sonne, sogar Schweiss im Schlaf"). Shown in Example 51, the melodic setting for the first part of this text is a long, descending nine-note line within which the first six pitches feature the "al-

most whole-tone" hexachord 6–22, the second six pitches produce another "almost whole-tone" hexachord, 6–21, and the first four pitches, at the words "Nichts als Arbeit," clearly project the same form of set 4-16 (normal order: 4, 5, 9, 11) that had appeared as the arpeggiated, then verticalized pitch-structural component of Marie's "waiting" motive in Act I/Scene 3. (The long-range significance of the tetrachord 4-17, repeated vertically in an ascending chromatic series scored for oboes, and also featured in the repeated viola-horn figure, will be discussed later. Note that the composite structure sustained for two and one-half beats in the orchestra at m. 113 (0, 1, 2, 4, 5, 8, 9, 10) constitutes another form of the large Wozzeck-set 8-19.)

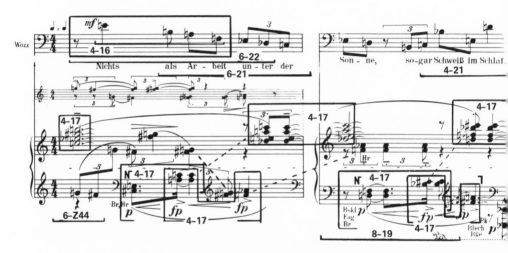

Example 51. Act II/Scene 1: mm. 112–13

Since a dramatic connection relating the occurrence of set 4-16 in Example 51 with its earlier appearance as the pitch-structural component of Marie's "waiting" motive does not immediately present itself, this may be the moment to stress a viewpoint that underlies in general my choice and treatment of examples. The frequency of occurrences throughout the opera of many of the pitch structures chosen for discussion is such that an effort to interpret every appearance of every set in terms of its dramatic-motivic function runs the risk of overlooking an important fact: whereas sometimes (as shown in abundance with the examples presented thus far in this and the preceding chapter) sets may be used to extend a network of motivic associations, at other times sets may reappear simply because they have a characteristic and integral role in the overall harmonic organization of the work, which is to say that they represent components of the complex but tremendously cohesive musical language of *Wozzeck* in much the same way that the central character Wozzeck represents the all-pervasive fundamental issues of the drama. The appearances of set 4-16 in Example 51 and in the two examples to follow provide a case in point. These three excerpts do *not* display the kind of network of interlocking associations shown, for instance, by the series of examples that pertained to Wozzeck's set 4-19; however, an appreciation of the harmonic importance of set 4-16, whose pervasive role reflects Marie's integral relationship to the drama, can be gained after all of the examples in the series under discussion have been examined in the light of each other.

3. The third example in this series (Ex. 52) shows in its entirety the passage that accompanies the single appearance of the Idiot (the tavern: Act II/Scene 4, mm. 649–68); immediately preceding the excerpt shown in Example 42, this is the passage at the end of which the Idiot's words "Ich riech Blut!" (mm. 667f: "I smell blood!") incite Wozzeck to "see red" and propel him ever closer toward the murder of Marie (review Ex. 42 and the corresponding comments). George Perle has asserted that deletions of the other appearances of the Idiot in the Franzos edition of the play, used by Berg, leave this single appearance unmotivated in the opera. Perle objects in particular to the loss of context for the Idiot's reference to blood, a context that would have been established by the excised scenes in which the Idiot is heard "innocently babbling words that belong to the child's world of fairy tale and counting rhyme, words—'Blut!', 'Wasser!'—that are fearfully transformed in Wozzeck's mind, and the portents of his fate" (Perle 1967b, p. 216; see Scenes 16 and 27 in the Lehmann reconstruction [Schmidt translation, 1969]). Certainly, however, the image of blood has been prepared early in the opera by the blood-red sunset at the end of the open-field scene. Wozzeck perceives this as the fire from a gigantic furnace, he describes the vision to both Marie and the Doctor, and he later associates it with Marie herself (Act II/Scene 3, mm. 381–83: "Aber Du hast einen roten Mund, einen roten Mund—keine Blase drauf?" ["But you have a red mouth, a red mouth—no blister on it?"]; Act II/Scene 4, mm. 534–37: "Das Weib ist heiss! ist heiss! heiss!" ["The woman is hot! Hot! Hot!"]). The even more straightforward connection between the image of blood and the *actual fate* of Marie, as well as the need to compensate for the absence of a stronger dramatic context for the appearance and text of the Idiot, may explain, moreover, why the composer is careful to choose pitch structures for the Idiot's passage that are "motivated" by earlier appearances and in fact originate in material associated with Marie.

Example 52. Act II/Scene 4: mm. 649–68

Compare the repeated melodic pattern in the ascending clarinet figuration that announces the Idiot's appearance at m. 650 (Ex. 52) with the opening of Wozzeck's descending melodic statement at Example 51. Brackets added to the examples for each of these excerpts will aid the reader in ascertaining that the arpeggiated tetrachord (normal order: 11, 0, 4, 6) coinciding with the Idiot's appearance is a transposed form (t = 5) of Wozzeck's melodic statement at Example 51, itself a restatement of the fixed form (normal order: 4, 5, 9, 11) of Marie's "waiting" motive. The similarity between these two melodic presentations of set 4-16 is made stronger at m. 660 (Ex. 52), where the clarinet restates the same arpeggiation in descending rather than ascending form.

The allusion to Marie's attitude of waiting, oblique at m. 650, is clarified at m. 653, where the fiddlers, who have violins with all four steel strings tuned up one tone (written in the score as sounded), are "waiting around" for the next bout of dance music and killing time in a simulated effort to tune their instruments; both fail at first to find their correct series of perfect fifths A♮-E♮-B♮-F♯, the first fiddler at first producing instead the exact pitch content of Marie's own "waiting" motive A♮-E♮-B♮-F♮, the fixed form itself of set 4-16. In fact the correct series of fifths, finally achieved at m. 655 after the first fiddler has groped his way through the quarter tone between F♮ and F♯ and the second fiddler has adjusted his B♮, further reinforces the allusion to Marie: the set name for the "fifths-chord," known literally inverted as a "fourths-chord," is 4-23, the set heard in Act I/Scene 3 along with set 4-16 as a vertical component of Marie's "Komm, mein Bub!" motive, then transplanted, as discussed earlier, to serve with set 4-20 as the harmonic component of the Lullaby.

The fiddlers, having found their fifths, presumably inspire the guitar player to follow their example. Now the "E-minor" orientation of the correct guitar series, achieved at m. 660 and proudly displayed, note by note, in descending arpeggiation at m. 662) ⌐E♮-B♮-G♮⌐ D♮-A♮-E♮⌐) retrospectively sheds light upon the composer's choice of an E-minor triad as the chord to which the accordion player continues to return throughout this passage; meanwhile the bombardon player nonchalantly provides added coherence by choosing E minor as the key in which he will repeat his bass line from the opening of the *Don Giovanni* minuet heard at the beginning of the scene (compare mm. 656–57 with mm. 439–42). Superimposed upon these non-concerted yet "accidentally harmonious" elements, the musical setting for the first of the Idiot's two utterances (mm. 658–59: "Lustig, lustig . . . " ["jolly, jolly . . . "]) is a simple reordering of the pitch-class content from the clarinet figuration in m. 650—an arrangement of set 4-16 in waltz rhythm whose first and last pitches (pcs 11 and 4) permit the Idiot, in blissful ignorance, to accommodate himself to the underlying E-minor tonality. At this point clarinetist, fiddlers, accordion player, guitarist, and bombardonist each meander "independently" toward an improvised cadence, bringing to its rough conclusion an interlude made unforgettable by its "gypsy" instrumentation and its unmotivated "E-minor" melancholy, in bizarre contradiction with the Idiot's "jolly" text.

The Idiot, however, has not finished. Having crept quite close to Wozzeck, he is now mysteriously impelled to utter his even more bizarre second and final statement of the opera; in the eerie high range of unaccompanied falsetto recitative, the Idiot's portentous claim that he "smells blood" (mm. 665–68) is given a distinctive setting that arises "cunningly" ("listig") out of the clarinetist's arpeggiated triplets and once again displays the predominant set 4-16. Now, however, this set is exhibited at an entirely new transpositional level and with a bold new contour that features the ascending diminished octave A♮-A♭, iterated three times in dramatic preparation for the keyword "Blut!" The newly transposed form of set 4-16 (normal order: 8, 9, 1, 3) supplies three of the four pitch classes (8, 1, 3, 10) *not* present in the preceding six measures of the instrumental interlude, where the complement of the "fourths-chord"—set 8-23—has been prolonged; the twelve-tone cycle is completed at m. 666 with the very first note (pc10) of Wozzeck's response.

Before turning to the last of our series of excerpts that feature set 4-16, it might be mentioned that, like 4-16, the "fourths-chord" set 4-23 plays a diversified role throughout the opera, about which the composer himself had the following to say:

The other result of my inquiries to date is the manner in which I have done justice to the necessity of conveying the popular and songlike [*Volkstümlich-Liedmässiges*], from which arises the necessity of establishing a relationship between art music and folk music in my opera— something that is a matter of course in tonal music. Within the so-called atonal harmony it was not easy to make these levels of distinction clear. I believe that I succeeded by means of composing everything that, musically speaking, extends to the domain of the popular with an easily understood primitiveness that is also practicable within atonal harmony. As such one finds: preference for symmetrical constructions of periods and sections, *the placing into relief of harmonies of thirds and especially of fourths, and also of a type of melody in which the whole-tone scale and the perfect fourth play a large role*, whereas in the atonal music of the Vienna School, diminished and augmented intervals dominate. [From Berg's 1929 lecture, in Redlich 1957a, pp. 317–18; emphasis my own.][3]

Berg continues by citing as examples from Act I the Military March, with its primitive "polytonality," created by means of "'wrong basses'" (which moreover provide the characteristic marching-band fourths in quarter-note oscillation) and Marie's Lullaby, with its "harmonies in fourths" (featured in the form of set 4-23 not only in the opening four measures as discussed earlier, but also again at mm. 378–79 and at mm. 380 and 382, where it serves as the fundamental harmony of the "Eia popeia" refrain [see Ex. 59]; consider below, moreover, the prominent ascending-fourth series in the horn and harp that summarizes the fourths-motive of this scene while providing a link at m. 395 to the reprise of the "Eia popeia" material at m. 396).

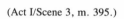

(Act I/Scene 3, m. 395.)

To Berg's own comments it may be added that the "fourths-chord" feature of the Lullaby becomes all the more outstanding at the point in Act II/Scene 1 where the Lullaby reappears transformed and transposed to become the Gypsy Song (see Ex. 62): there the vertical component, set 4-23, is arpeggiated and further displayed repeatedly within the sixteenth-note theme in the violins that serves as countersubject to Marie's Gypsy (Lullaby) tune. In the complex Interlude that completes the sonata recapitulation and provides the coda for that scene, the same fourths-dominated countersubject returns augmented in striking juxtaposition with a contracted tune, and both are now ingeniously counterpointed against the "earrings" theme (see Act II, mm. 150–65). We may also note that like the role of set 4-23 in the Lullaby and in the Gypsy Song, the role of this set as it occurs in the vocal line at the fourth measure of Andres's Song in Act I/Scene 2 (see Ex. 16a, m. 216) is clearly the role of set 4-23 as conveyor of the "folk" idiom. Similarly the first appearance of this set in the opera—as the set that is formed by the first four notes of the Captain's theme (Ex. 3)—helps to cast the Captain in a chattering and mundane, if not "folkish," light.

By contrast, the consecutive vertical presentations of set 4-23 in variation 20 of the Doctor's scene (see Ex. 15f, from Act I/Scene 4, mm. 620–23) do *not* play a "folk" role but rather represent a third stage within the ostentatious piling-up of fourths that culminates in a verticalized eight-note cycle (the "fourths-chord" complement 8-23)—a music-theoretical symbol for "eternity" that will be understood by cognoscenti to "mock" the Doctor's extraordinarily pretentious, obsessive notion that his "theory" will win him everlasting renown.[4] Likewise, earlier in Act I/Scene 1, the Captain's less-than-profound definition of "eternity" (mm. 34–35: " 'Ewig,' das ist ewig!" [" 'Eternal,' that is eternal!"]) is parodied (m. 33) by a "profoundly eternal" cycle of descending fourths (in horn and contrabass tuba, doubled by harp), that is, an eight-note fourth-series presented in "straightforward descent to the most profound depths of musical space" (Perle 1971, p. 304). To summarize, whereas the appearances of set 4-16 in the series of examples under discussion function as at least oblique if not direct references to Marie, the "folk" role of set 4-23 and its membership as a subset within the cycle of fourths (fifths) clearly take priority over its association with Marie as a component of the "Komm, mein Bub!" motive and the Lullaby.[5]

4. The fourth and final example in this series (Ex. 53) has been chosen not only because it contains yet another texted, melodic statement of set 4-16 but also because it can serve as the preface to a survey of the most important of all the tetrachords associated with Marie—set 4-18.

Example 53 shows an excerpt from the first large section of the barracks scene—the Introduction to the *Rondo marziale* movement of Act II/Scene 5. Wozzeck has just come from the tavern. There the sight of Marie dancing with the Drum Major had removed every last doubt about her infidelity; now that image will take on the quality of a nightmare vision that strips Wozzeck of the one remaining source of relief from obsession—sleep (mm. 744–49: "Andres! Ich kann nicht schlafen. Wenn ich die Augen zumach', dann seh' ich sie doch immer, und ich hör' die Geigen immerzu, immerzu. Und dann spricht's aus der Wand heraus—Hörst Du nix, Andres? Wie das geigt und springt?!" ["Andres! I can't sleep. When I shut my eyes, I still keep seeing them, and I hear the fiddles, going on and on, on and on. And then a voice from out of the wall—Don't you hear anything, Andres? The fiddling and the dancing?!"]).

Brought to closure at the point where the Drum Major enters (m. 761) to taunt Wozzeck by flaunting his own success with Marie, the Introduction to the *Rondo marziale* is innovatively framed (mm. 737–43; mm. 759–60) by

Example 53. Act II/Scene 5: mm. 747–50

the sounds of snoring soldiers (Berg's own addition to Büchner's setting)—
sounds that in juxtaposition with Wozzeck's sleepless moans underscore the
soldiers' indifference to his plight and throw into relief his estrangement from
"normal" fellow humans in full possession of their natural body comforts.
The soldiers' five-part "snoring" chorus—a restatement (at $t = 6$) of the three
five-part "hallucination" chords from the open-field scene (see Ex. 29)—
serves as preparation for the return of another "hallucination" theme, shown
in Example 54 as it originally appeared in Act I/Scene 2; this theme now
reappears melodically unaltered at the moment when Wozzeck once again
asks Andres if he can hear the sounds in his nightmare (m. 748: "Hörst Du
nix, . . .). Interposed with allusions to material from the preceding tavern
scene itself—that is, to the Ländler theme (compare Ex. 55 with m. 750 of
Ex. 53) and to the "immerzu" motive (as indicated in Ex. 53), introduced at
the very point where Wozzeck first sees Marie waltzing with the Drum Major
(Act II/Scene 4, m. 504)—these references to the open-field scene establish
an association between Wozzeck's current nightmare and his earlier visions
that has been interpreted by Leo Treitler as follows:

> In this way the music leads us to refer the tavern scene—which is in
> Wozzeck's consciousness—back to the scene in the field and suggests
> that the contents of the second scene are transformed from Wozzeck's
> unconscious, concretized as the episode on the dance floor, realized as
> the working out of what was portended. [Treitler 1976, p. 260.]

A clear-cut rhythmic connection between the "hallucination" theme and
the "immerzu" motive lends further support to Treitler's notion of the "pene-
tration of the implicit or unconscious meaning of events in Wozzeck's mind
onto their explicit, surface meaning" (ibid.). As background for our examination of the contents of Example 53, Treitler's comments warrant consideration:

> Just before the great lighting display in the second scene, Wozzeck says
> to Andres, "Listen! Something down below is moving with us." The
> horns are the principal orchestral voice at that moment, and they rise
> quickly and hysterically to a climax [Ex. 54]. In the barracks scene,
> describing his nightmare visions to Andres, Wozzeck sings a develop-
> ment of that line. His words are "I keep seeing them and hearing the
> fiddles, 'Immer zu, Immer zu'" [Ex. 53]. With the words "Immer zu"
> Wozzeck is aping Marie and the Drum Major dancing and singing in the
> tavern. . . . There the rhythm of those words had fallen right in with the

Example 54. Act I/Scene 2: mm. 273–77

Example 55. Act II: mm. 412–13 (Interlude preceding Scene 4)

waltz rhythms of the stage band. But now as Wozzeck recalls them, it is in the musical context in which they originated, that fearful moment in the second scene. . . . Now we recognize that the waltz has had implanted in it the germ of that earlier music and that the waltzing plays out in Wozzeck's mind what that music portended. [Treitler 1976, p. 268; for Treitler's example numbers in parentheses I have substituted my own in brackets.]

Treitler's interpretation of the passage shown in Example 53 may be augmented by the following observations. First of all, motivic details give recognition by musical means to the towering presence of *the Drum Major* in the nightmarish vision from the tavern that Wozzeck cannot obliterate. The rhythm of the Drum Major's motive, shown in Example 56 as it first appeared just prior to Act I/Scene 5, makes a contracted but protrusive appearance in the first violins and xylophone at m. 749, as indicated in Example 53. Meanwhile, beneath this figure, bass clarinet, bassoons, contrabassoon, contrabass tuba, timpani, and harp all pound out the tremolo pedal point G♮-A♮, heard in the Largo movement, Act II/Scene 3, when Marie tried to deny her involvement with the Drum Major; there that pedal point affirmed her guilt by recalling the G♮ pedal point that had dominated the beginning (Interlude) and end of the seduction scene itself (see Examples 11, 17b, and 57, from Act I/Scene 5). At these points in the seduction scene, the G♮ appeared as the lower component of the perfect fifth G♮-D♮, whose role throughout the opera was previewed in chapter 2. In Act II/Scene 3 as in Example 53, the pairing of G♮ with A♮ may have some relationship to the fact that A♮ has become strongly associated with Marie by virtue of its presence in her "waiting" motive and its function as a pedal point in the Interludes that frame her first scene—Act I/Scene 3 (see mm. 317–32 [Ex. 60]; mm. 484–88 [Ex. 33]). In fact in the Interlude that precedes Act I/Scene 3 (mm. 317–32), the pedal point A♮ supports first one, then a second sustained vertical structure whose lowest-sounding tones compose as an ordered fourths-series all three pitch classes in question— A♮-D♮-G♮. Later, at the precise point where Marie succumbs to the Drum Major in Act I/Scene 5 (m. 709), timpani, low brass, and low winds violently interject the pedal point A♮-G♮ and sustain it until Marie and the Drum Major disappear through her doorway. Finally, the reader will recall that all three pitch classes—the A♮ as well as G♮ and D♮— are present in the final 8-element structure with which the three acts end and Act II begins (see Examples 11, 12, and 69).

The presence of specific references to the Drum Major with Marie on an audible level of construction in Example 53 may help to persuade the reader

Example 56. Act I: mm. 665–66 (Prelude to Scene 5)

that the Drum Major is also represented in this passage by elaborately concealed set-structural means. The set structure of the Drum Major's motive as introduced in Act I/Scene 5 (Ex. 56), though abandoned in Example 53, is maintained in so many of its numerous appearances elsewhere in the opera (including its appearances in the *Rondo marziale* of the barracks scene itself; see mm. 761ff) that it may be regarded as the fundamental Drum-Major structure. As shown in Example 56, the set name for that structure is 5-Z18, whose interval vector is [212221]. The reader will recall that Z-sets do not have unique interval vectors; in the case of set 5-Z18, another 5-element set, namely 5-Z38, though unique with respect to normal order, possesses the same total interval content as that of set 5-Z18, represented of course by the same vector [212221]. Now note that the chromatically ascending pentachords in the strings (*tremolo col legno*) at m. 749 of Example 53—just at the point where Wozzeck describes the "fiddling and the dancing"—each reproduce a form of that set which is Z-related to the Drum Major's 5-Z18, set 5-Z38.

From the set-structural as well as dramatic viewpoint, the composer's choice of pentachord here could not have been more appropriate. An examination of the Hauptstimme melodic component of the "hallucination" theme, in relation to which the ascending statements of this pentachord serve as accompaniment, reveals the following set-structural features (the H⁻ melody as shown in Ex. 53 and diagrammed below begins on the downbeat of m. 748 and concludes with the G♮ (pc7) on the third beat of m. 749):

$$\begin{array}{c} \overbrace{}^{\text{5-Z38}} \quad \overbrace{}^{\text{5-Z38}} \\ \text{pcs:} \; \underline{1\;3\;(1)\;6\;4\;0}\;\underline{8\;7},\;3\;9\;0\;\overline{\;6\;11\;2\;5\;7\;} \\ \underline{}_{\text{7-Z38}} \end{array}$$

The reader will note, first, that two inversionally related forms of the pentachord 5-Z38 reinforce the ascending sequential aspect of the melody and.

second, that the first seven discrete pitches of the "hallucination" melody produce the complement of that pentachord—set 7-Z38. Finally, observe that at the point shown in Example 53 where Wozzeck describes the "fiddling and the dancing" (m. 749: "Wie das geigt und springt?"), his part doubles but also staggers somewhat behind the second presentation of set 5-Z38 within the "hallucination" melody, thus drawing further attention to that discrete climactic segment of the line.

Now by comparing Example 53 with Example 54 from the open-field scene, the reader will see that the "hallucination" melody—with its "immerzu" rhythm (♩♪♪♪) and its set-structural components 7-Z38 and 5-Z38—constitutes only one of the features held in common between the two passages; the ⌐G♮-A♮⌐ pedal point and the chromatically ascending statements of set 5-Z38 in the barracks scene, not to mention the unquestionably perceptible crescendo and the rhythmic accelerando, have also all been transplanted from the earlier passage. In short, these two passages are virtually, though not metrically, identical; or rather, the earlier passage has become a Leitsektion.[6] To conclude, if the vision of the Drum Major with Marie is represented by set-structural as well as motivic means in the passage from the barracks scene, but if all of the same musical dimensions were already concealed within the composer's musical representation of Wozzeck's first visions, then by extraordinarily careful compositional planning, the composer has developed these set-structural as well as motivic components in such a way that between Act I/Scene 2 and Act II/Scene 5 the domain of their associations grows increasingly more specific (i.e., set 5-Z38 becomes connected with the Drum Major via set 5-Z18, the ⌐G♮-A♮⌐ pedal point becomes inextricably associated with the seduction); this aspect of the compositional scheme remarkably parallels Wozzeck's gradual development from vague subconscious fears to despair resulting from concrete facts.

Since the justness of this observation hinges in part on whether the relationship between the Drum Major's set 5-Z18 and the 5-Z38/7-Z38 aspect of the "hallucination" theme was recognized by the composer himself, let me dare to offer a speculative opinion. In order to appreciate the relationship between these sets as it has been presented here in theoretical terms, Berg would simply at some point have had to calculate the total interval content of each of these pitch structures. In light of a recently published letter to Schoenberg in which Berg describes his painstaking twelve-tone calculations in preparation for the *Lyric Suite*,[7] it is not inconceivable that the same composer submitted himself to similar kinds of pitch-structural manipulations in his earlier work; however, a simpler, more plausible explanation for the composer's choice of set structures 5-Z18 and 5-Z38/7-Z38 can be posed. All three of these sets contain the tetrachord whose significance in association with Marie and whose general importance throughout the opera will become incontestable in the next portion of this chapter—set 4-18 (prime form: 0, 1, 4, 7; inverted form: 0, 3, 6, 7).[8] A linear display of the pitch components (1) for the Drum Major's theme from Example 56, (2) for Wozzeck's vocal line at the words "Wie das geigt . . . " from Example 53, and (3) for the opening segment of the "hallucination" melody is offered below in order that the reader may examine this shared inclusion property firsthand:

Note, first of all, that set 7-Z38 contains not just one but three discrete forms of set 4-18. Recognition of the symmetrical diminished-triad subset that gives both prime and inverted forms of set 4-18 their characteristic sounds may help the reader to hear the similarity among the three larger sets 5-Z18, 5-Z38, and 7-Z38. I propose not only that Berg too heard that similarity, but also that he arrived at the five- and seven-note structures by the process of building larger collections from a single fundamental pitch-structural idea— set 4-18. I further maintain, then, that a motivic association between the Drum Major's pitch structure and the chromatically ascending statements of 5-Z38 in Examples 53 and 54 was fully intended. This view will be further substantiated in the next section of the chapter, whose purpose will be to establish beyond all doubt that set 4-18 functions throughout the opera as a compositional "building-block" comparable in importance to none other than Wozzeck's all-pervasive set 4-19. As for the latter set, it should come as no surprise that 4-19 is *not* included in the Drum Major's sets 5-Z18 and 5-Z38 but that a clear-cut presentation of the Wozzeck-set may be heard in Wozzeck's own "hallucination" melody (see Ex. 53, m. 748, and Ex. 54, m. 276: pcs 4, 0, 8, 7).

Before leaving Example 53, let us examine Andres's sleepy response, at m. 750, to Wozzeck's outcries. Here we have the promised melodic and texted presentation of Marie's "waiting" motive set 4-16; like the references to the Ländler theme and to the "immerzu" motive in this passage, Andres's (pcs 9, 4, 2, 10) is clearly a reminiscence of the music at the tavern—a transposed quotation from the clarinet figurations heard in the Idiot's passage (review Ex. 52) and discussed earlier at length. A vertical statement of the same four-note collection in strings *tremolo col legno* accompanies Andres's falsetto. The voice-leading sketch below shows that, as with Marie's paired tetrachords 4-20, 4-16 in Act I/Scene 3 (see the voice-leading reduction on p. 130), only one carefully chosen pitch needs stepwise alteration in order for set 4-16 to become set 4-18. This is the voice-leading motion that produces the change of harmony in the strings on the last strong beat of m. 750. Finally, an examination of the total pitch content (normal order: 9, 10, 1, 2, 4) of the harmonic progression yields yet another significant relationship based upon inclusion. Together sets 4-16 and 4-18 here produce an additional form of 5-Z18; this is to say that the Drum Major's 5-Z18 contains both tetrachords associated with Marie:

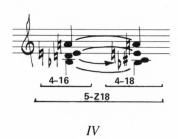

IV

Like all the other dimensions of the passage from the barracks scene discussed in the preceding pages, the pairing of the tetrachords 4-16 and 4-18 has its origin in a much earlier moment of the opera. That moment, shown in Example 57, occurs in a passage from the ten-measure Interlude that serves as Prelude to the last scene of Act I—the seduction scene. With this and several of the next examples in the series that will represent a fourth stage in our examination of tetrachords associated with Marie, it ought to become clear that the pairing of Marie-tetrachords constitutes a characteristic compositional feature of the opera.

By virtue of the ascending perfect fourth, the eighth-note motion, and the articulation scheme of the upper voices (♪ ♪ ♩) as well as the texture and instrumentation of the passage as a whole, the excerpt shown at Example 57 may be regarded as a development of the first and fundamental idea of the Prelude, shown in chapter 2 at Example 17b; that idea derives in turn from the Drum Major's rising "fanfare" motive, heard at the beginning of Marie's Act I/Scene 3 and shown in Example 58. The dimensions held constant among these three passages (in chronological order, Examples 58, 17b, and 57)—

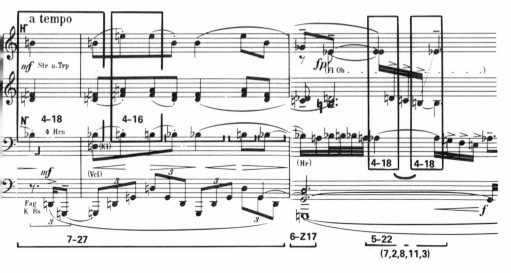

Example 57. Act I: mm. 661–63 (Prelude to Scene 5)

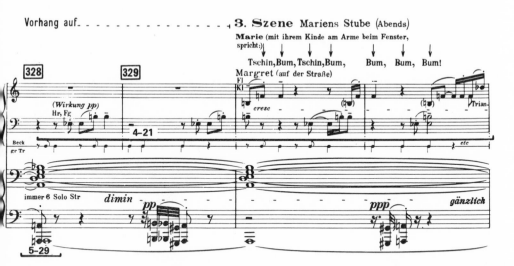

Example 58. Act I: mm. 328–31

that is, the presence of a pedal point and the rhythmic, articulative, and contour similarities—should be obvious, but certain less obvious changes of melodic, harmonic, and set-structural details from one passage to the next are worthy of brief examination.

Note, first of all, that the melodic component of the four-bar "fanfare" motive (Ex. 58) unfolds one of the whole-tone tetrachords, set 4-21, and displays the "fateful" tritone ⌞B♮-F♮⌟. These features are abandoned at the opening of the Prelude to Act I/Scene 5 (Ex. 17b), the tritone now contracting to become the perfect fourth, whose role in association with the folklike Lullaby elements of Marie's Act I/Scene 3 has been established in the interim. Example 17b shows, moreover, that the adjacent second and third harmonic structures in the first bar of the Prelude (m. 656) respectively represent forms of the Z-related hexachords 6-Z19 and 6-Z44—hexachords whose importance in the opera as a whole has grown increasingly evident in the course of our study of pitch structures associated with Wozzeck and Marie. Finally, in the third passage, at Example 57, variety within the continuity is achieved by a new harmonization imposed upon the old pedal point ⌞G♮-D♮⌟ heard at the beginning of the Prelude. Above that sustained-arpeggiated pedal point (in 'cellos, basses, and low winds) upper strings, trumpets, and horns produce repeated statements of sets 4-18 (normal order: 10, 11, 2, 5) and 4-16 (normal order: 4, 5, 9, 11) in an oscillating pattern that incorporates and accommodates the embellishing fourth-motion of the tune. The association here of set 4-16 with Marie is unequivocal: the form of the set featured in this passage is the same as that heard in Marie's "waiting" motive itself (review Ex. 28). Furthermore, two pitch classes are held invariant by the single forms of set 4-18 and 4-16 presented here, and these are none other than the components of the "fateful" tritone ⌞B♮-F♮⌟, the interval that only two bars later (m. 665) will be sounded naked and fortissimo in low strings at the precise point where the curtain rises to reveal the Drum Major with Marie. Last of all, note that the Hauptstimme shown in Example 57 comes to rest upon a second, inverted form of set 4-18 (8, 11, 2, 3), created by the pitches sustained in the strings at m. 663 along with the quarter-note A♭ (pc8) upon which the horns finally settle.

The passage shown in Example 57 returns abbreviated but at the same transpositional level just before the curtain falls at the end of the scene (Act I/Scene 5, m. 713). There it becomes apparent that this figure has been developed to prepare the final oscillating 8-element structure with which this act as well as Acts II and III are concluded (see Ex. 11): the rhythmic-articulative disposition, the ⌞G♮-D♮⌟ pedal point, and five of the eight pitch classes of the final structure (pcs 2, 5, 7, 9, 11) have all been carefully planted within the passage at Example 57.

For a summary of occurrences elsewhere in the opera of the opening measure from the Prelude to Act I/Scene 5 (Ex. 17b), with its vertical set structures 6-Z19 and 6-Z44, see Perle (1971, p. 293). Two later appearances of the excerpt shown in Example 57 help to confirm beyond question the association of this passage and of the paired tetrachords 4-18, 4-16 with the seduction of Marie. As mentioned earlier in connection with the G♮-D♮ pedal point, this passage reappears, once again untransposed, during the moment in Act II/Scene 3 (m. 390) when Marie tries to deny her involvement with the Drum Major. Then, in the immediately subsequent tavern scene, the same untransposed unit becomes incorporated in the waltz at the point where Wozzeck responds to the sight of Marie with the Drum Major by uttering the words: "Weib! . . . Das Weib ist heiss!" ("Woman! . . . The woman is hot!"). Added to the series of examples in the preceding section of this chapter, the passage from Example 57, so straightforwardly linked with the seduced Marie, gives strength in retrospect to the proposition that at least one of the harmonic components of that passage—set 4-16—really does serve in its appearances elsewhere, however indirectly or subtly, to imbue seemingly disparate events and moments of the opera with an underlying acknowledgment of Marie's importance to the drama. More especially, set 4-16 becomes invested with the power to point not only to Marie's attitude of waiting but also to the direct outcome of that accessibility, that loss of commitment and vague desire for change that her waiting represents—the seduction. As for the choice of set 4-18 as the other member of the harmonic pair in Example 57, here the question should arise, To what extent does set 4-18, independent of set 4-16, have a direct association with Marie?

V

The answer may be found by returning to our point of departure in this chapter, the moment in Act I/Scene 3 when we are brought for the first time into Marie's private world. Thus far we have approached the subject of the role of set 4-18 primarily by reference to the inclusion of this set within important larger sets (5-Z18, 5-Z38, 6-Z19/6-Z44, 7-Z38) and to its appearances in immediate juxtaposition with set 4-16. Like 4-16 as well as all the other sets associated with Marie and discussed so far (3-3, 4-20, 4-23), set 4-18 makes several prominent appearances in the form of discrete melodic and harmonic units during Marie's very first moments alone onstage. These units will now be examined in support of the argument that set 4-18 acquires an independent association with Marie and serves as the fundamental "building-block" in the construction of the above-mentioned larger sets.

From among the sets that constitute Marie's pitch-structural matrix, set

4-18 distinguishes itself by virtue of the fact that it does *not* present itself in a segmentally obvious manner within Marie's "Komm, mein Bub!" motive (Ex. 45); instead the first memorable statement of set 4-18 is saved for the opening melodic unit of the Lullaby, as shown in Example 46. At this point a property of the set that is crucial to its importance throughout the opera reveals itself in the simplest and most clear-cut fashion. The reader will recall that the three-note setting for Marie's words "Komm, mein Bub!" (pcs 2, 11, 10)—a form of set 3-3—becomes literally incorporated within the opening statement of the Lullaby tune; since the first complete statement of the tune displays a formation of set 4-18 (normal order: 10, 11, 2, 5), then 4-18 can be seen at Example 46 clearly to contain the "Komm, mein Bub!" set 3-3. Now it can be observed that the very same form of set 4-18 that appears at the opening of the Lullaby tune really was already present, however concealed, within the "Komm, mein Bub!" motive at Example 45: the single pitch class F♮ (pc5) added to the "Komm, mein Bub!" motive (pcs 2, 11, 10) at the opening of the Lullaby (Ex. 46) was also heard in the orchestral soprano line at m. 363, immediately preceding Marie's statement of the motive (Ex. 45). Thus a hidden but contiguous composite segment at Example 45 forecasts the fundamental melodic idea of the Lullaby and lends further support to the notion that the "Komm, mein Bub!" passage provides the formal exposition of Marie's pitch-structural matrix.

In the bridge passage that connects the "Komm, mein Bub!" motive at mm. 363–64 with the Lullaby proper at m. 372, several additional formations of sets 3-3 and 4-18 further prepare the appearances of these sets in the Lullaby tune. By consulting the full score, the reader will note, first of all, that the initial pitch of the Lullaby tune—the B♭—has been sustained in the same register throughout the preceding seven measures as a pedal point (in the solo violin at first, then doubled and ornamented by a trill [pcs 10, 11] in the horn [mm. 368–69], then reinforced by flutter-tonguing flutes [mm. 369–70]). Beneath the B♭ pedal point, a chromatically descending "minor six-four chord" series perpetuates the basic four-voice texture and creates the tetrachordal sequence 4-17, 4-22, 4-18 in m. 365, literally repeated in diminution at m. 366 (Ex. 45). The upper three pitches of the vertical structure 4-17 at the downbeat of m. 365

$$\overbrace{1, \underbrace{6, 9, 10}_{3\text{-}3}}^{4\text{-}17}$$

constitute a new form of the "Komm, mein Bub!" set 3-3; in other words, set 4-17 contains set 3-3, a fact that may explain the appearance of set 4-17 (the "major-minor chord") in the section of the sonata movement, Act II/ Scene 1, that concerns Marie and her child—the Bridge Section (see Ex. 65).[9] The form of set 4-18 that is the harmonic goal of the tetrachordal series ⌊4-17, 4-22, 4-18⌋ is the contour inversion of the form that appears in the Lullaby, constructed "beneath" rather than "above" the axis ⌊B♭-B♮⌋:

Meanwhile, notice that Marie's vocal line at m. 365 features yet another form of the "Komm, mein Bub!" set 3-3 (pcs 5, 4, 8), disguised by the jagged contour as shown in Example 45.

Finally, at m. 370 (Ex. 46), just before the beginning of the Lullaby, the syllabic setting for Marie's unforgettable "Eia popeia . . . " ("Rockaby . . . ") marvellously exemplifies a structural relationship between Wozzeck's set 4-19 and Marie's set 4-18 that provides a new technical explanation for the overwhelming importance of these two sets throughout the opera. As shown below, the "Eia popeia" phrase exhibits interlocking forms of the Wozzeck-set and the Marie-set, with three pitch classes held in common between the two:

$$
\begin{array}{cc}
\text{(vocal line,} & \overbrace{3\text{-}3}\\
\text{Ex. 46, m. 370)} & \underbrace{8\ \overbrace{4\ 1\ 0}}\ 7\\
& \underbrace{}_{4\text{-}19}\\
\end{array}
$$

4-19

4-18

The common 3-element set is none other than the basic "Komm, mein Bub!" cell, set 3-3. Needless to say, this is the trichord whose outstanding role in Act I/Scene 3 is established in the context of a direct reference to the child, who in turn represents the one binding link between his mother and his father. Should the notion of a set-structural correlate for the dramatic situation not appeal to the technique-oriented reader, then the inclusion of set 3-3 in both sets 4-19 and 4-18, considered in light of the all-pervasive nature of these sets in the work as a whole, may be taken simply as a new manifestation that the large-scale harmonic organization of the opera is tremendously cohesive. Just the same, that Marie's set 4-18 shares the child-related subset 3-3 with Wozzeck's most distinctive set acquires special significance in light of the fact that set 3-3 is *not* included in any of the other tetrachords associated with

Marie and discussed so far (4-16, 4-20, 4-23). This fact will be interpreted after we have completed our survey of pitch structures associated with Marie.

Before leaving the "Eia popeia" phrase at Example 46, let us briefly consider the five-voice harmony sustained throughout m. 370 in support of Marie's vocal line. The set name for this harmony is 5-31, a set that can be constructed by adding *any* discrete pitch class to a form of the symmetrical tetrachord 4-28, otherwise known as the "full-diminished-seventh chord."[10] A form of set 4-28 is represented in m. 370 by the pcs 1, 4, 7, 10, to which pc8 has been added. The choice of pc8 in this case not only effects the inclusion within the complete five-voice harmony of an inverted form of Marie's set 4-18 (pcs 1, 4, 7, 8) but also creates a representative of the form of set 4-27 that in tonal theory is called the "half-diminished-seventh chord" (the inverted form of the set is the "dominant-seventh chord"). Heard most distinctly on the downbeat of m. 370 (pcs 1, 4, 8, 10), set 4-27 has been mentioned earlier in connection with Marie (see chapter 3, sections II and VII), and that connection will be further substantiated as we continue.

At the end of the opening eight-bar sentence of the Lullaby, the "Eia popeia" phrase returns to assume the capacity of a refrain, transposed and expanded as shown in Example 59, and newly harmonized by means of the "fourths-chord" set 4-23 mentioned earlier, which appears here in alternation with one of the whole-tone tetrachords, set 4-25. The listener will hear that the original five-note syllabic setting for "Eia popeia" remains unaltered except for the transposition; now, however, a varied repetition of the original setting at the words "süsser Bu'" (mm. 382–83: "dear boy") results in a new inverted statement of set 4-19 (pcs 2, 10, 6, 5). Note, moreover, that the sixth pitch class added at m. 381 to the original five-note setting produces the hexachord 6-Z19 (pcs 2, 10, 7, 6, 1, 9). Here the linear unfolding of this very important hexachord exposes two of its characteristic properties. First of all, observe that the formation of set 6-Z19 in mm. 380–81 appears to be the result of a melodic extension from the fundamental sets 4-19 and 4-18, both of which the larger set includes. Second, the setting for set 6-Z19 shown at Example 59 demonstrates that the set may be constructed by juxtaposing two minor triads—or two major triads—that stand one semitone apart from each other, as with the I-♭II (Neapolitan) tonal progression (in this case, the triad ⌊7, 10, 2⌋ at m. 380 is juxtaposed with the triad ⌊6, 9, 1⌋ at m. 381.) Considered in addition to the fact that set 6-Z19 is the Z-related complement of the "musical signature" (set 6-Z44) of Schoenberg, Berg's teacher (see Forte 1978b), this second characteristic of the hexachord may in part account for the frequency of its appearances in the works by Schoenberg and Berg that are representative of their transition from the tonal to the atonal idiom.[11]

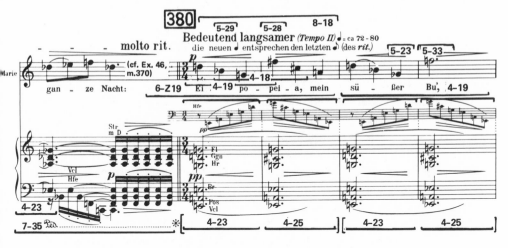

Example 59. Act I/Scene 3: mm. 379–83

Measures 388–99 of Act I/Scene 3 present an expanded, varied repetition of the Lullaby and its refrain; accordingly, the extended "Eia popeia" phrase makes one final appearance, again altered melodically to accommodate the new text: "Lauter kühle Wein muss es sein!" (mm. 396–99: "[Only] clear, cool wine will be fine!"). Now, at m. 400–03, as shown in chapter 2 at Example 17a, a new closing phrase that provides the setting for a repetition of the "Lauter . . . " text dramatically expands the role of sets 4-18 and 4-19 in the original "Eia popeia" melody. The initial contour and the interlocking presentation of these sets are now abandoned in favor of a long, disjunct descent from the upper to the lower limits of the soprano range, within which each of the two sets is given a distinctive and discrete statement. As shown in Example 17a, the first four pitches of Marie's eight-note descent yield a representative of set 4-19 (pcs 10, 6, 2, 11), while the last four pitches provide a final inverted formation of Marie's own set 4-18 (pcs 8, 4, 1, 7)—in fact the same form of the set that was embedded within the original five-voice harmony at m. 370 (Ex. 46). The importance of the set structure created by the first six pitches of the descent—set 6-34—was discussed in chapter 2; in addition, it will now be appropriate to observe that the entire eight-note line represents the complement of Marie's set 4-27—8-27.

VI

In coordination with other set-structural features, the distinctive contour of the closing phrase of the Lullaby permits this melodic phrase to serve as an important link within a motivic chain associated with the two leading characters. From the perspective of contour, the chain originates with the second of the two Austrian military calls—the "Abgeblasen" (see Reich 1963 [trans., 1965], p. 127)—announced by clarinet ("imitating the trumpet") in the preceding Interlude (Ex. 60), just before the sounds of the military "fanfare" (Ex. 58). Although the first two pitches of the descending "Abgeblasen" line (pcs 10, 6) will become the point of departure for Marie's closing phrase in the Lullaby (Ex. 17a), the subsequent interval series and the set structures are not the same. As indicated in Example 60, the first four pitches of the "Abgeblasen" tune (10, 6, 3, 11) produce a form of set 4-20, perhaps forecasting the prominence of that "major-seventh chord" set as the adumbration of Marie's "waiting" motive in her forthcoming scene (Ex. 48). By examining the sequential contiguous four-note subcomponents of the descending line at Example 60,[12] we shall discover that the second and third tetrachordal collections within the line represent interlocking inverted forms of Wozzeck's 4-19:

$$
\begin{array}{c}
\overbrace{}^{\text{7-21}} \\
\overbrace{}^{\text{4-20}} \\
\text{(clarinet line, Ex. 60:)} \quad 10 \underbrace{\;6\;\;3\;\;11}\;\;7,\;\;2\;\;9 \\
\underbrace{4\text{-}19} \\
\underbrace{4\text{-}19\;(t=10)}
\end{array}
$$

As mentioned in chapter 2 section II, where the presentation in this passage of the fixed form 7, 2, 9, 6, 3, 11 of set 6-31 as shown in Example 60 was identified as a component of the 8-element structure at the close of each act, the inclusive 7-element structure, simultaneously sustained as a vertical sonority in the strings and arpeggiated melodically by the clarinet, is a form of set 7-21. Since this set is a subset of the large Wozzeck-set 8-19, it should come as no surprise that 8-19 makes its own brief appearance at m. 319, when the C♯ in the solo violin is sounded against the seven-note pedal point. In keeping with the fact that the Interlude serves not just as the transition to Marie's Act I/Scene 3 but also as the conclusion for the scene where Wozzeck, the army man, has been fulfilling his military duties in the open field, the set structures featured in the military call give priority to Wozzeck, not to Marie. Thus the absence of a display of Marie's set 4-18 as a contiguous segment in the military call, and thus the intervallic changes in the closing phrase of the Lullaby that permit set 4-18 to emerge once Marie has become the center of our attention.

The reader may wish to compare the slower, repeated descent in mm. 321–

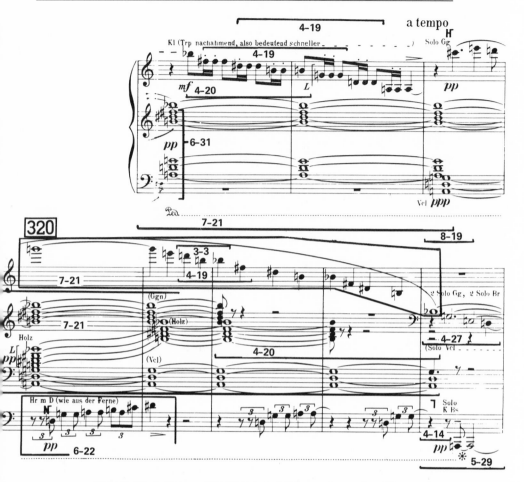

Example 60. Act I: mm. 317–24 (Interlude between Scenes 2 and 3)

23 at Example 60 with the preceding "Abgeblasen" line. The second descent
holds six pitch classes invariant with the first (pc4 is substituted for pc9);
despite the change in the total pitch content and changes in the interval series,
the complete seven-note descent reduces to another form of set 7-21. Note,
moreover, that the alteration of the interval pattern at mm. 321–22 yields the
pitch sequence 2, 11, 10—an adumbration at t = 0 of the "Komm, mein Bub!"
motive.

Returning to the closing phrase of the Lullaby at Example 17a—now
understood as the second link in the motivic chain under discussion, we may
proceed by observing that the first five pitch classes of Marie's descending

line yield a form of set 5-26; this pentachord in turn results from interlocking formations of Wozzeck's 4-19 and Marie's 4-27:

(vocal line, Ex. 17a:)

$$
\begin{array}{c}
\overset{\displaystyle 5\text{-}26}{\overline{\rule{0pt}{0pt}\hspace{5em}}} \\
\overline{10\ \ 6\ \ 2\ \ 11\ \ 8} \\
\underline{\hspace{4em}} \\
4\text{-}19 \\
\underline{\hspace{5em}} \\
4\text{-}27
\end{array}
$$

The same tetrachords in disjunct descent, now both inverted and interlocking in reverse order to produce the inverted set 5-26, provide the syllabic setting for Marie's remorseful "Ich bin doch ein schlecht Mensch" ("I really am a bad person") at the end of the heated development of Act II/Scene 1 (Ex. 40):

(vocal line, Ex. 40:)

$$
\begin{array}{c}
\overset{\displaystyle 5\text{-}26\ (t = 10)}{\overline{\rule{0pt}{0pt}\hspace{5em}}} \\
\overline{7\ \ 4\ \ 1\ \ 9\ \ 5} \\
\underline{\hspace{3.5em}} \\
4\text{-}27 \\
\underline{\hspace{5em}} \\
4\text{-}19
\end{array}
$$

My discussion of that excerpt in chapter 3 included an interpretation of the presence of Wozzeck's set 4-19 in the setting for Marie's self-indictment. Now it is possible to stress that Marie too is fully represented here by motivic-referential means. Although the more immediate source for Marie's private confession is the ascending retrograde presentation of the same set structures at the point where Marie challenges Wozzeck with "Bin ich ein schlecht Mensch?" (Ex. 39: "What am I—a bad person?"), both the descending contour and the specific set structures as shown in Example 40 refer the listener backward to that *first* scene (Act I/Scene 3) in which Marie is likewise found alone with her thoughts—thoughts only of a somewhat less troubled nature. Thanks to the attentions of the Drum Major and then the seduction itself, Marie's life has changed significantly since that earlier moment, and this may or may not be reflected in the subtle reversal of the interlocking tetrachords. On the other hand, Marie herself has not changed much at all. In the Lullaby of Act I/Scene 3, with its allusions to deprivation, isolation, and imposed self-reliance (mm. 372–79: "Mädel, was fangst Du jetzt an? Hast ein klein Kind und kein Mann! Ei, was frag' ich darnach, Sing' ich die ganze Nacht" ["Maiden, now what are you going to do? You have a small child and no husband! Ei, what do I care? I'll sing the whole night long"]), juxtaposed with folktale images of virility and strength (mm. 388–91: "Hansel, spann'

Deine sechs Schimmel an, Gib sie zu fressen auf's neu" ["Hansel, saddle up your six horses, give them something new to eat"]) as well as one reference to "the better life" (mm. 396–403: "Lauter kühle Wein muss es sein!" ["Only clear, cool wine will be fine!"]), Marie betrays her longing for change in the sense of release. By Act II/Scene 1 a drastic change has been accomplished, but only at the expense of Wozzeck's already precarious sanity. As a result, Marie is fundamentally no happier and certainly no freer now than she was before; her sense of guilt is at least as strong if not stronger than the pleasure she has enjoyed ever so briefly. There may be a fine touch of irony concealed in the fact that Marie's self-indictment is expressed as a slightly warped version of the dreamy closing phrase of her Lullaby; the more Marie changes her circumstances and then hates herself, the more she is the same. Like Wozzeck, Marie is not in a position—be it economical, historical, psychological, existential—to control the direction of her life. The motivic and set-structural chain within which Marie's "Ich bin doch ein schlecht Mensch" is a third link reinforces Büchner's implication that all the factors that lead to Wozzeck's and Marie's decline have been present as if predetermined from the very beginning of their story. Just as Marie's seduction is interpreted by Wozzeck as the predestined reality that brings about the destruction prophesied to him in the open fields, Marie's self-disgust in Act II/Scene 1 is the unfortunate outcome of one change that she longed for in the Lullaby but to which she has succumbed in final awareness that her attempted resistance was futile (Act I/Scene 5, mm. 708–09: "Meinetwegen, es ist Alles eins!" ["For all I care; it makes no difference!"]).

Two more links in the motivic chain ultimately clinch the association of the descending line with Marie and with her downward fall in the course of the drama. In the very last scene of the opera, a transposed and rhythmically altered but otherwise exact replication of the closing phrase of the Lullaby returns in company with Marie's "waiting" motive at the precise point where Marie's child is informed that his mother is dead (Act III/Scene 5, mm. 378–80; see the analysis of this scene in section X of this chapter). Prior to that final statement, in Wozzeck's drowning scene, the descending line appears in a context even more explicitly associated with the "reasons" for Marie's death. There, as Wozzeck stumbles upon Marie's corpse in an aborted effort to retrieve the murder weapon, he regards with surprising composure the bloody "red cord" (Act III/Scene 4, m. 240: "eine rote Schnur") around her neck and asks of the dead Marie: "Hast Dir das rote Halsband verdient, wie die Ohrringlein, mit Deiner Sünde!" (Ex. 61: "Have you earned the red necklace, like the little earring, with your sins?").

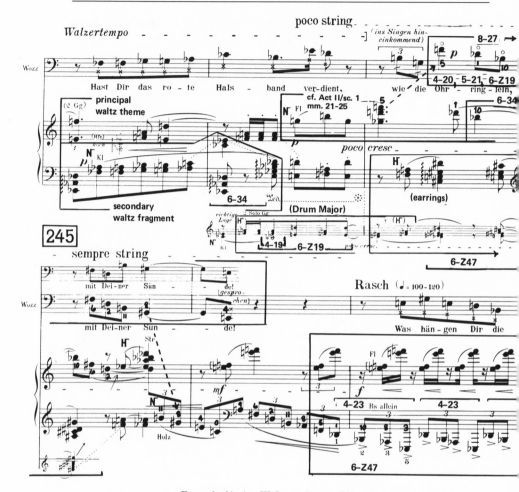

Example 61. Act III/Scene 4: mm. 242–47

The array of motivic references that accompany this text is reminiscent of, though not quite so complex as, the instantaneous juxtaposition of motives associated with Marie that earlier portrayed the notion of her life flashing before her at her actual moment of death (see Act III/Scene 2, mm. 104–07). As shown in Example 61, the passage as a whole is given the waltz tempo from the tavern scene and begins with a simultaneous contrapuntal presentation of two of the waltz fragments; the primary waltz tune itself, with its "built-in" rhythmic reference to the Drum Major, is now transformed explicitly to produce the melodic fourths-contour of the Drum Major's motive at m. 243. With the words "wie die Ohrringlein" (m. 244), the Drum Major's motive elides with a distorted reference to Marie's "earrings" theme (Ex. 41), while flutes present a disjunct descending statement that incorporates the first six pitches (6-34: 10, 6, 2, 11, 8, 4) of the descending phrase from the Lullaby (Ex. 17a); these are duplicated at t = 0 in Wozzeck's vocal line, which at first trails behind the flutes, then catches up, then again staggers behind. No longer a mere eight-note descent, but rather now extended to become a nineteen-note plummet from the high regions of the flute register through the middle and low registers of the clarinets, bass clarinets, and bassoons to the lower regions of the double basses, this penultimate link in the motivic chain that had originated with the "Abgeblasen" tune has now become a vivid musical representation of the actual "reward" Marie has earned with her "sins"—the death itself.

For easier inspection, the nineteen-note descending line from Example 61 has been translated into pc integers and displayed below along with some of its set-structural properties. The bracket with the label 6-34 delimits that segment of the descent which duplicates Marie's descending Lullaby statement (Ex. 17a) at t = 0. As with the initial segments of all of the antecedents in the motivic chain under discussion, the most obvious pitch-structural characteristic of this complete descent is the seemingly haphazard alternation of major and minor thirds, represented respectively by "M" and "m" below. The absence of repeated patterns of M and m suggests either that the line unfolds by the simple random addition of single minor or major thirds or that the line was constructed by the assembling of specific but unordered larger pitch structures. The set-structural method reveals the latter rather than the former to be the case:

(descending line, Ex. 61, mm. 244–47:)

M m M M m m M M m m M m m m M m

6-34

5 1 10 6 2 11 8 4 0 9 6 2 11 8 5 1 10 8 3 (1 10 8 3)

8-27(5-21,6-Z19):   4-20 , 4-27 , 4-27 , 4-27 , 4-23

8-21:   4-19 , 4-19 , 4-26 , 4-26

8-21(5-26,6-34):   4-19 , 4-19 , 4-27 , 4-26

8-27(5-34,6-34):   4-27 , 4-27 , 4-28

8-27(5-26,6-Z44,7-34):   8-17:

8-27(7-34):   8:26

8-27(5-26,6-34,7-34):

8-27(5-34,7-34):

8-18(7-31):

Tonal theorists will recognize that the twelve-pitch-class system permits seven distinct seventh-chord formations, that is, four-note chords whose elements can be ordered to produce three contiguous major and/or minor thirds. In set-theoretical terms, these seven formations can be distinguished as forms or inverted forms of five discrete sets: 4-20 (the major-seventh chord), 4-26 (the minor-seventh chord), 4-27 (the dominant-seventh chord, or, inverted, the half-diminished-seventh chord), 4-28 (the full-diminished-seventh chord), and 4-19 (the minor triad with added major seventh, or, inverted, the augmented triad with added major seventh). As one might expect, all seven formations, hence all five of these sets, are represented in the nineteen-note descent at Example 61. What concerns us here, then, is that three of the five "seventh-chord" sets are given priority over the other two by virtue of their placement within the series and the number of times they are represented. The set-structural display presented above indicates that of the sixteen discrete contiguous 4-element groups, four tetrachords are forms of Wozzeck's set 4-19 and six represent formations of Marie's set 4-27; moreover, as with the "Abgeblasen" tune at Example 60, the structure formed by the very first four notes of the descent is Marie's set 4-20. To summarize, the texted first eight notes of the long descent feature elaborately interlocking formations of sets that have predominated throughout the motivic chain—sets that have played outstanding roles in association with Wozzeck and with Marie, whose "sins" and the "reward" they have received from Wozzeck himself are the textual issues here. It has become a commonplace to note that Berg is fond of tertian harmonies. As a compendium of the available seventh-chord formations, Example 61 supports the view that Berg's use of seventh-chord structures in this opera may be more precisely described as follows: Berg gives special priority to only three of the five distinct tetrachords that can be treated as seventh-chords—4-19, 4-20, and 4-27; he favors these tetrachords by assigning them a distinctive role in the development of motivic networks associated with the two leading characters.

Of the two remaining "seventh-chord" tetrachords represented in Example 61, set 4-26, which is featured contiguously three times, and set 4-28, featured just once, appear only in the second half of the long descent, after the relatively explicit reference to the eight-note descending line from the Lullaby has been completed. Since these tetrachords do not have a motivic role in the opera as a whole, it seems clear that their first appearances here serve to provide contrasting links to the rhythmically more prominent statement of set 4-27 with which they interlock. The final tetrachord of the series is not a seventh-chord formation but rather the "fourths-chord" set 4-23. As indicated by the parentheses in the set-structural display above, a single form of set 4-23 (pcs 1, 10, 8, 3) marks the end of the long descent by thirds; this collection then assumes the role of ostinato within a triplet configuration, to be repeated from m. 247 to m. 249. The appearance of set 4-23, the set from the "Komm, mein Bub!" matrix and the Lullaby that is associated with Marie but more closely linked with folk elements in the opera, may be best explained here in terms of its inclusion within the hexachord that serves as the fixed ostinato basis for the drowning scene as a whole—set 6-Z47 (see chapter 2 for a discussion of this hexachord that focuses upon the passage shown at Ex. 22—the passage immediately following the excerpt at Ex. 61). In fact the fixed form of set 4-23 that marks the end of the nineteen-note descent also signals the resumption of the basic fixed form of set 6-Z47 (pcs 1, 10, 8, 3, 4, 5), completed by the addition of pcs 4 and 5 in the sixteenth-note flute figure at m. 247.

All of the contiguous 8-element pitch structures in the nineteen-note descent have also been identified in the set-structural display presented above—for reasons that should become apparent upon perusal. Note that of the eleven 8-element collections displayed, six are forms of set 8-27—the complement of Marie's set 4-27. As for the contiguous five-, six-, and seven-note groups, sets mentioned earlier have been included in parentheses in order that the reader may now appreciate their tertian nature—a characteristic that may not have been quite so clearly exposed in other passages where these sets were featured. Note in particular that the hexachord formed by the very first six pitch classes of the descent—6-Z19—is the set that was featured at the opening of the "Eia popeia" refrain (Ex. 59), whose direct set-structural relationship to the second link in the motivic chain under discussion, the closing phrase of the Lullaby, was examined earlier. In both cases, but perhaps more obviously in the case at Example 61, set 6-Z19, which maximizes ic4 (its interval vector is [313431]), appears as the result of a juxtaposition of two semitone-related triads (Ex. 61: $\underline{5, 1, 10}$; $\underline{6, 2, 11}$).

Finally, should it come as a surprise that Marie's set 4-18 does *not* appear as the component of a contiguous segment in either Example 61 or in any of the preceding links within the motivic chain save the closing phrase of the Lullaby, remember that even though 4-18 nearly maximizes ic3 [102111], it cannot be arpeggiated as a seventh-chord formation. It seems clear that set 4-18 has been abandoned because the initial descending-thirds feature of the motive as it originated with the "Abgeblasen" tune is that feature which has instead been chosen for developmental extension. Accordingly, as with the setting for Marie's "Ich bin doch ein schlecht Mensch" (Ex. 40), set 4-27—

a seventh chord—assumes the aspect of substitute set-structural representative for Marie. Just the same, a single esoteric vestige of the prominent role set 4-18 played in the closing phrase of the Lullaby can be seen in the set-structural display for Example 61 presented above: one of the eleven contiguous 8-element collections within the descent is the complement of Marie's 4-18—set 8-18. For a more distinctive statement of this large Marie-set that may give greater significance to its single appearance in the nineteen-note descent, see Example 63 and the corresponding discussion below.

VII

Having traced from its point of origin to its final link a motivic chain brought to our attention by the unforgettable descent of the closing phrase of Marie's Lullaby, we shall now turn from the final to the first phrase of the Lullaby (Ex. 46) for one last observation and its ramifications. In each of the two sequentially treated statements of the fundamental melodic idea of the Lullaby, a fifth pitch introduced after the opening set 4-18 (see mm. 373 and 375) serves as a connective and upbeat to the subsequent bar. The absence of that connective in the passage from Act II/Scene 1 where the Lullaby tune is transformed and transposed to become the Gypsy Song (Ex. 62) justifies the importance we have conferred upon set 4-18 as the fundamental pitch-structural idea of the tune in its original setting. But since the inclusion of Marie's 4-18 within the Drum Major's set 5-Z18 has already been demon-

Example 62. Act II/Scene 1: mm. 43–44

strated, it should now be of further interest to note that that inclusion relation is once again clearly exemplified at mm. 374–75 of the Lullaby tune: there the fifth pitch (pc6) added to the 4-18 segment (pcs 1, 2, 5, 8) creates an inverted form of the Drum Major's 5-Z18. The last two pitches of the resultant line (pcs 1, 6) moreover forecast at t = 0 the embellishing fourth-motion that will characterize the soprano line of the Drum Major's motive when it first appears at the beginning of Act I/Scene 5 (cf. Examples 46 and 56). These admittedly inaudible suggestions of a connection between Marie's Lullaby tune and the Drum Major's motive may be taken more seriously in light of the fact that the Drum Major's motive itself is treated to contour inversion when it reappears to play a dominant role in the barracks scene:

(Act II/Scene 5: m. 765, hns.)

By reassembling the pitches at mm. 374–75 of the Lullaby tune, we can without difficulty recreate the inverted Drum Major's motive at t = 1 as follows:

Whether the pitch-structural connection was intended or "accidental," the fact of the eventual physical relationship between Marie and the Drum Major need not be labored, and the absence of that kind of relationship in Marie's life at the moment she sings the Lullaby is the very subject of her lament at the point where the Drum Major's set appears: "Hast ein klein Kind und kein Mann!" (mm. 374–75: "You have a small child and no husband!").

In fact we have every reason to suspect that Marie is already thinking specifically of the Drum Major as she begins the Lullaby. After all, she has just seen him for the first time—strutting by her window at the head of the military band, even greeting her while ignoring Margret, undoubtedly aware that he has attracted the attentions of both these women. At the moment just prior to the Lullaby when Marie slams down her window and throws her attention upon the child, it seems clear that she is making a vehement effort not only to cut off the crude remarks her behavior toward the Drum Major has elicited from Margret, but also to drive away the reminder that Wozzeck, the disturbed father of her child, can no longer fulfill her sexual desires. Although Marie ostensibly sings the Lullaby in order to console and distract her child, it is Marie who needs to be consoled.

Our interpretation of Marie's state of mind as she sings the Lullaby is naturally colored by her behavior at the very beginning of the scene, when we see her and hear her speak for the first time: having just laid eyes on the Drum Major, Marie makes no effort to conceal her attraction to him. From the set-structural point of view, the setting for this critical moment can shed light upon the role of set 4-18 in the Lullaby and its connection with the Drum Major's motive. As shown in Example 63, Marie's first utterance in the drama—"Er steht auf seinen Füssen wie ein Löw'" (m. 339: "He stands on his feet like a lion")—coincides with a shrill piccolo figure whose total pitch content (pcs 7, 10, 1, 6) represents a new form of the same set—4-18. Meanwhile, read as a flamboyantly expansive single melodic unit, the broad, legato marching tune in horns and trumpets, marked as Hauptstimme in the full score at m. 337, produces a form of the complement 8-18, whose apex pitches (pcs 6 and 7) anticipate and then double the piccolo at m. 339. At the very moment Marie describes the Drum Major, the accompanying instruments of the military band supply the figure that will become the rhythmic component of the Drum Major's motive in Act I/Scene 5 (♩♪♫ ♫ ♩). In fact these instruments in combination with the bass and the tune reproduce in toto the pitch content of the piccolo figure, providing a harmonic statement of set 4-18 that supports the melodic presentation of the same set form on the downbeat at m. 339. Finally, when the entire two-bar idea is repeated with distinctive melodic and harmonic changes at mm. 340–41, the piccolo figure and the harmony at the downbeat of m. 341 take the form of set 4-27 (pcs 6, 11, 2, 8)—the tetrachord we have observed elsewhere as a substitute for 4-18.

The apex pitches of the marching tune at m. 339 (Ex. 63)—pcs 6 and 7— reappear ten bars later to serve the same function in the texted opening phrase of the Trio, shown at Example 64. That similarity between these two passages, otherwise strongly contrasted with respect to harmony, rhythm, and character, is reinforced by the fact that the shared pitch classes participate in the formation of an inverted form of the same set structure—once again, 4-18 (in Ex. 64, set 4-18 is represented by pcs 0, 3, 6, 7). And once again, the text exposes Marie's appreciation of attractive men. Undaunted by Margret's snide comments ("Ei was freundliche Augen, Frau Nachbarin! So was is man an ihr nit gewohnt! . . . " [mm. 341–42: "Ooh, what friendly glances, neighbor! We're not used to that from you! . . . "]), Marie boldly observes that

Example 63. Act I/Scene 3: mm. 337–41

"soldiers are handsome fellows" (mm. 345–50: "Soldaten, Soldaten sind schöne Burschen!").

If the appearance of set 4-18 in the Lullaby tune can be interpreted in the light of its occurrences in the two earlier passages shown at Examples 63 and 64, then we have three instances where set 4-18 appears in contexts that involve not simply the presence of Marie but more specifically the presence of Marie as sensual woman, whose physical attraction to the Drum Major will lead to her own downfall as well as Wozzeck's. When we remember that Marie's 4-18 is a subset of the Drum Major's 5-Z18 and that 4-18 reappears as a prominent harmonic component of the seduction material itself (Ex. 57), these three examples suggest that the motivic domain of set 4-18 includes a direct association with at least one determinative aspect of Marie's multifaceted character—her unrelinquished sexual longing. But just as it would be a mistake to overlook other equally characteristic sides of Marie's nature, it would be an injustice both to technique and to metaphor were we to circumscribe the domain of set 4-18 in such a specific and limited way. As the first case in point, it cannot be forgotten that set 4-18 contains the child-related

Example 64. Act I/Scene 3: mm. 345–50

set 3-3 from the "Komm, mein Bub!" motive and that this property of the tetrachord has been audibly exploited in the dramatic-musical context of the Lullaby. The child is physically present in only four of the fifteen scenes of the opera (Act I/Scene 3, Act II/Scene 1, Act III/Scene 1, Act III/Scene 5), the first of which is the Lullaby scene; and except for the very last scene of the work, where the child is alone but his mother's death is the fundamental textual issue, the child is always seen in company with Marie. With the next group of examples, each from one of the scenes where the child is present, it will be demonstrated that like its connection with Marie-and-the-Drum Major, the association of set 4-18 with Marie as the child's mother is sustained over the large span of the opera.

VIII

We turn first to the passage from the work in which set 4-18 defines the harmonic area of an entire unit within the large formal design. The design in question is the sonata-allegro movement that constitutes Act II/Scene 1, and the unit is the Bridge Section of the First Exposition that effects the transition from Principal to Subordinate themes. Even though several excerpts from the First Exposition have been shown and discussed earlier (Examples 12, 41, and 62), the First Exposition has been reproduced in its entirety at Example 65; the complete example will be needed in a discussion of the distinctive pitch-structural features of the Bridge Section that includes a more general survey of its formal context.

Berg explains that the sonata form was chosen for Act II/Scene 1 because it could provide a musical correspondence for the textual design, based in turn on the interaction of the three members of the Wozzeck family—Marie, the child, and Wozzeck himself (see the 1929 lecture in Redlich 1957b, p. 274). Accordingly, Principal, Subordinate, and Closing Sections provide formal settings for those portions of the text that concern respectively Marie, who is seen alone with the child, admiring her earrings from the Drum Major as the curtain rises (Ex. 65, m. 7); the child, whom Marie tries to distract with the Gypsy Song (Ex. 65, mm. 43–53); and Wozzeck, whose entrance at the close of the Second Exposition is forecast by the juxtaposition of his "entrance" theme with the imagined entrance of the "gypsy boy" at mm. 53–59. The Bridge Section for both First and Second Expositions begins at the point where the child stirs, inadvertently interrupting Marie's reverie and eliciting her efforts to put him to sleep. In the analysis that follows, all references to the score by measure number will be references to Example 65 unless otherwise indicated.

Like all the passages that concern the child, the Bridge Section, shown at mm. 29–42, does not "represent" the child as much as it reflects Marie's generally ambivalent attitude toward him. In fact, since the boy's only words in the entire opera are his "Hopp, hopp!" in the last scene, and since his behavior throughout appears to be only representative of the behavior of any very small child, we know the child only as the offspring of Marie and Wozzeck, too young to serve within the dramatic structure as much more than a projection of Marie's thoughts. With the Lullaby Marie certainly made an effort to soothe the child, but her song also served as a vehicle for the expression of her own sense of deprivation. Here at the Bridge Section, even though it is a bright, sunny morning, Marie again wants the boy to go to sleep: "Schlaf, Bub! Drück die Augen zu, fest. Noch fester! Bleib so! Still, oder er holt Dich!" ("Sleep, boy! Shut your eyes tight. Tighter! Stay that way! Quiet, or he'll come and get you!"). Her efforts are contradicted by the elfish, even edgy nature of the characteristic motive of the passage—a staccato and ac-

Example 65. Act II: mm. 1–59

(Vorhang auf) _ ⊣ **1. Szene** Mariens Stube (Vormittag, Sonnenschein)

(Example 65 *continued*)

(Example 65 *continued*)

(Example 65 *continued*)

(Example 65 *continued*)

cented eighth-note pair featuring a verticalized, repeated minor second, a figure made sharp and dry by xylophone and strings at the point of the bow; hardly soothing, this figure instead betrays Marie's annoyance with the child's very presence and her impulse not so much to lull him to sleep as to frighten him by the notion of a gypsyboy goblin (cf. mm. 45–46), so that he will close his eyes *and not see her*.

Likewise the Bridge Section does not introduce set structures that could be construed to have a unique association with the child; indeed, *such set structures do not exist*, a fact that conforms with the dramatic characterization of the child as dependent in every respect upon Marie. Instead, considered in light of its association with Marie's Lullaby, Marie's attraction to the Drum Major, and even Marie's seduction, the generative set structure of the Bridge Section, like the characteristic motive itself, can be understood figuratively to represent Marie's point of view. As indicated by the boxes placed in the score at mm. 29–42, every pitch element within the passage except for the chromatic extensions at mm. 32 and 37–38 participates in a series of inverted forms of set 4-18. The transpositional pattern of the series at mm. 29-36, which features ascending fourths, is reversed in the second half of the passage (mm. 37–42), as clarified in the following reduction:

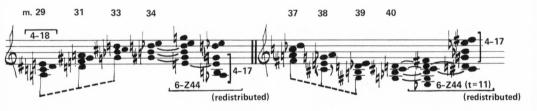

Inverted forms of set 4-18 naturally produce inverted forms of its subset 3-3—the "Komm, mein Bub!" set through which a connection between Marie's 4-18 and the child was originally established. Note that the predominantly three-voice texture of the Bridge Section and especially the arrangement of pitches in the first bar of each of its halves (m. 29, m. 37) give particular emphasis to the presence of the inverted 3-3. Now consider the six-voice harmony created at the end of each half of the Bridge Section by the addition of two pitch classes to the sustained but redistributed 4-18 collection. The 6-element structures at mm. 34–36 and at mm. 40–43 are transpositionally equivalent forms of set 6-Z44, whose importance elsewhere in the opera as a set which multiply contains 4-18 has already been demonstrated and whose significance in this scene will be displayed below. In keeping with the concealed contour-inversion scheme that informs the relationship between first and second halves of the Bridge Section, the redistribution of pitch elements at the end of each half, thrown into relief by the entrance of the horns, results first in the subimposing, then in the superimposing of a new tetrachord—the "major-minor chord," set 4-17. This is the tetrachord that contains not one but two inversionally related forms of the "Komm, mein Bub!" set 3-3, represented at mm. 34–36 by the pitch classes ⌊4, 7, 8⌋ and ⌊7, 8, 11⌋. Of special interest is the fact that the latter form of set 3-3— ⌊7, 8, 11⌋, which shares two of its three elements with the form of set 4-18 heard at m. 34 (pcs 8, 11, 2, 3)—is the very form of set 3-3 that appears at the end of the Prelude (m. 6) to serve as upbeat to the Principal Section of the sonata proper.

The Prelude also provides exquisite preparation for the preeminence of set 4-18 in the Bridge Section. In chapter 2 (Examples 11 and 12) we saw that the opening measures of Act II sustain an untransposed version of the 8-element structure (set 8-24) that had marked the end of the preceding act and that will reappear at the ends of Acts II and III. These opening measures have a connective as well as introductory function, then, on both the immediate and the very long-range levels. In the remaining measures of the Prelude a middleground connection is established: with the neighbor-motion figure in trumpets at mm. 4–5, doubled by violas and marked in the full score as *Nebenstimme* ("subordinate voice") but inevitably heard above the pianissimo sixteenth-note triplet ascent in the violins, we hear, accented and reiterated, the very same inverted form of set 4-18 (pcs 9, 0, 3, 4) that will mark the beginning of the Bridge Section at m. 29. The figure congeals at the second beat of m. 5 and is sustained until the fourth beat, conveniently facilitating comparison with the first vertical configuration in the reduction of the Bridge Section presented above. Meanwhile, note at m. 5 that the violins themselves momentarily come to rest upon their own inverted but non-intersecting form of the same tetrachord, represented by pcs ⌊3, 6, 9, 10⌋.

It is the lowest and the highest pitch within the more prominent form of set 4-18 in trumpets and violas, however, that now serve as point of departure for a descending fifths-series in 'cellos and harp $\frac{(E\natural-A\natural-D\natural-G\natural)}{(A\natural-D\natural-G\natural-C\natural)}$—a series that parallels in slower contrary motion the 'cello ascent at the opening of the Prelude. Above this, horns, trumpets and celesta reiterate an augmented version of the tremolo figure from m. 2 (set 6-34), whose tetrachordal components have grown in significance since this figure was last discussed in chapter 2: the tremolo consists of alternating statements of Marie's 4-27 (pcs 9, 3, 6, 11) and the whole-tone tetrachord 4-24 (pcs 11, 5, 9, 1), whose augmented-triad subset will ensure recognition of this set as an important feature of the Principal Section to follow (see the melodic component of the "earrings" theme itself [mm. 7–9] as well as the downbeat verticals at mm. 8 and 11). The Prelude is concluded when the slow-motion tremolo figure comes to rest upon set 4-24 and the fifths-series has been completed as well as sustained; the resulting vertical sonority at the fermata is a gigantic "circle-of-fifths" chord plus one "wrong" note—the D♯. As indicated in mm. 5 and 6, this massive eight-note harmony (set 8-26) clearly contains a form of set 6-Z47, the set that will become the basis for the pitch-structural content of the drowning scene in Act III (see Ex. 23).[13] Finally, the outer boundaries of the final eight-note structure—the perfect fifth C♮-G♮ in the basses and the E♮ in the treble—forecast the startling C-major triad sustained at the end of the Development (mm. 116–27) and the C-major harp glissandi that will demarcate the beginning and the end of the subsequent Interlude. To summarize, the Prelude to Act II, on the one hand a perfectly self-contained unit framed by the fifths-series and the tremolo figure, on the other hand not only anticipates the Bridge Section but also incorporates pitch structures whose importance on immediate, intermediate, and long-range levels we can acknowledge with growing appreciation.

Given the assumption that in an atonal sonata movement, atonal pitch structures will serve as analogues for tonal centers in the establishing, delimiting, and interrelating of harmonic areas, at least one important question concerning the Bridge Section should now be raised: as a form-generating dimension, to what extent is the harmonic region defined by set 4-18 in the Bridge Section *distinctive from and/or related to* the harmonic disposition of the other sections of the First Exposition? For answers to that question, the reader will most certainly wish to consider the following observations in coordination with a study of George Perle's detailed analysis of "basic cells and aggregates of basic cells" featured in Act II/Scene 1. Inasmuch as Perle's analysis is not only very detailed but also available in three publications (Perle 1967a, pp. 223–39; abridged version, 1968 [3d ed. 1972], pp. 35–37; adaptation, 1980, pp. 145–55), it would be inappropriate to duplicate his information here except for the purpose of placing his observations about Act II/Scene 1 within the larger scope of our study of pitch combinations that have an integrative role in the opera as a whole.

Perle's Cells and Aggregates, Act II/Scene 1:   Forte's Set Names

Cell A (Principal Section):
features the augmented triad.

4-19

Cell B (Bridge Section):
features the diminished triad.

4-18

Cell C (Subordinate Section):
features the major triad.

4-20

Cell D (Closing Section):
features the major triad.

4-19

Basic Pentad in "home key"
(t = 0), m. 162:

5-22
(⊃ 4-19, 4-18)

Pentad X_p (t = 0), m. 7:
(see mm. 105, 126:
"Bin ich ein schlecht Mensch?")

5-26
(⊃4-19, 4-24)

Pivotal harmonic center (fixed form of the augmented triad;
component of Cell A, pentad X, the basic
pentad, and the aggregate hexads A and B at t = 0,4,8; see
mm. 1-2, 6,7,8,16)

3-12

Hexad B_p (t = 10),
mm. 40–42:

6-Z44
(⊃ 4-19,
      4-18,
      4-20,
      5-22)

Hexad A_p (t = 0);
final aggregate,
m. 166:

6-Z19
(⊃ 4-19,
      4-18,
      4-20,
      5-22)

(The subscript "p" represents "prime," as opposed to "inversion" ["i"].)

Perle demonstrates that "Principal Section, Bridge Section, Subordinate Section and Closing Section are each characterized by a special harmonic cell" and that "the movement as a whole is based on aggregates of the different cells" (Perle 1967a, p. 227). Since Perle does not use Forte's set-theoretical apparatus, a summary of Perle's "basic cells and aggregates" that coordinates these with Forte's set names has been provided to facilitate comparison of the pitch components of this scene with pitch combinations discussed elsewhere in this study. At a glance the reader will ascertain that all but one of Perle's "basic cells and aggregates" are forms of sets whose outstanding importance in association throughout the opera with Wozzeck and/or Marie has been the central issue of this and the preceding chapter. The only pitch structure that has not yet been discussed is Perle's "basic pentad," set 5-22; this is the structure that is reiterated in a chromatically ascending series toward the end of the Subordinate Section (see Ex. 65, m. 48) and then announces the beginning of the Closing Section at m. 55. As shown by Perle, the importance of the "basic pentad" in this scene rests upon the fact that this structure is an "aggregate" of cells A, B, and D, and is moreover contained in hexads A and B; or, in set-theoretic terminology, set 5-22 contains 4-19 and 4-18 and is contained in 6-Z19 and 6-Z44.

Note that Perle's cells A and D are inversionally related forms of the same set—4-19; in the language of set theory, we would say, then, that set 5-22 contains 4-19 twice. Although Perle acknowledges the inversional relationship between cells A and D and concedes by footnote that "inversional forms of the basic cells play a subordinate role" (he sometimes refers to "inversional forms" as "complementary forms" [1967a, p. 231]), his primary concern is to demonstrate that the harmonic design of the sonata movement depends upon *fixed forms* of pitch structures to which he ascribes primary and subordinate transpositional levels as analogues to "home key" and "digressions" from the "home key." With respect to Act II/Scene 1, Perle's position is tenable as well as convincing and should by all means be studied. With reference to the opera as a whole, our concern throughout this work has been to show that *not only fixed forms and transposed forms but also inversionally related forms of sets play interchangeable roles* both in their association with the principal characters and as integrative features of the overall design. This position can be maintained even in respect to the sonata movement, as the following observations will demonstrate.

As a first example, not only does set 5-22 contain 4-19 twice, it also contains two discrete inversionally related forms of set 4-18, only one of which is Perle's cell B. This property of set 5-22 is made perfectly clear by the

vertical arrangement of pitch classes at the point toward the end of the Subordinate Section where the set is presented in the chromatically ascending
series:

$$
\left.\begin{array}{r}
4 \\
11 \\
8 \\
5
\end{array}\right\} \quad a): \text{4-18}
$$

(pcs, downbeat vertical structure, m. 48:)   0

$$\underbrace{\qquad}_{\text{5-22}}$$

4   *a*): 4-18
11
8
5   *b*): 4-18 [I-related to *a*)]
0

Perle does not draw attention to the presence of the normal form of set 4-18,
labeled *a*), because he has exclusively defined his cell B as the inversionally
related form of the set, labeled *b*)—the fixed form that predominates in the
Bridge Section. As shown in the above summary of Perle's "basic cells,"
Perle moreover chooses the major-seventh chord, our set 4-20, as the characteristic cell C of the Subordinate Section, even though the sequentially
treated harmonic progression of this Gypsy-Song Section features not just
one but two tetrachords, 4-20 and 4-23, and even though the repeated melodic idea of the Gypsy Song—adapted, like the harmonic progression, from
the Lullaby—is a transposed normal form *a*) of set 4-18. (The Gypsy-Song
Subordinate Section, shown in part at Ex. 62, may now be examined in full
at Ex. 65, mm. 43ff.) The presence of form *a*) as well as form *b*) of set 4-18
in the ascending 5-22 series at m. 48—just two measures after we have heard
the Gypsy tune twice—exemplifies the integration of melodic and harmonic
dimensions, an outstanding characteristic of the composer's technique that
most certainly warrants consideration here.

   In the remaining bars of the Subordinate Section in the First Exposition
(mm. 49–54), Perle's cell C—set 4-20—is no more prominent, in fact even
less predominant, than his cell B—set 4-18—as well as the "fourths-chord"
set 4-23 (see the thirty-second-note arpeggiations in fourths at mm. 50–51).
Cell C appears only once, as the expansive setting (minus the portamento
triplet) for the first part of Marie's "Fort ins Zigeunerland" ("Away into Gypsyland") at mm. 49–51 (pcs 9, 5, 2, 10). Meanwhile, at mm. 49–50, we
hear for the first time an adumbration of Wozzeck's "entrance" theme; this
figure forecasts Wozzeck's actual entrance at the end of the Second Exposition (see Ex. 17d), but it appears here as a reflection of the fear Marie has by
now induced in the child by describing the imagined entrance of the gypsy
boy, who she threatens will carry the child off into Gypsyland. Accordingly,
at mm. 49–50 the predominant tetrachord (pcs 2, 5, 8, 9) is not a Wozzeck-

set but rather Marie's 4-18, Perle's cell B. The same form of the same set 4-18 reappears included within none other than the Drum Major's set 5-Z18 at m. 53, where the "fear-of-entrance" figure is reiterated. Only in the measure just before Wozzeck's "real" "entrance" theme emerges in violas and 'cellos (cf. Ex. 65, mm. 55–56, and Ex. 17d, from the close of the Second Exposition), marking the beginning of the Closing Section, does the predominant tetrachord become a form of Wozzeck's own 4-19, Perle's cell D. Serving as the climactic harmonic goal for the horns at m. 55, that tetrachord is now sustained for five measures and creates in combination with the complete "entrance" theme itself a form of the large Wozzeck-complement, 8-19.

The "aggregate" function of the "basic pentad," set 5-22—heard as the first composite vertical structure at the beginning of the Closing Section (pcs 6, 7, 10, 1, 2), where Wozzeck's "entrance" theme elides with the horn tetrachord 4-19—takes on new significance in light of the audible presence of set 4-18 in the preceding Subordinate Section. As the container of two inversionally related forms of Marie's 4-18 (6, 7, 10, 1; 7, 10, 1, 2) and two inversionally related forms of Wozzeck's 4-19 (6, 10, 1, 2; 7, 10, 2, 6), set 5-22 dramatically marks the elided boundary between the passage dominated by Marie with her child (Subordinate Section) and the passage that presages Wozzeck's arrival (Closing Section). Beyond this and in general of even greater significance, the distinctive harmonic designs of the two sections—Marie's Subordinate Section and Wozzeck's Closing Section—admirably conforms with, moreover reinforces, all that we have already observed about the ever clearer association of sets 4-18, 4-20, and 4-23 with Marie and the outstanding role of set 4-19 in association with Wozzeck.

If we can agree that Marie's set 4-18 plays just as "characteristic" a role in the Subordinate Section as Perle's cell C and as the "fourths-chord" 4-23, we are also now in a position to note that set 4-18 provides one of two links between the Subordinate Section and the preceding Bridge Section, likewise dominated by Marie with her child: by definition a link to the Subordinate Section, the Bridge Section not only introduces the staccato eighth-note motive that will be maintained and developed in the Subordinate Section, it also features inverted forms of the very set—4-18—that "uninverted" will become the fundamental melodic component of the Gypsy Song. It must be understood, finally, that this observation is *not* based upon an unsupported and strictly theoretical notion that inversionally equivalent sets play interchangeable roles; on the contrary, the set-theoretical connection between the Bridge Section and the Subordinate Section finds all of its strength in the indisputable fact that both prime and inverted forms of set 4-18 appear here as elsewhere throughout the opera in unquestionable association with Marie.

For one final example that illustrates the importance of inverted as well as normal forms of set 4-18 in Act II/Scene 1, we may turn to the concluding measures of the movement (mm. 160–69), from the section that functions both as Interlude and as completion of the sonata Recapitulation, begun at m. 128. Perle has noted that "in the concluding bars of the Recapitulation of the principal theme, immediately after the curtain falls, the harmonic material is greatly simplified and the basic harmonic ideas clearly and emphatically exposed" (Perle 1967a, p. 236). He supports this observation with reference to mm. 145–46, which feature "parallel lines generating successive statements of the augmented triad" (ibid.), the most pervasive harmonic feature of the Principal Section. He also points to mm. 147–49, where cells A, B, and C—our sets 4-19, 4-18, and 4-20—all appear as vertical formations within a thick nine-voice texture that features motivic fragments from the Principal Section (m. 147) and a new rhythmically augmented, tetrachordally harmonized version of the Gypsy-Song countersubject (mentioned in section III of this chapter) against the "earrings" theme in the basses (mm. 148–52). Like these examples, mm. 162–63 from the passage at the end of the Interlude shown in Example 66 "emphatically expose" a "basic harmonic idea" of the movement—not Perle's cell B, but instead transposed replications of the "uninverted" forms of set 4-18 that were featured in the Gypsy tune. As displayed in Example 66, mm. 162–63 recapitulate in four-part parallel motion Wozzeck's "entrance" theme from the Closing Section of the First Exposition (mm. 55–56). Here the combined forces of four instrumental choirs—the flutes, the clarinets, the trumpets, and the violins—are employed to present the "uninverted" 4-18 in a blaring triple-forte series. A fifth pitch class sustained by violas against each reiterated 4-18 collection once again creates the "basic pentad" 5-22, with its interlocking inversionally related 4-18 structures; thus the reference at mm. 160–61 to the chromatically ascending 5-22 series heard toward the end of the Subordinate Section is now completed within the descending pattern. Simultaneously, the augmented Gypsy-Song countersubject in horns, trombones and 'cellos drives toward its conclusion at m. 165, culminating in a climactic statement of cell C—set 4-20.

As duplicated in Example 66, Perle demonstrates the presence of "a linearization of the basic pentad at T-2," a "series of passing chords," and "hexad A$_i$" (Perle 1967a, pp. 231–32). To this we shall add, as shown in Example 66, that Perle's "series of passing chords" in fact yields interlocking trans-

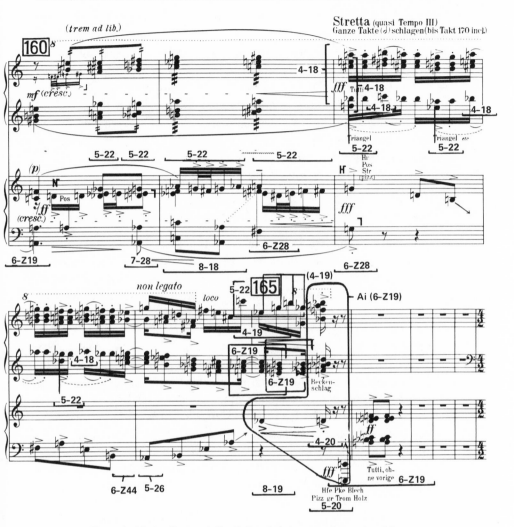

Example 66. Act II: mm. 160–69 (Interlude between Scenes 1 and 2)

posed forms of his own hexad A_p, which the reader will recognize as the structure that can be created by juxtaposing two semitone-related minor triads— set 6-Z19. As Perle notes, the eighth-note pair that punctuates the very end of the movement presents the same hexad in its "home key." Earlier in this study I proposed that the importance of set 6-Z19 in this opera can best be understood in light of the fact that 6-Z19 contains three forms of Wozzeck's 4-19, two forms of Marie's 4-18, and the first of the "hallucination" chords,

5-Z17 (review Examples 28 and 29). We can now add one form of set 4-20 (cell C), one form of the tetrachord 4-17 (review the end of each half of the Bridge Section), and the "basic pentad," set 5-22, to the remarkable list of prominent components of this scene and of the opera as a whole that find their summary representation in the final chord of this movement. In conclusion, note the presence of a form of the large Wozzeck-set 8-19 at m. 165; and, most amazing of all, observe that the pitch classes juxtaposed by the chord of climax at m. 165 and the triple-forte upbeat to m. 166 combine to produce precisely the same form of set 5-20 (pcs 2, 4, 5, 9, 10) that was heard as the very first sonority of the opera (see Ex. 3).

IX

Since many divergent issues concerning Act II/Scene 1 have been considered within the context of the role of set 4-18 in this scene, it may be useful at this point to remind the reader that our analysis of Examples 65 and 66 has been placed within the broader context of a study of occurrences of set 4-18 in the scenes where the child is present and where the association of this set with Marie as the child's mother is reinforced. After Act II/Scene 1 the child is not seen again until the first movement of Act III, Marie's Bible-reading scene. In this movement, as at both the beginning and the end of Act II/ Scene 1, Marie is alone with the child; and this time Wozzeck's *absence* is brought to our attention as a significant substitute for his by now expected entrance (mm. 42–44: "Der Franz ist nit kommen, gestern nit, heut' nit . . . " ["Franz hasn't come, not yesterday, not today . . . "]). These parallels between the introductory scenes of Acts II and III can account for two references in the later scene to the earlier scene—one concealed and the other boldly drawn. The following examples will illustrate.

From part 1 of section III above, the reader may recall that set 4-18 did not figure among the pitch-structural components of the thematic material upon which the variation design of Act III/Scene 1 is based. This may correspond in part with the fact that when the scene opens, Marie has now become so entirely absorbed in her search for relief from remorse that she appears to be oblivious to the child's presence until he once again inadvertently distracts her. At that moment, and only at that moment in this scene, a new version of the characteristic motive of the Bridge Section, with its "basic cell" B, the inverted 4-18, appears in piccolos, flutes, harp, and celesta as shown in Example 67; here the motive is uniquely set in counterpoint with transposed, imitative statements of the thematic component #1 in the strings.

Note at m. 22 that the biting minor-seconds motive from the Bridge Section becomes the basis for a chromatically ascending adumbration of component #5—the "knife" component, itself stated at m. 23, where Marie admits that the child gives her "a stab in the heart."

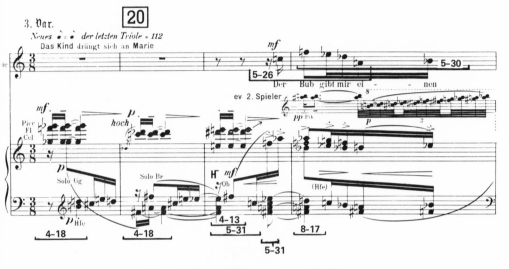

Example 67. Act III/Scene 1: mm. 19–22

This fleeting reference to Act II/Scene 1 serves as preparation for the large-scale similarity in point of function, harmonic construction, and overall textural design between the Interludes with which Act II/Scene 1 and Act III/Scene 1 conclude. Whereas the Interlude at the close of Act II/Scene 1 served to complete the sonata Recapitulation begun twelve measures before the descent of the curtain, the Interlude at the end of Act III/Scene 1 completes in stretto the double fugue based on components #1 and #3, likewise begun twelve measures earlier. As shown in Example 68, the fall of the curtain at the end of Act III/Scene 1 coincides with successive and overlapping entrances of component #3, presented in parallel minor sixths by horns and trombones, component #1, contracted in oboes and clarinets, and component #1 inverted as well as contracted in harp, low strings, and low winds. As with Wozzeck's "entrance" theme in the Interlude at the end of Act II/Scene 1 (Ex. 66), the statement of component #1 in oboes and clarinets at mm. 64–65 is treated to four-part parallel motion, and the resulting tetrachordal texture features successive statements of the "uninverted" 4-18. At mm. 66–67 the rhythmic scheme is simplified and the counterpoint inverted (i.e., component #3 is placed in the treble and component #1 in the bass), and now component #3 makes its final appearance in a new four-part setting that features cell C (set 4-20), while component #1 marches toward its climax in parallel statements of the whole-tone tetrachord 4-21. The Interlude begins to dissipate at mm. 69–70, where, as shown in Example 68, the Marie-related tetrachords 4-18, 4-20, and 4-27 as well as the tetrachord 4-26 (see Ex. 61) and the large Marie- and Wozzeck-sets 8-18 and 8-19 all make brief vertical appearances. Finally, with the insidiously quiet and deep entry of the B♮ pedal point at mm. 71–72, we have the single pitch class that at this very moment has begun to assume the role of idée-fixe ostinato for the forthcoming murder scene. Revealing the abrupt shift from Marie's candlelit room to the locale of the murder—a dusk-lit forest path by a pond, the curtain now rises to the accompaniment of an arpeggiated replication (in flutes, harp, strings, and celesta) of the very hexachord that had marked both the end of Act II/Scene 1 (transposed here at t = 7) and the end of the first phrase of this scene (see Ex. 50, mm. 6–7)—6-Z19.

Example 68. Act III: mm. 64–72 (Interlude between Scenes 1 and 2)

(Example 68 *continued*)

X

The remaining scene in which the child is present is of course the very last scene of the opera. This is the scene where all of the essential motives and pitch structures associated with Marie throughout the work are definitively brought together in recognition of Marie's outstanding importance—to Woz-zeck, to the child, and to the overall dramatic and operatic structure. In an effort to give a semblance of completeness to the inexhaustible subject of Marie's material, and with appreciation for the brevity and poignancy of Act III/Scene 5, I have reproduced the entire scene at Example 69. As with a number of other examples presented in this study, Example 69 contains some set-analytical information that for organizational reasons cannot be treated verbally below but has been included in order that the reader may have a comprehensive presentation at his disposal. Although the first issue at hand continues to be the role of set 4-18 in its association with Marie as the child's mother, we shall move from that issue toward a general summary of the predominant Marie-related components of the scene, placing stress upon the extent to which these help to articulate the formal design. Before proceeding with the analysis of this scene, the reader may wish to review notes 7 and 8 of chapter 3, which concern relationships between the ending of this scene and the opening of the opera and the textual origin of the "Ring-around-a-Rosy" game the child's peers are playing as the scene opens. In the discus-sion that follows, all references by measure number will be references to Example 69 unless otherwise indicated.

We need only turn to the orchestral accompaniment that supports the chil-dren's "Ring-around-a-Rosy" song at the beginning of the scene for confir-mation that in this last scene of the work set 4-18 fulfills its obligation as the essential pitch-structural component of a long-range motivic chain that trans-mits Marie's bond with the child. The ostinato subject for this sixth Invention-movement in the series that composes Act III is a triplet eighth-note *moto perpetuo*, scored at the outset for the flute choir and pizzicato violins in their ethereal register, with the total pitch content of each strong beat reinforced by rolled celesta chords. Here, as throughout the scene, the utterly transpar-ent orchestration, the dearth of low instruments (no trombones, bassoons, double basses), and the ongoing triplet motion—treated *molto rubato* and gradually retarded, but fundamentally inexorable—reinforce the hypnotic ef-fect of the child rocking on his hobby horse and recreate the atmosphere of a merry-go-round, underlining with irony the harsh fact that the child's mother lies dead by the pond while "normal" life goes on and on, untouched and

Example 69. Act III/Scene 5 (complete)

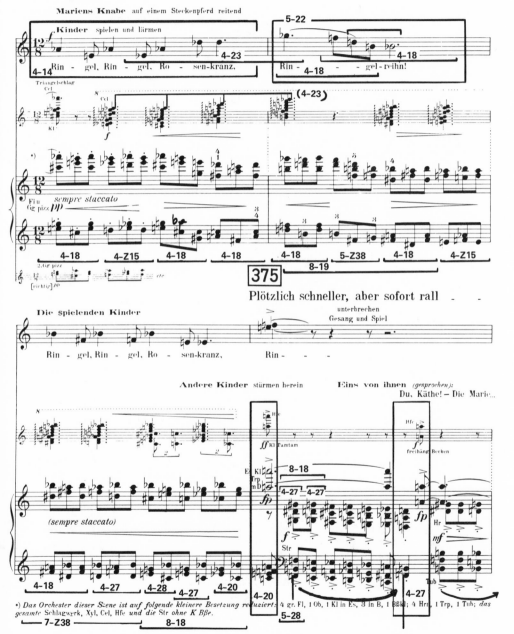

5. (letzte) Szene Vor Mariens Haustür (Heller Morgen, Sonnenschein)

Fließende Achtel, aber mit viel Rubato

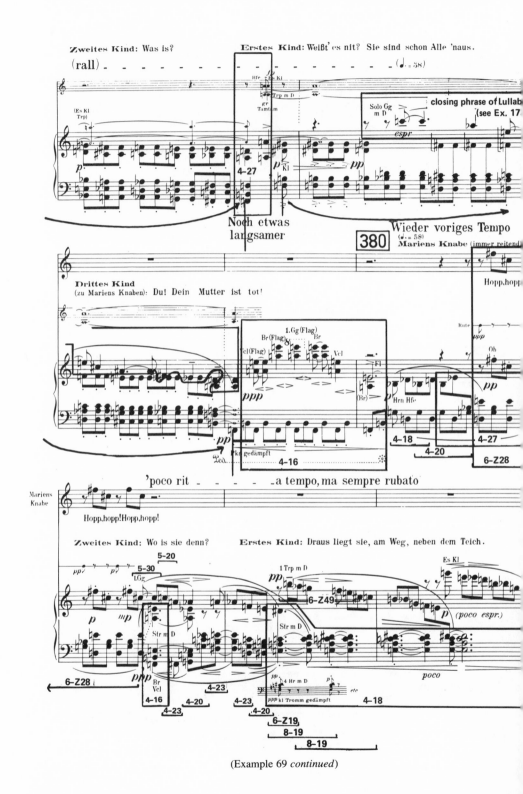

(Example 69 *continued*)

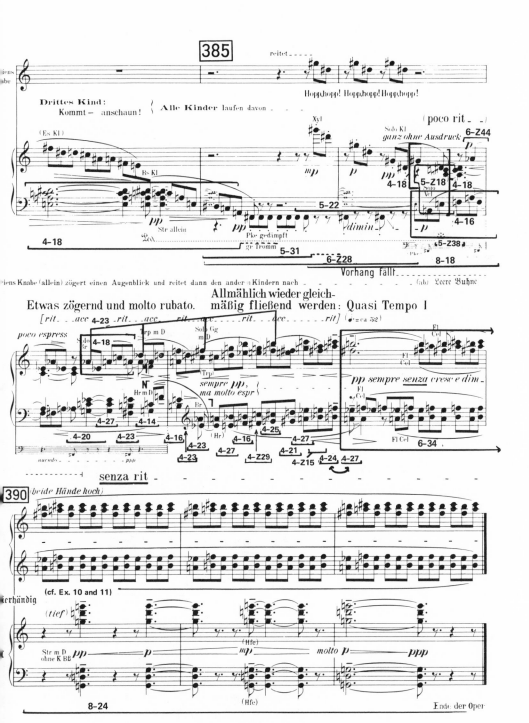

(Example 69 *continued*)

indifferent. The celesta chords clarify both the pitch-structural and the motivic underpinning of the opening three measures. Although the tetrachords
4-Z15 (see chapter 5), 4-18, 4-28, 4-27, and 4-20 all participate, the most
frequently repeated tetrachord is Marie's inverted 4-18; it is this set whose
successive transpositions support the ascending fourths-motion (set 4-23) in
the children's tune at mm. 372–73. By now the set and the fourths-motion
itself have become the transmitters of referential associations that are so numerous and multi-leveled as to defy classification. We can recall, for instance, that the same combination of vertical and horizontal components
characterized the Bridge Section of Act II/Scene 1 (Ex. 65), where Marie
tried to negate the child's presence by putting him to sleep; but the ascending
fourths-motion also constituted a melodic variant of the first seduction theme
(see mm. 673, 677, 679, and 681 of Act I/Scene 5), whereas the "uninverted" set 4-18 appeared vertically in combination with oscillating fourths
as part of another thematic component of the seduction material (Ex. 57).
Finally and most certainly, the fourths-motion in the tune for the children's
nursery rhyme fulfills its general role as conveyor of the folk idiom.

Example 70. Act III: m. 371
    (Interlude between Scenes 4 and 5)

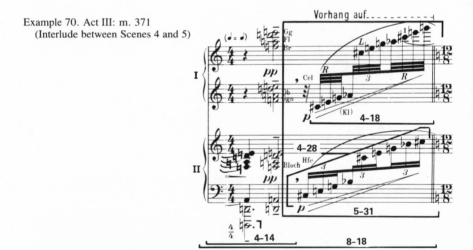

The ascending fourths aspect is only one of several features of the nursery
tune that warrant comment. On the local level, the tune may be regarded as
an outgrowth of two pitch-structural components heard in the pivotal bar
that, shown at Example 70, provides both the final, fundamental chord of the
preceding Interlude and the upbeat to this scene. The first of these compo-

nents is the cadential chord itself, the D-minor triad with added ninth that frames the final Interlude (cf. Ex. 16b) and accounts for the otherwise superficial description of this Interlude as an "Invention on a Key." The set structure represented by the cadential chord (pcs 2, 4, 5, 9) is 4-14. As clarified in the following reduction, the total pitch content of the opening measure of the nursery tune at m. 372 yields a statement of the same set, transposed down one semitone:

m. 371   m. 372

The second pitch-structural component of interest in the pivotal measure at Example 70 is a constituent of the brusque ascending arpeggiation that accompanies and "describes" the swift ascent of the curtain in the instant before the scene begins. While the harp provides a full-diminished seventh-chord glissando composed of pcs ⌞1, 4, 7, 10⌟, celesta and clarinets present an arpeggiation of the pitch classes ⌞1, 4, 7, 8⌟, whose set structure should by now be easily identified as an inverted form of Marie's 4-18. Note, incidentally, that the combined arpeggiations reproduce the very form of set 5-31 (pcs 1, 4, 7, 8, 10) that was heard in the orchestral accompaniment to Marie's first utterance of the "Eia popeia" refrain in Act I/Scene 3 (Ex. 46); note, moreover, that the total pitch content of m. 371 (Ex. 70) yields a form of the large Marie-complement 8-18. Just as the cadential chord at m. 371 becomes the basis for the first bar of the nursery tune at m. 372, so the ascending arpeggiated 4-18 finds its consequence in the second bar of the tune, where interlocking inversionally related forms of set 4-18 appear in descent as follows:

$$
\begin{array}{c}
5\text{-}22 \\
\overline{6\ 5\ 2\ 11}\ \ 10 \\
4\text{-}18 \\
\underline{} \\
4\text{-}18
\end{array}
$$

(pcs, vocal line, m. 373:)

The larger 5-element set at m. 373 is a transposed form of Perle's "basic pentad" from Act II/Scene 1—set 5-22. With the second of the two interlocking forms of set 4-18, we have an explicit pitch-structural reference to the Lullaby tune from Act I/Scene 3 (Ex. 46): the pitch content of this form of the set (pcs 5, 2, 11, 10) is exactly the same as that of the opening of the

Lullaby tune, with the original "Komm, mein Bub!" melody (pcs 2, 11, 10) reappearing in precisely the same vocal register.

The first sectional unit of this tiny scene elides with the second at m. 375, where the children's game is interrupted by the entrance of other children who have just come from the pond. The arrival of these children, callous couriers of the news about the dead Marie, is announced in clarinet, trumpet, harp, and viola by a forte series of representatives—in three successive octave registers, from high to low (mm. 375–78)—of the single pitch class exclusively associated with Marie, the A♮ (see comments in section III above). The A♮ series participates here within the broader, only somewhat less obvious, context of Marie's "waiting" motive. The tetrachord heard as the downbeat vertical of m. 375 is none other than the exact form of set 4-20 (pcs 4, 5, 9, 0) that had served as the pitch-structural adumbration of the "waiting" motive in Act I/Scene 3, as discussed at the beginning of this chapter with reference to Example 48. Once again this form of set 4-20 provides a long-range preparation for the entry of the "real" "waiting" motive at m. 379; the two "waiting"-motive harmonies thus effect a frame for the second section of the movement, which elides with the third section at the precise moment the child is told that his mother is dead. In the long-range motion from the fixed form of the "adumbration" set 4-20 at m. 375 to the fixed form of the "waiting" set 4-16 at m. 379, a passing chord that takes the half-diminished seventh-chord form of another Marie-set, 4-27, permits the fundamental voice-leading of this passage to be just slightly more complex than that of the corresponding passage in Act I/Scene 3 (mm. 412–25). Compare the following reduction with the reduction discussed on p. 130:

Now by examining the score itself for mm. 375–79, the reader will see that the passing chord 4-27 is itself prolonged by a thrice-stated descending chromatic figure (heard first in the strings *am Frosch* ["at the heel of the bow"], then in the stopped horns, and finally in the clarinets), within which each representative of the set remains a half-diminished-seventh chord, with the bass motion chromatically filling in the space between F♮ and B♮, the components of the "fateful" tritone. Notice as indicated in the score that each pair of semitone-related seventh chords creates interlocking forms of Marie's large set 8-18. The intrusive chromatic descent, at first forte, accented, and staccato, recalls the "knife" motive (see section III above), and the complete passage exemplifies the notion of a written-out "harmonic" ritardando, with each discrete vertical component of the descending series reiterated first once (m. 375), then twice (mm. 375–76), then four times (mm. 376–79), until finally the word "dead" ("tot!") is pronounced and the ultimate "resolution" of Marie's "waiting" is accomplished. In the final stage of the ritard (mm. 378–79), a muted solo violin recalls with utmost tenderness the closing phrase of Marie's Lullaby, now more than ever enriched and made painful by its aspect of descent toward "tot" and its added association with Marie's own recognition that she is, after all, "ein schlecht Mensch."

On the basis of our set-structural reading from the opening of the scene to m. 379, we can describe the passage from m. 380 to the middle of m. 381 as a telescoped summary of the fundamental harmonic events thus far. Framed by the iterations of the child's uncomprehending "Hopp, hopp!" response to the news about his mother (mm. 380–81; mm. 385–86), the penultimate section of the scene unfolds from the "waiting" motive, with the oscillating B♮-F♮ tritone giving way to the oscillating perfect fourth G♮-D♮ in anticipation of the cadential structure at the end of the scene. Now the compound soprano voice in horns and harp at m. 380 recalls with inverted contour the chromatic wedge motion from the fixed point B♭ in the children's nursery tune and in the triplet figure at m. 374. As the ascending component of the line moves from D♭ through D♮ and E♭ to E♮ against the B♭ pedal point and the oscillating G♮-D♮ in the bass, set 4-18 (pcs 2, 7, 10, 1), featured at the opening of the movement, is succeeded by sets 4-20 (pcs 2, 7, 10, 3) and 4-27 (pcs 2, 7, 10, 4), once again on their way toward the "waiting" set 4-16, which now reappears in its fixed form (pcs 5, 11, 4, 9) on the third beat of m. 381.

Meanwhile, the last of the perfect-fourth "Hopp, hopp!" figures at m. 381 becomes the point of departure for a direct reference in muted violins to the first orchestral statement of the "Komm, mein Bub!" motive from Act I/ Scene 3 (Ex. 45), transposed at t = 4 and rhythmically altered to accommodate the ostinato triplet motion. The reader will remember that the harmonic component of the "Komm, mein Bub!" motive is the tetrachordal series 4-16, 4-23, 4-20. The same harmonic series obtains here, with the "waiting" set 4-16 dually serving as the goal of the harmonic progression at m. 380 and the point of departure for the reference to "Komm, mein Bub!" Now, however, the "Komm, mein Bub!" motive begins with a 5- rather than 4-element chord, with the "correct" first bass pitch F♯ sliding into place only after the fixed form of the "waiting" set 4-16 (5, 11, 4, 9) has finished substituting for the "required" form (6, 11, 4, 0) within this transposition of the motive. Note, incidentally, that the initial 5-element chord of the motive (pcs 5, 11, 4, 9, 0) and the immediately preceding 5-element chord (pcs 5, 11, 4, 9, 1) respectively yield sets 5-20 and 5-30, pentachords that have been paired earlier at a most important moment, namely, in the opening measure of the opera (Ex. 3).

As in Act I/Scene 3, the "Komm, mein Bub!" series is repeated sequentially on the first beat of m. 382, with the original four-voice texture as well as the initial pitch content of the motive (cf. Ex. 45, m. 363) now resumed. This time, however, the tetrachordal series is extended toward a new harmonic goal—the tetrachord that takes preeminence over all the others associated with Marie, set 4-18. Appearing in the inverted form heard at the beginning of the Bridge Section in Act II/Scene 1 (4, 9, 0, 3), this tetrachord will now be sustained in muted strings and reinforced with eighth-note repetitions in muted horns from m. 382 until the second "Hopp, hopp!" phrase has been completed at m. 386. Above the 4-18 pedal point, the muted trumpet and then the clarinet, overlapping at m. 384 with the bass clarinet, present two successive long dolce legato descents; each of these begins unequivocally with an iteration of the descending "Komm, mein Bub!" melody, and each continues as an uninterrupted extension of that trichord figure in which both original and inverted forms of the trichord—set 3-3—interlock with ever-increasing regularity:

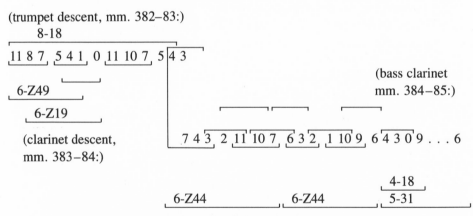

(trumpet descent, mm. 382–83:)

The unlabeled brackets displayed above delimit transpositionally and inversionally equivalent forms of the "Komm, mein Bub!" set 3-3. Among the many larger pitch structures that unfold contiguously within the two descents, the ones labeled above have been chosen for the following reasons:

1. Note that the first eight pitch classes of the trumpet descent provide a form of Marie's 8-18, a set that in fact contains no fewer than seven forms of 3-3, four of which appear here contiguously; since all of the 29 8-element sets save 8-23 contain at least four discrete forms of set 3-3, and since 11 of these large sets contain at least seven forms of that trichord, the choice of Marie's 8-18 from among all the other possibilities has significance here.

2. The clarinet descent features two successive statements of set 6-Z44, the second of which duplicates the interval series of the first at $t = 1$. Set 6-Z44 contains 3-3 four times, and all four discrete forms are presented contiguously here. Notice that the choice of semitone as transposition operator yields two additional intersecting forms of set 3-3 at the point where the two hexachords overlap ($\underline{10, 7, 6}$; $\underline{7, 6, 3}$); note, moreover, that the complement of set 6-Z44—6-Z19— is represented contiguously in the trumpet descent as shown above. The constructive role of the Z-related hexachords 6-Z19/6-Z44 in the two descents may shed light on the choice of initial pitch classes in the trumpet line: as shown in Example 69 at m. 382, the first two trumpet pitches (11, 8) in combination with the sustained 4-18 tetrachord (4, 9, 0, 3) produce yet another form of the all-important 6-Z19. Finally, two interlocking forms of set 8-19 result from the interaction of the trumpet descent and the sustained tetrachord at m. 382; the appearance of 8-19 is not surprising in light of the fact that 8-19 is the only 8-element set that contains as many as nine discrete forms of the "Komm, mein Bub!" set 3-3.

3. Whereas the opening pitches of the trumpet and clarinet descents reproduce the "Komm, mein Bub!" melody in its original shape, the overlapping bass-clarinet line at m. 384 begins with an inverted form of the trichord, whose pitch content happens to duplicate three components (4, 3, 0) of the sustained tetrachord 4-18. Reminding us that 4-18 also contains the "Komm, mein Bub!" set 3-3, the bass clarinet reinforces the sustained tetrachord by means of descending arpeggiation and concludes on the pitch class F♯; that pitch passes in turn to the timpani and is reiterated against the 4-18 pedal point, effecting a final vertical presentation of set 5-31 as displayed above and in Example 69. Only two occurrences of this pentachord have been discussed earlier (review Examples 46 and 70), but both of those appearances in coordination with the one demonstrated here confirm the association of this set with Marie.

Now as the child's perfect-fourth "Hopp, hopp!" figure returns transposed up a major second, giving closure to the penultimate section of the scene, the set-structural product of the interaction of three pitch components at mm. 385–86—the sustained 4-18 tetrachord (9, 4, 0, 3), the pedal point F♯ (pc6), and the child's figure (8, 3)—once again attests to the composer's extraordinary control of pitch materials: the hexachord that results is 6-Z28, and this is the very hexachord that was heard at the first "Hopp, hopp!" phrase, even though the interacting pitch components at the earlier statement of the child's figure were *not* the same. By turning to mm. 380–81 in Example 69, the reader will see that at the first "Hopp, hopp!" statement, set 6-Z28 results from the interaction of the child's perfect fourth ⌐6, 1⌐ with Marie's tetrachord 4-27 in the form ⌐2, 4, 7, 10⌐. Clearly set 6-Z28 contains both 4-27 and 4-18 as well as 5-31, and all of these sets relate to Marie; that property of the hexachord has been exploited for the purpose of effecting a deep-structural harmonic relationship between the two "Hopp, hopp!" phrases while at the same time achieving considerable variety on the surface.

The role of set 6-Z28 in this scene can be further demonstrated by the following chain of Marie-sets, all related by inclusion—a chain that can be compared with the chain of Wozzeck-sets at which we arrived at the end of chapter 3:

$$3\text{-}3 \subset 4\text{-}18 \subset 5\text{-}31 \subset 6\text{-}Z28$$

On the audible level coherence is accomplished in the passage from m. 380 to m. 386 by means of the all-pervasive melodic role of the "Komm, mein Bub!" figure, whose set structure is the basic element of the chain; the relationships represented by the chain suggest that the "Komm, mein Bub!" set controls the long-range harmonic plan of the passage as well. To this observation can be added that the hexachord 6-Z28 contains all the sets to its left in the chain not just once but twice.

One final comment about the initial portion of the trumpet descent at m. 382 will now be of interest: the first six pitch classes of the descent provide a form of the Z-related complement of 6-Z28, set 6-Z49. The identity of 6-Z49 in respect to 6-Z28 is expressed in the fact that 6-Z49 does not contain the pentachord 5-31; however, 6-Z49 does contain four forms of set 3-3 as well as two forms each of Marie's tetrachords 4-18 and 4-27, and of course the total interval content of 6-Z49 is identical with that of its complement 6-Z28.

We may turn now to the elided closing section of Act III/Scene 5 (mm. 386–92). Like the preceding section, the closing section is differentiated by the predominance of a single motivic idea and by a unifying contour design; and as with the elisions into the second and third sections of the scene, the elision at mm. 385–86 is accomplished not only by virtue of the ongoing triplet motion but also by motivic and set-structural means. The single motivic idea—Marie's Lullaby tune—simultaneously grows out of the child's perfect-fourth figure (see the soprano voice [clarinet] at m. 386) and emerges complete in the solo 'cello, whose point of departure is the lowest tone of the sustained 4-18 tetrachord, E♮. As shown in Example 69 and further clarified below, the pivotal set structure at mm. 385–86 is set 5-22, the "basic pentad" of Act II/Scene 1, the set which in that scene as here results from interlocking inversionally related forms of Marie's 4-18:

$$4\text{-}18 \begin{bmatrix} 8 \\ 3 \\ 0 \\ 9 \\ 4 \end{bmatrix} 4\text{-}18$$

5-22

The form 4, 9, 0, 3 of 4-18 represented in the composite vertical 5-22 collection is of course the form of the set that has been sustained as a pedal point from m. 382 to m. 386; the other 4-18 collection— 9, 0, 3, 8 —will be horizontalized by solo viola in the shape of the Lullaby tune at m. 387. Remembering that the original Lullaby tune (Ex. 46) featured a form of set 4-18, the reader will now notice that the solo 'cello statement at the pivotal bar 386 provides the shape of the tune but not the original interval series. In the guise of the Lullaby tune, the 'cello instead presents the fixed set-structural form of Marie's "waiting" motive—set 4-16 (11, 4, 5, 9).

Most remarkably, the total pitch content of the pivotal bar 386 produces the complement of the preeminent 4-18, set 8-18. As indicated in Example 69, the interaction of pitch components in m. 386 draws attention to several outstanding properties of Marie's 8-18: this large set contains not only the "waiting" set 4-16 but also the Drum Major's sets 5-Z18 and 5-Z38 as well as the all-important Z-related hexachords 6-Z19 and 6-Z44—representatives of Marie's bond with Wozzeck (in fact 8-18 contains three discrete forms of Marie's 4-16, five forms of Marie's 4-27, two forms of each of the hexachords 6-Z19 and 6-Z44, and three forms each of the pentachords 5-Z18 and 5-Z38). Like all of the 29 8-element sets, 8-18 is the container of a very large number of smaller sets, many of which are not featured whatsoever in the opera; of significance at m. 386, then, is the fact that those inclusion-related smaller sets that appear as discrete components of the motivic and pitch-structural design are the very sets that have played a distinctive role throughout the opera in association with Marie as the Drum Major's sexual partner, Marie as Wozzeck's mistress, and Marie as the child's mother.

In contrast to the descending contour of the preceding section, the closing section of the scene features an ascent in all voices that culminates at m. 389 with the oscillating tetrachords (4-27 and 4-24) heard in the same vertical arrangement and register at the end of Act I and at the beginning of Act II. The ascent takes its shape from the abbreviated sequential iterations of the Lullaby tune, first in viola, then in trumpet, then in violin, with each successive melodic statement of the Lullaby set 4-18 beginning at the perfect fourth above the preceding (see the extended beamed stems at mm. 387–88 in Example 69). The overt reference to the Lullaby is made complete at m. 387 by a four-part harmonization in the strings that supplies the original Lullaby progression ͵4-20, 4-23͵. When viola and then trumpet respectively complete their solo Lullaby statements, they successively join the horn in a chromatic ascent that supports the solo-violin melody, perpetuates the four-part texture, yields a succession of verticalized tetrachords which have all played outstanding roles in the opera (4-14, 4-16, 4-23, 4-27, 4-Z29, 4-25, 4-21, 4-Z15, 4-24), and reminds us that our survey of pitch materials associated with Marie began with the observation that Marie's first appearance coincided with a predominantly tetrachordal texture.

The last two pitches of the final Lullaby statement by the violin (m. 388) are harmonized by the fixed forms of 4-24 and 4-27 that will now be stabilized and then conjoined with the perfect fifth ͵G♮-D♮͵ to yield the final 8-element cadential structure 8-24. Up to this point the scene has been entirely dominated by motivic and set-structural references to the child's dead mother; as the Lullaby tune now merges with the final cadential harmony, references to Marie lose their identity as they become absorbed within the broader domain of that harmony—the structure whose significance as the largest collection within a chain of sets that represents the fundamental pitch-structural matrix of the opera was demonstrated at the end of chapter 3. Vestiges within the final sonority of the outstanding role of Marie's pitch materials in this scene and throughout the opera take the form of two clearly defined components at mm. 390–92—the tetrachord 4-27 and the dyad ͵G♮-D♮͵, especially featured in the seduction material, whose function as a pedal point here was anticipated at mm. 380–81. To this it can be added that on the inaudible level the final 8-element configuration in fact contains four discrete forms of 4-27 and of 4-16 as well as six forms of the "Komm, mein Bub!" set 3-3 and two forms each of the Marie-tetrachords 4-17, 4-18, and 4-20. Finally, the reader will note that the fixed pitch components of the closing sonority include not only the motivically important dyad ͵G♮-D♮͵ (review chapter 2) but also the "fateful" tritone ͵B♮-F♮͵, Wozzeck's "Jawohl" D♭ from Act I/Scene

1, Marie's A♮ (review p. 152), and the predominant first pitch class of the Doctor's passacaglia theme from Act I/Scene 4, the E♭ (see Examples 33 and 34). This accounts for every single pitch component of the cadential chord save the F♯, whose role in the final scene as a component of the child's first "Hopp, hopp!" figure and as a pedal point from m. 385 to m. 387 has been treated above.

XI

With the foregoing study of Act III/Scene 5, our survey of the role of set 4-18 in the four scenes that expose Marie's role as mother comes to a finish. In a final effort to demonstrate the overriding importance of Marie's 4-18 in the overall harmonic and dramatic design, I shall return now to a viewpoint introduced in chapter 3 and further developed earlier in this chapter. Using references to Büchner's own writings (see chapter 3, section I) and Leo Treit-ler's reading of the philosophical context of *Woyzeck* as a point of departure, I have suggested that Wozzeck's need to invest incomprehensible events with purpose, made explicit by his effort to interpret his visions as portents of doom, is portrayed in the opera not only by networks of motives (see Treitler 1976) but also by networks of set structures; these help to transmit the fatal-istic undercurrent of the drama—an undercurrent that finds its clearest expression in Wozzeck's sense that the things that happen were bound to happen from the moment of his very first revelation in the open field. In this view, irony serves as the fundamental dramatic device. We as witnesses are shown that all the unjust and insufferable conditions of Wozzeck's existence as well as the futility of his demise point to the absurdity of the Enlighten-ment doctrine that man inevitably progresses toward a higher good by virtue of his reason. Meanwhile, Wozzeck—an unwitting victim of that doctrine, or better, a humble believer in the Christian doctrine of salvation secularized by the Enlightenment—becomes all too rapidly convinced that he has been called by forces outside of himself to execute punishment for sin. He ends by destroying not the Drum Major, the immediate agent of his despair, nor any of the other inhuman elements of his world as represented by the pro-gressivist Doctor and the callous Captain, but rather the one source of hap-piness that had temporarily given meaning to an otherwise wretched exis-tence—Marie. To summarize: "In his mind what happens must happen, and so he causes it to happen in reality" (Treitler 1976, p. 255).

We have examined the manner in which the seduction pedal point G♮-A♮, the Drum Major's set structures, and the "immerzu" rhythm of the first tavern scene were implanted in Wozzeck's "hallucination" theme from the open fields (review Examples 53 and 54); these concealed features of the compositional scheme have been interpreted as musical correlatives for Wozzeck's need to believe that the visions of the open field must contain a mysterious and horrifying message about future events. It remains to show that the person whose act of betrayal initiates the chain of events that Wozzeck comes to interpret as the fulfillment of the prophecies from the open field is also represented by set-structural means in the hallucination material itself.

Example 71 shows the central passage of the episode from the open-field scene that separates the first and second versions of Andres's Song. The oscillating trombone figure at m. 226 is a reiterated statement in diminution at t = 0 of the harmonic progression with which the scene opens—the progression that introduces the first two of the three "hallucination" chords upon which the pitch materials of the scene will be based (cf. Ex. 29: 5-Z17, 5-19, 5-Z17). An instant after the trombones have completed their written ritardando and become silent, the first of the two "hallucination" chords reappears untransposed in the strings, now providing the impetus at m. 227 for a new "hallucination" motive that will unfold as Wozzeck points to the strange sign above the toadstools (mm. 227–34: "Do you see that shining streak over there across the grass, where the toadstools are growing? That's where a head rolls at night"). The outstanding melodic feature of the new motive is the augmented-second embellishing motion A♭-B♮-A♭ —an outgrowth of the trombone figure at m. 226, whose uppermost part in turn reproduces the opening melodic statement of the scene. Of foremost interest here is that the complete melodic component of the new "hallucination" motive yields the form 8, 11, 4, 5 of Marie's most pervasive tetrachord—4-18.

Several additional Marie-sets play a concealed role in the passage shown at Example 71. Having heard no fewer than six iterations of the fixed "hallucination" chord-pair 5-Z17, 5-19 in mm. 225–26, we expect to hear the same basic form of set 5-19 immediately after the statement of the fixed 5-Z17 at m. 227; instead we hear not one but two successive inversionally related vertical statements of Marie's "waiting" set 4-16. Note that the Drum Major's sets 5-Z38 and 5-Z18 make vertical appearances in mm. 228 and 230; and remember that these pentachords each contain one form of Marie's 4-18. Finally, when the "hallucination" motive is repeated at mm. 228–29, the initially altered harmonization yields one new vertical statement of 4-18 in the form 1, 5, 10, 4 just before the downbeat of m. 229. Like the visions themselves, the occurrences of sets 4-18 and 4-16 within the "hallucination" motive at Example 71 cannot be interpreted as references to Marie until in

Example 71. Act I/Scene 2: mm. 226–32

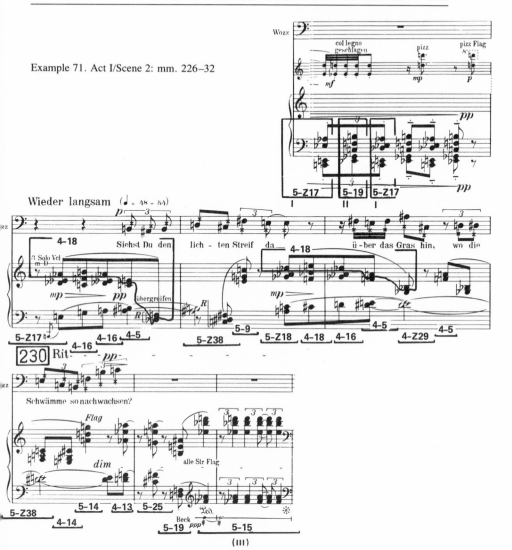

the next scene these sets begin to be explicitly associated with her by virtue of their prominence in the "Komm, mein Bub!" motive and then the Lullaby. The dramatic parallel can surely be regarded as more than coincidental: only after Marie makes her first move toward the Drum Major in the next scene can Wozzeck even begin to think that the visions were warning him specifically of Marie's betrayal.

If from the vantage point of analytical hindsight we can suspect that the

occurrence of Marie-sets in the passage at Example 71 is not without significance, then our suspicions are heightened by the manner in which the "hallucination" motive of Example 71 is further developed in the passage shown
at Example 72. Having found the spot where "a head rolls at night" (mm.
233–34), Wozzeck now terrifies Andres by telling him that "somebody once
picked one up [mm. 237–38], thought it was a hedgehog [Ex. 72, mm. 238–
39]; three days and three nights, and he was lying in a coffin [mm. 239–42]."
Wozzeck's disclosure is accompanied by a brief canonic treatment of the
four-note figure announced as Hauptstimme by the English horn at mm. 238–
39. Note that the first three pitches of the figure in the English horn preserve
the embellishing motion $\underline{A^\flat\text{-}B^\natural\text{-}A^\flat}$ of the earlier motive. The continuation,
however, is new: gone is the complete melodic statement of Marie's 4-18,
but in its place we hear a subset of that tetrachord, presented as an adumbration by means of contour, interval series, and hence set structure of the fundamental melodic idea of the forthcoming scene—the melodic component,
set 3-3, of Marie's "Komm, mein Bub!" motive. At m. 240 the altered fourth
canonic entry in the oboe permits two composite vertical statements of each
of the two most important tetrachords of the opera—Marie's 4-18 and Wozzeck's own 4-19.

In Act I/Scene 3, in the Doctor's Act I/Scene 4, and in the barracks scene
of Act II, at points where Wozzeck gropes toward his ultimate interpretation
of the visions, either the "hallucination" motive shown at Example 71, or an
extended version of the same introduced at m. 233 and/or the canonic development of the motive shown at Example 72 recurs untransposed as a Leitsektion. This network of recurrences has been traced and admirably interpreted
by Leo Treitler (1976), and it need not be reexamined here. What does need
to be clarified, however, is the fact that before any of the "hallucination"
passages return, we are given a chance at the beginning of Act I/Scene 3 to
meet Marie and to hear the matrix of pitch structures that will be inextricably
linked with her from that point forward. Hence by the time the canonic passage at Example 72 returns in Act I/Scene 3 (mm. 442–46), now emerging
from an intensified reiteration of the embellishing motion $\underline{A^\flat\text{-}B^\natural\text{-}A^\flat}$ accomplished by bassoon tremolando (mm. 442–43), the careful listener is thor-
oughly prepared to make an association between, on the one hand, the interval pattern and the descending-contour presentation of the motive of the first
two canonic entries, and on the other hand, the reiterated statements earlier
in this scene of the same motive in the same shape—the motive heard as the
"Komm, mein Bub!" melody (Ex. 45) and as a component of the Lullaby
tune itself (Ex. 46).

One later excerpt confirms beyond all doubt the planned connection be-

Example 72. Act I/Scene 2: mm. 238–43

tween the canonic "hallucination" motive at Example 72 and the "Komm, mein Bub!" melody. By returning to Example 32, from Act I/Scene 4, the reader can review the only moment in the opera where Wozzeck himself sings the "Komm, mein Bub!" melody. Like the Leitsektion from Act I/Scene 3, this moment is prepared by an $A\flat$-$B\natural$-$A\flat$ tremolando, rescored here for 'cello; and now the pitch content of the melodic statement "Ach, Marie!" incorporates the same fundamental melodic feature of the "hallucination" material from the open field: Wozzeck's "Ach, Marie!" is set to the pitch classes $B\natural$-$A\flat$-$G\natural$. At this point, if only by reference to the preceding dramatic events, the viewer might fully predict something that has begun to emerge in Wozzeck's mind but will remain unclear even after he sees the earrings (Act II/Scene 1) and is warned of Marie's infidelity by the Doctor and the Captain (Act II/Scene 2): the viewer is in a position to understand that the disaster Wozzeck senses in the open fields will become concrete to him in the actuality of Marie's betrayal. And the acute listener may also realize that by means of carefully planned pitch-structural associations, the composer has taken every measure first to conceal and then gradually to clarify the role that Marie will play in the fulfillment of the prophecy Wozzeck imagines to have received.

The inevitable consequence of the fulfilled prophecy is of course the murder of Marie. One final link between Wozzeck's canonic "hallucination" motive and Marie's "Komm, mein Bub!" melody suggests that even that consequence was portended by pitch-structural means in the second, third, and fourth scenes of the opera. Among the countless occurrences of set 3-3 throughout the work, two take priority for the following reasons: the form shown in Example 32— B♮-A♭-G♮—is Wozzeck's fundamental version of the set, regarded as such in comparison to his only other statement of the "Komm, mein Bub!" melody (Act I/Scene 4, mm. 606–07: "Ach, Marie!") because it is adumbrated in his open-field scene and reiterated at the beginning of the two Leitsektion recurrences of the canonic episode. The form D♮-B♮-B♭, sung by Marie at the beginning of Act I/Scene 3, constitutes the only statement of the "Komm, mein Bub!" motive that is explicitly set to the text "Komm, mein Bub!," and it is chosen over all the other iterations of the set at the opening of the scene to be transplanted into the first phrase of the Lullaby (cf. Examples 45 and 46). A single pitch class is held in common between these two most prominent forms of the set—the B♮. This is the pitch class that will serve as the all-pervasive ostinato of the murder scene.

As a farewell gesture to Marie, let us finally examine two passages from her last scene on stage. The opening measures of the murder scene—Act III/ Scene 2—are shown at Example 73. In the immediately preceding passage that accompanies the rising curtain (Ex. 68), double basses, with their lowest string tuned down one semitone, have called attention to their sustained B♮ by means of a twice iterated crescendo-decrescendo, the second swelling to forte; now as we see Marie and Wozzeck entering onto the forest path, the all-important B♮ is passed quietly, almost imperceptibly, to a single trombone, with the result that its presence is more sensed than heard. Above the pedal point a lonely bassoon at first gropes upward, then hastens nervously toward a point of rest. The resting-point—a sustained C♯—marks the first stage in an ascending vertical construction of the five-note collection B♮-C♯-F♮-B♭-D♮, achieved by the second beat of m. 74 and sustained until m. 75. As the stopped horns, then the violins abruptly jut into the scene, completing the construction with embellished *fp* additions to the collection, Marie—the first to speak—senses trouble and urges Wozzeck to hurry with her back to town.

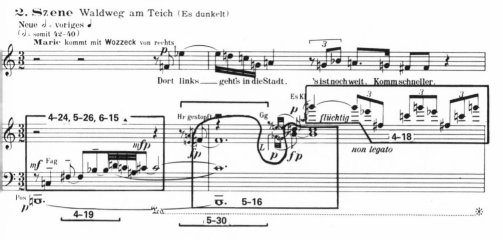

Example 73. Act III/Scene 2: mm. 73–74

A set-structural reading of the passage reveals that whereas sets that obliquely refer to Wozzeck are given some priority in m. 73, these contrast sharply with at least one straightforward Marie-representative at m. 74. The opening ascent in the bassoon (0, 6, 10, 2) is a whole-tone formation represented by the set name 4-24; the reader may recall that 4-24 maximizes the major third (ic4) and that the only other tetrachord with this property is Wozzeck's 4-19. The first five pitch classes of the bassoon line provide a statement of set 5-26. Along with 4-24, this pentachord appeared in an entirely different me-lodic shape at the opening of the "earrings" theme in Act II/Scene 1 (Ex-amples 41, 65); it also resulted from interlocking statements of 4-19 and 4-27 in Marie's "Ich bin doch ein schlecht Mensch" (Examples 39, 40). The complete bassoon line is a form of the hexachord 6-15, a set that contains one form of Marie's 4-18 and two forms of Wozzeck's 4-19. Though none of these contained tetrachords is made prominent in the shape of the line, a contiguous segment of the line interacts with the pedal point B♮ to produce a fleeting composite statement of Wozzeck's 4-19 (11, 6, 10, 2). Finally, and perhaps of greatest interest, the bassoon line comes to rest on Wozzeck's C♯ from Act I/Scene 1. I place particular stress on this last observation because, like the C♯ and the B♮ pedal point, the remaining three pitch classes of the sustained pentachord that coalesce at m. 74 have acquired a special signifi-cance during the course of the opera. In juxtaposition with the B♮ pedal point, the F♮, which enters just before the downbeat to m. 74, creates an exposed and now tremendously ominous representative of the "fateful" tritone, the appropriateness of whose appearance here need not be labored. Finally, the pentachord 5-16 that results from the addition of the dyad ⌊B♭-D♮⌋ in the violins contains no fewer than three forms of Marie's "Komm, mein Bub!" set 3-3, and the form exposed by the outer voices of the pentachord—the ⌊B♭-D♮⌋ in combination with the pedal point B♮—is none other than Marie's fundamental form of the set, discussed above.

As Marie's "Komm schneller" ("come faster") at m. 74 betrays her uneasiness, obscured pitch-structural associatives of the near murderer and his trapped victim give way to a sharply defined, by now recognizable reference to the speaker: in sympathy with Marie's urge to run away, a constrained E♭ clarinet (marked piano in its brightest register) presents a repeated triplet figure—marked *flüchtig* ("fugitive"; "fleeting")—within which an out-of-phase four-note pattern circles above and below a centrally placed C♮, trying to flee but going nowhere and finally stopping short; the four-note collection is the form ⌊7, 3, 6, 0⌋ of Marie's 4-18.

Outstanding features of our final example fulfill the expectation set forth by the E♭ clarinet that Marie's 4-18 will play a significant role in the music that accompanies her remaining moments on stage. Example 74 shows the beginning of the second of the two large sections of the murder scene, isolated from the first by the longest absolute silence that occurs within the three acts, and further set into relief by its correspondence with the stage direction "der Mond geht auf" ("the moon rises"). As the full string choir now sustains the portentous B♮ in seven discrete octaves, the remaining eleven pitch classes are ordered to produce a spacious quarter-note pianissimo ascent initiated by a single deep, muted first trombone and imitated canonically at the unison by the other three muted trombones, with Marie providing a final fifth entry. When the first trombone enters his extreme high register, the last two pitches of the eleven-note ascent are passed to the muted first trumpet, who comes to rest at m. 98 on Marie's A♮ and then sustains that pitch until the middle of m. 101. The other trombones follow suit, passing continuations of their ordered series to the other three trumpets. Meanwhile, however, the temporal distance between entries decreases by one quarter note with each successive entry, and all instrumental voices come to rest on the fifth beat of m. 99; thus the eleven-note ascent is completed only by the first trombone with the help of the first trumpet, and the remaining trombone-trumpet ascents conclude respectively on the tenth, ninth, and eighth pitches of the series. In other words, the tetrachord that congeals in the trumpets at m. 99 consists of the last four notes of the series—pcs 10, 3, 6, 9; having emerged from the depths of musical space while the moon rises from below the horizon, this tetrachord is the sonority that will now be set into shimmering reverberation by the flutter-tonguing trumpets as Marie completes her six-note portion of the series, the syllabic setting for "Wie der Mond rot aufgeht!" ("How red the moon is rising!"). The shimmering tetrachord—sustained into m. 101—is an inverted form of Marie's 4-18.

Not only do the last four pitches of the eleven-note ascent constitute a 4-18 formation, in fact the first four pitches have been ordered to produce the same. Once again, moreover, 4-18 interlocks at the beginning of the ascent with Wozzeck's 4-19, this time effecting a new presentation of the "basic pentad" 5-22 from Act II/Scene 1. These and other 4- to 8-element set structures formed by contiguous segments of the ordered series are displayed below:

```
                          8-27
                 ┌──────────────────────┐
                      4-27
                 ┌──────────┐
              8-27
         ┌──────────────┐
                             5-Z18
                          ┌──────────┐
              7-Z38
         ┌──────────┐
pcs:     7 1 4 8 0 2 5 10 3 6 9 (11)
         4-18          4-18  ·
         └──────┘      └──────┘
            4-19
         └──────┘
         5-22      6-Z19
         └────┘ └──────────┘
    →  6-Z17      6-Z43
       └──────┘ └──────────────┘
         6-15
       └──────────┘
            4-24
          └──────┘
            5-26
          └──────┘
            6-34
          └──────────┘
```

It should be apparent at a glance that the ascent at mm. 97–98 provides a compendium of pitch-structural formations that have played an outstanding role throughout the opera in particular association with Wozzeck and Marie. Note especially that the complete ascent features interlocking forms of Marie's 8-27, within which the complement Marie-set 4-27 is embedded and the Drum Major's sets 7-Z38 and 5-Z18 are moreover contiguously displayed. In Example 74 the sets formed by the first seven pitches of the ascent in combination with the pedal point B♮ have also been indicated. There it can be seen that the first composite four-note segment provides yet another form of Marie's 4-27; the large eight-element composite set is none other than the complement of the predominant 4-18, set 8-18.

Finally, the arrow in the above display draws attention to the fact that the first six pitches of the ascent—Marie's segment as sung at mm. 98–99—

Example 74. Act III/Scene 2: mm. 97–102

have been given to her for a very special purpose. In response to Marie's observation about the redness of the rising moon, Wozzeck provides a chilling complementary view that is syllabically set to the last five pitches of the original ascent and now reaches its apex on his idée fixe—the B♮. It follows that the setting for Wozzeck's "Wie ein blutig Eisen!" (m. 100: "Like a bloody blade!") must be the literal pc complement of Marie's "Wie der Mond rot aufgeht!" The Z-related complementary hexachords are 6-Z17, for Marie, and 6-Z43, for Wozzeck. The same Z-related hexachords provided the pitch-structural basis for the Doctor's twelve-tone passacaglia theme in Act I/Scene 4 (Ex. 33). More significant, however, is the fact that Wozzeck's 6-Z43 was introduced in the beginning of the open-field scene at the point where the single pitch class C♮ (pc0) was added to the fixed form (5, 9, 4, 11, 3) of the third "hallucination" pentachord (see Ex. 29). The resulting fixed collection reappeared at mm. 270–71 of the same scene, where Wozzeck stamped his foot on the ground and found that "Everything is hollow! A gulf! It quakes" ("Alles hohl! Ein Schlund! Es schwankt"). The collection was again reiter-

(Example 74 *continued*)

ated in dramatic forte ascent (mm. 291–92) at the moment when Wozzeck saw "a fire" ("ein Feuer"). That moment corresponded with the great lighting display of the scene ("The sun is just setting. The last penetrating ray bathes the horizon in the most glaring sunlight, from which twilight follows, as if suddenly, with the effect of deepest darkness, to which the eye gradually becomes accustomed" [mm. 286–95: "Die Sonne ist im Begriff unterzugehen. Der letzte scharfe Strahl taucht den Horizont in das grellste Sonnenlicht, dem ziemlich unvermittelt die (wie tiefste Dunkelheit wirkende) Dämmerung folgt, an die sich das Auge allmählich gewöhnt"]). The same fixed form of 6-Z43 returns in Act I/Scene 3, as shown at Example 49. Finally, the figure from the lighting display in the open-field scene recurs in the tavern scene of the second act, where Wozzeck cries out "Warum löscht Gott die Sonne nicht aus?" (mm. 516–19: "Why doesn't God blot out the sun?"). These connected earlier appearances of the hexachord 6-Z43 "shed light" on Wozzeck's presentation of the set in Example 74; as the bloody rays of the moon now remind him of his purpose, the mission toward which he has been called ever since the visions of the open field, Wozzeck at last draws the knife.

The physical appearance of the knife at m. 101 has been anticipated in m. 100 not only by Wozzeck's allusion to the "bloody blade" but also by its corresponding "knife"-motive accompaniment—the chromatic figure in stopped horns and muted contrabass tuba that insidiously juxtaposes its descent against the rising B♮-series in low strings. Now Marie's "Was zitterst?" ("Why are you quivering?") reveals cold-blooded terror, further transmitted in a reiteration of her figure by oboes, xylophone, and pizzicato strings (compare the setting for Wozzeck's "Das Messer?" in Act III/Scene 4, m. 222). The "Was zitterst" figure—announced an instant before Marie's death—serves as a conclusive example of the outstanding role of 4-18 in association with her. As shown in Example 74, the figure emerges from the sustained shimmering 4-18 tetrachord in the trumpets, throwing this fixed form of the set and a new inverted vertical formation of the same— 2, 5, 8, 1 —into reiterated mezzoforte relief. Marie's end is now seconds away. Wozzeck's actual moment of entry into Marie with the knife at m. 102 has been shown and discussed earlier (Ex. 43). It remains to mention that as Wozzeck finally announces his intentions at m. 102 ("Ich nicht, Marie! Und kein Andrer auch nicht!" ["If not me, Marie, then no one else!"]), Marie's "waiting" set 4-16—to be heard in its fixed form just after she has expired (mm. 106–08)—is promised with ruthless irony by trombones and pizzicato 'cellos. Unlike Marie, we have known for some time now that Marie's "waiting" will, in the words of the composer, "find its end only in her death."

5 CONCLUSIONS: THE SET COMPLEX

As we approach the final stage of this study, it will be useful to take a retrospective view of the set-theoretic tools employed in the preceding chapters and briefly assess what has been accomplished by their means. Thus far, diverse analytical observations about relationships within and among a wide range of passages from the opera have been made with reference only to a very few fundamental set-theoretic principles—equivalence under transposition and inversion, inclusion, complementation, and invariance. Although we have by no means exhausted the subject of relationships between pitch-class set structures and the dramatic design, the reader can be assured at this point that should he wish to apply the set-analytic method to other passages of the work on his own, he will without difficulty find further confirmation that certain by now familiar pitch-structural formations pervade the opera; he will moreover discover anew that those outstanding formations are the very sets that have been shown to serve as associatives of the central character Wozzeck, of Marie, and of the unhappy bond between them that determines their fate.

With a very limited array of analytical techniques, we have arrived, then, at the point where it should be possible to summarize fundamental aspects of the harmonic language of *Wozzeck*. The basic vocabulary of pitch structures that characterizes this language has been established. Inasmuch as the examination of invariant subsets and inclusion relations has led to the notion of the formation of sets from smaller sets, morphological features of that vocabulary have been probed. And by establishing referential associations between specific sound-combinations of the language, that is, specific pitch structures, and specific extramusical elements—characters, images, and dramatic issues—I have further attached "meaning" to some components of the language; that is, with discretion I have established some semantic relationships. It should be stressed here that an attempt to formulate syntactical relationships in this work cannot be made outside of a more detailed study of voice-leading and phrase structure in relationship to the logical unfolding of the text; if on this basis I have touched upon syntactical issues, in doing so, I have obviously not tried to present a study of musical syntax. Nor have I yet attempted to characterize the essential nature of the atonal harmonic language that is uniquely Berg's language of *Wozzeck*, to be distinguished, for instance, from Berg's harmonic language in *Lulu*, or Stravinsky's harmonic language in *The Rite of Spring*, or Schoenberg's harmonic language in *Erwartung*. Though distinctions or comparisons of this kind will not fall within the scope of this study, some steps in the direction of a general characterization with respect to *Wozzeck* can be taken, and here an introduction to the concept of the set complex will be appropriate. (For comments about the extent to which the pitch-structural vocabulary of *Wozzeck* reflects general compositional tendencies as exemplified in Berg's earlier works, review note 1 of chapter 4.)

The notion of the set complex is based upon a fundamental association between the inclusion relation and the complement relation that can be expressed very simply as follows: if set A is included in set B, then the complement of B (notated $\overline{B}$) will be included in the complement of A (notated $\overline{A}$). In other words, A is a subset of B iff (if and only if) $\overline{B}$ is a subset of $\overline{A}$; or, in mathematical notation,

$$A \subset B \text{ iff } \overline{B} \subset \overline{A}$$

Following Allen Forte (1964, 1973a, 1978a), I shall now describe the set complex as a group of sets related by inclusion to a single set, called the *nexus set*. There will be two types of set complexes: "a large all-inclusive type called K and a more restrictive type [a subcomplex] called Kh" (Forte 1978a, p. 12). (The choice of the letter K obviously derives from the first phoneme of the word "complex"; the "h" of "Kh" serves to distinguish the subcomplex from the complex and has no added significance.) Membership within the set complex K will be defined as follows: the set complex K about a nexus set A will consist of all the sets that are in an inclusion relation with either A or $\overline{A}$. More formally, set B and its complement are members of the set complex K about set A and its complement if and only if (1) B can contain or be contained in A, OR (2), B can contain or be contained in the complement of A. In mathematical notation the preceding statement is written as shown below:

$$B/\overline{B} \ \epsilon \ K(A,\overline{A}) \ \text{ iff } \ B \supset\subset A \mid B \supset\subset \overline{A}$$

$B/\overline{B}$ is read "B and its complement"; the Greek letter ϵ (epsilon) stands for "is a member of"; the symbol $\asymp$ is read "can contain or be contained in"; the symbol | represents logical *or*.

Two conditions on B and A will be added: (1) sets B and A will contain no fewer than 3 and no more than 9 elements; that is, the null set, the universal set of twelve pitch classes, the 6 interval classes, and the six 11-element sets will not be considered as nexus sets or as members of a set complex. (2) Set B will not have the same number of elements as set A, nor will B have the same number of elements as the complement of A; in other words, for example, the set complex K about a 4-element set excludes 4-element and 8-element sets. This of course does not mean that inclusion relations between 4-element and 8-element sets cannot be considered in an analysis; relations precisely of this kind as well as inclusion relations between 5- and 7-element sets have in fact already played a significant role in this study of *Wozzeck*.

Before proceeding to the more restrictive subcomplex Kh, I shall further demonstrate the set complex K-relation by means of an example that is pertinent to our analysis of the opera. Let us determine whether the all-pervasive Wozzeck-set 4-19 (prime form: 0, 1, 4, 8) is a member of the set complex K about the whole-tone pentachord 5-33 (prime form: 0, 2, 4, 6, 8) and its complement 7-33 (prime form: 0, 1, 2, 4, 6, 8, 10). Our first question must be whether the set-type 4-19 is itself contained in 5-33; in other words, can the prime form of 4-19 or any of the other twenty-three transpositionally and inversionally equivalent forms of the set be mapped onto the prime form of 5-33? Whereas the comparison of some sets in this respect might necessitate an inspection of all available transpositionally and inversionally equivalent forms of the smaller set, in this case the answer to the question can be determined in a flash: that the interval content of set 4-19 [101310] includes a semitone rules out the possibility of any mapping onto the whole-tone pentachord [040402]. Having ascertained that 4-19 is not a subset of 5-33, we now ask whether 4-19 is contained in the complement of 5-33, set 7-33. Here the answer is affirmative, as demonstrated below:

$$
\begin{array}{c}
4\text{-}19 \\
\overbrace{} \\
7\text{-}33 \text{ (prime form): } 0\ 1\ 2\ 4\ 6\ 8\ 10 \\
\underbrace{} \\
4\text{-}19
\end{array}
$$

In fact the prime form of 7-33 contains both the prime form and an inverted form of 4-19. This inclusion relation suffices to make 4-19 and 8-19 members of the set complex K about 5-33 and 7-33; in mathematical notation, the following statement is therefore true:

$$4\text{-}19/8\text{-}19 \in K(5\text{-}33, 7\text{-}33)$$

Since the set names 8-19 and 7-33 can be determined from their complements 4-19 and 5-33, the statement can be abbreviated to:

$$4\text{-}19 \in K(5\text{-}33)$$

Now if 4-19 is a subset of 7-33, then 5-33 will be a subset of 8-19:

$$4\text{-}19 \subset 7\text{-}33 \text{ iff } 5\text{-}33 \subset 8\text{-}19$$

Finally, since on this basis the relation determined by the definition of set-complex membership is symmetric, it follows that:

$$5\text{-}33 \in K(4\text{-}19)$$

Now on the one hand, it can be stated without hesitation that extended pure whole-tone passages are *not* a characteristic feature of *Wozzeck* and that set 7-33 does *not* play a significant role in the opera. On the other hand, we have seen firsthand that sets 4-19 and 8-19 have a central place in the pitch materials of this work; moreover, among the 54 sets that are members of the set complex K(5-33,7-33), the following 16 have figured prominently in passages discussed at length in chapters 1 through 4: 3-3, 3-12, 4-12, 4-Z15, 4-16, 4-19, 4-21 and 4-24 (two of the three whole-tone tetrachords), 4-27, 4-Z29, 6-21, 6-22, 6-34, 8-19, 8-24, and 8-27. Accordingly, an examination of the set complex K about the whole-tone pentachord 5-33 and its complement can serve as the first step toward an assessment of the role of whole-tone material in relationship to the overall harmonic design: whereas it would be entirely inaccurate to say that the harmonic language of *Wozzeck* is characteristically whole-tone, it can be said with authority that the "almost whole-tone" feature of the prominent hexachords 6-21, 6-22, and 6-34 discussed in chapters 2 and 3 is a distinctive harmonic trait of the opera that is further reflected in the large number of other sets prominent in *Wozzeck* that belong to the set complex K-family about the whole-tone pentachord 5-33. For the reader who finds this observation to be discouragingly abstract, it may be helpful to mention that all of the above-mentioned 4-element sets from *Wozzeck* that are members of K(5-33) contain a form of the whole-tone segment that is known as the augmented triad (set 3-12: 0, 4, 8) or a form of set 3-8 (0, 2, 6), another segment of the whole-tone scale (the tetrachord 4-24 contains both 3-8 and 3-12). I will return to the whole-tone issue after the more restrictive Kh-relation has been explored.

As exemplified by K(5-33), K-families tend to be large. Consider the fact that 22 of the 29 8-element sets contain representatives of all of the twelve trichord set-types; this means that set complexes about those 8-element sets

and their complements will contain 24 discrete 3- and 9-element sets alone—
the twelve trichords and their twelve complements. Note, moreover, that of
the K-families about the twelve trichords, 7 contain all 58 4- and 8-element
sets (29 + 29). The unwieldy size of many K-families constitutes one of two
aspects of the K-relation that limit its usefulness as an analytic concept. The
second of these is the absence of what Forte calls the *reciprocal complement
relation*: as shown above, to qualify for membership about $K(A,\overline{A})$, set B
need only contain or be contained in either A OR $\overline{A}$. Thus 4-19/8-19 ϵ K
(5-33,7-33) and 4-19 is a subset of 7-33, but 4-19 is not a subset of 5-33;
and since 4-19 is not a subset of 5-33, it follows that 7-33 is not a subset of
8-19. As a response to the limitations of the K-relation, Forte's subcomplex
Kh arises with the imposition of a single additional restriction on the set-
complex relation that introduces reciprocity with respect to complement relations and thus effects a reduction in the sizes of set complexes. The new
restriction is expressed by the change from OR (|) to AND (&) below:

$$\text{K-relation: } B/\overline{B} \in K(A,\overline{A}) \text{ iff B} \quad \asymp \quad A \mid B \quad \asymp \quad \overline{A}$$
$$\text{Kh-relation: } B/\overline{B} \in K(A,\overline{A}) \text{ iff B} \quad \asymp \quad A \And B \quad \asymp \quad \overline{A}$$

To clarify further: set B and its complement will not be members of the
subcomplex Kh about a nexus set A unless (1) B can contain or be contained
in A, AND (2) B can contain or be contained in $\overline{A}$.

Two examples will demonstrate. Like the set complex K about 5-33, these
have been chosen for their outstanding relevance to *Wozzeck*. (1) The reader
will have no difficulty recalling that the Wozzeck-set 4-19 is a subset both of
6-Z19 and of its Z-complement, 6-Z44. (2) The same was shown to be true
of Marie's most important tetrachord, 4-18; that is, 4-18 $\subset$ 6-Z19 AND
4-18 $\subset$ 6-Z44. It follows that both 4-19 and 4-18 qualify for membership
within Kh(6-Z19,6-Z44). And since the reciprocal complement relation now
obtains, all the relationships notated below are understood in the preceding
statement:

$$4\text{-}19 \subset 6\text{-}Z19 \And 4\text{-}19 \subset 6\text{-}Z44$$
$$6\text{-}Z19 \subset 8\text{-}19 \And 6\text{-}Z44 \subset 8\text{-}19$$

$$4\text{-}18 \subset 6\text{-}Z19 \And 4\text{-}18 \subset 6\text{-}Z44$$
$$6\text{-}Z19 \subset 8\text{-}18 \And 6\text{-}Z44 \subset 8\text{-}18$$

The composer's exploitation of these inclusion relations and the long-range
role of the hexachords 6-Z19 and 6-Z44 have already been amply demonstrated (for a review, see the discussions that accompany the following: Ex-

amples 28, 36, 43, 50, 59, 65, 66, 68, 69). As we move in this chapter from specific examples to general considerations, it will now be useful to examine the entire Kĥ-family about 6-Z19/6-Z44. In the list provided below, complementary sets do not appear by set name but are understood to participate as members of the family; thus, for example, the set name 3-3 indicates that both 3-3 and 9-3 are members of Kh(6-Z19,6-Z44):

> members of Kh(6-Z19,6-Z44):
>
> > 3-3; 3-4; 3-5; 3-8; 3-10; 3-11; 3-12
> > 4-7; 4-8; 4-17; 4-18; 4-19; 4-20
> > 5-21; 5-22

Of the 15 sets and their complements about the nexus 6-Z19/6-Z44, 11 have been shown to figure significantly in *Wozzeck*: 3-3, 3-12, 4-17, 4-18, 8-18, 4-19, 8-19, 4-20, 5-21, 7-21, and 5-22. (Set 4-8, not discussed, is featured repeatedly in the Ländler tune, shown at Example 55.) On the basis of the preeminence of the hexachords 6-Z19 and 6-Z44 in scenes where Marie and Wozzeck are shown together and in conflict, as well as in light of the fact that each of these hexachords multiply contains Wozzeck's 4-19 and Marie's 4-18, I have proposed that 6-Z19 and 6-Z44 provide pitch-structural correspondents for the fatal bond between the two leading characters. That proposal now gains further strength. Note that Kh(6-Z19,6-Z44) contains a rich assortment of sets associated with both Wozzeck and Marie: whereas Marie is represented not only by 4-18 and 8-18 but also by the sets 4-17, 4-20, and 5-22 (the "basic pentad" of Act II/Scene 1, where it appears as the result of interlocking forms of Marie's 4-18), Wozzeck is represented by the augmented triad 3-12 (see chapter 3) and 4-19/8-19 as well as 5-21/7-21 (Examples 24, 26, 36, and 60); moreover, the third member of the Wozzeck family—the child who personifies the bond between Wozzeck and Marie—is represented in Kh(6-Z19, 6-Z44) by the "Komm, mein Bub!" set 3-3.

Kh-membership is considerably more exclusive than K-membership. It is understood, of course, that if set B is not in K-relation with set A, then it cannot qualify for Kh-membership about A. To demonstrate, whereas 54 sets qualify as members of K(5-33,7-33), only 10 of these—the ones listed below—and their complements belong to Kh(5-33,7-33):

> members of Kh(5-33,7-33):
>
> > 3-6; 3-8; 3-12
> > 4-21; 4-24; 4-25
> > 6-21; 6-22; 6-34; 6-35

(Note that all of the hexachords in Kh(5-33,7-33) are self-complementary.) It should come as little surprise that among the sets that remain after the reduction from K to Kh about the whole-tone pentachord 5-33 has been accomplished, we find only those trichords and tetrachords that are segments of the whole-tone scale; moreover, the only hexachords in Kh(5-33,7-33) are the whole-tone hexachord 6-35 and the three "almost whole-tone" hexachords 6-21, 6-22, and 6-34. For a list of all the subcomplexes Kh about sets of 4 to 6 elements, and for further information about the range of sizes of subcomplexes Kh, the reader may wish to examine Forte's appendix 3 (pp. 200–08) and his table at example 103 (pp. 99–100) in Forte 1973a. It will suffice here to note that the sizes of subcomplexes Kh about the 38 pentachords range from 7 to 18 sets and their complements. Before turning to set-complex relations among sets prominent in *Wozzeck*, it will also be appropriate to mention that whereas the subcomplex Kh about the whole-tone hexachord 6-35 contains only 7 sets (3-6, 3-8, 3-12, 4-21, 4-24, 4-25, 5-33) and constitutes the smallest subcomplex Kh among those about the hexachords, the subcomplexes Kh about the "almost whole-tone" hexachords 6-21, 6-22, and 6-34 each contain 28 sets, just three short of the maximum size (sets 6-15, 6-16, and 6-31 have subcomplexes Kh of 31 sets each).

Let us now give further consideration to the specific membership within two of the three Kh-families listed in their entirety thus far—Kh(6-Z19, 6-Z44) and Kh(5-33,7-33). On the basis of the reader's familiarity with inclusion relations among sets prominent in *Wozzeck* discussed at length earlier, it should be apparent that *within* the Kh-families about 6-Z19/6-Z44 and 5-33/7-33, certain members are further related to certain other members by inclusion. For a first example, I will again display the 11 members of Kh(6-Z19,6-Z44) that have important motivic roles in *Wozzeck*: 3-3, 3-12, 4-17, 4-18, 8-18, 4-19, 8-19, 4-20, 5-21, 7-21, and 5-22. It is hoped that the reader can vividly recall the fact that the "Komm, mein Bub!" set 3-3 is contained not only in 6-Z19 and 6-Z44 but also in Marie's 4-17 and 4-18 as well as in Wozzeck's 4-19 (for a review, see especially the "Eia popeia" phrase from Act I/Scene 3 [Ex. 46] and the Bridge Section from the sonata movement, Act II/Scene 1 [Ex. 65]); moreover, since 4-18 and 4-19 are both contained in the "basic pentad" 5-22, it follows of course that 3-3 is also contained in this 5-element set (and in fact 3-3 as well as 4-17, 4-19, and 4-20 are also all subsets of Wozzeck's 5-21). As a second example, since we know that all the members of Kh(5-33,7-33) contain or are contained in the whole-tone pentachord 5-33 and its complement, it should not be surprising to learn that all of the trichords (3-6, 3-8, and 3-12) and all of the tetrachords

(4-21, 4-24, and 4-25) that are members of Kh(5-33,7-33) are contained in all of the hexachords (6-21, 6-22, 6-34, and 6-35) within the same Kh-family; and since all of the hexachords are self-complementary, this means that all of the trichords and all of the tetrachords in Kh(5-33,7-33) are also members of Kh(6-21), Kh(6-22), Kh(6-34), and Kh(6-35).

These facts point to certain general properties of the Kh relation that can be summarized as follows:

1. In the Kh-family about any nexus set of 4 elements, all 3-element members will be in the relation Kh with all 5-element and all 6-element members.

2. In the Kh-family about any nexus set of 5 elements, all 3-element members will be in the relation K with all 4-element members, and all 6-element members will be in the relation Kh with all 3-element and all 4-element members.

3. In the Kh-family about any nexus set of 6 elements, each member will at least be in the relation K with all other members; and though no other general statement can be made, the possibility that Kh may hold between some members must not be excluded. For example, in Kh(6-Z19,6-Z44) set 3-3 will be in the relation K with all other members; set 3-3 also holds the more exclusive Kh-relation with 4-17, 4-18, 4-19, 5-21, and 5-22 (that is, 3-3 is contained in each of these sets as well as in their complements).

The reader is encouraged to examine Forte's proofs for these general Kh properties (see Forte 1973a, pp. 101–04); though the proofs need not be considered here, the properties themselves must be assessed before observations about the relation Kh can be fully appreciated. First, it must be recognized that the subcomplex Kh about 4-, 5-, and 6-element sets not only circumscribes the relationship of a group of sets to one nexus set; it also defines internal relations among members of each Kh-family. Second, it will be ascertained from the above that whereas some internal relations will always obtain within Kh-families about 4-, 5-, and 6-element sets, only the hexachords yield subcomplexes Kh within which every member of the family will also be in a set-complex relation (K or Kh) with every other member. In other words, subcomplexes Kh about hexachords alone possess what Forte calls the *closure property*; and in Forte's view, a subcomplex Kh that possesses this property can be regarded as a "self-contained and highly structured unit" (ibid., p. 101).

William Benjamin observes that Forte's proofs for the general properties of the Kh-relation outlined above "result, somewhat surprisingly, in yet another confirmation of the centrality of the hexachord in 12 pc music" (Benjamin 1974, p. 176). Abundant evidence that specific hexachords play a central role in the large-scale harmonic design of *Wozzeck* has already been uncovered without recourse to the Kh-relation. The subcomplex Kh simply provides one further means of demonstrating the preeminence of those specific hexachords, first in respect to local and intermediate levels of construction and then in relation to the most general and fundamental harmonic features of the work. No finer demonstration that the exploitation of Kh-relations can contribute toward a remarkably integrated harmonic design can be imagined beyond that which is provided in *Wozzeck* by the sonata movement, Act II/Scene 1 (Ex. 65). In chapter 4 the "basic cells" and "aggregates" of this movement described by George Perle were translated into set structures, and the interaction of these basic pitch materials was traced in relationship to the sequence of formal sections within the First Exposition as well as in relation to fundamental materials of the opera as a whole. By returning to chapter 4, section VIII, the reader can review Perle's "basic cells" and "aggregates," which appear as fixed and transposed forms of sets 3-12, 4-18, 4-19, 4-20, 5-22, 5-26, 6-Z19, and 6-Z44—sets that play outstanding roles elsewhere in the work. To this list, we shall add Marie's 4-17 (the "major-minor chord," containing two forms of set 3-3), isolated and emphasized by the horns as a discrete component within the larger 6-Z44 collections at the end of each half of the Bridge Section (Ex. 65, mm. 34–36; mm. 40–42; review the reduction on p. 183). Now it happens that with one exception, all of the sets listed above are members of Kh(6-Z19,6-Z44). And since the nexus set is a hexachord with its complement, this means that (with one exception) each of the basic sets of Act II/Scene 1 is related by the inclusion relation K or the more restrictive relation Kh to every other set in the subcomplex.

This general feature of the harmonic plan for Act II/Scene 1 can be shown very clearly by the table presented below. As explained by Forte, the stepped shape of tables of this kind reflects the fact that sets of the same or inverse-related number of elements are not compared. To read the K- or Kh-relations for, say, 4-17, first proceed left to right across the row labeled 4-17 and then proceed down the column labeled 4-17; "the entry at the intersection of any column and row gives the relation between sets named at the head of that column and row" (Forte 1973a, p. 100):

	3-3	3-12	4-17	4-18	4-19	4-20	5-22	5-26
4-17	Kh	K						
4-18	Kh	K						
4-19	Kh	Kh						
4-20	K	K						
5-22	Kh	Kh	K	Kh	Kh	K		
5-26	Kh	Kh	K	K	Kh	K		
6-Z19/Z44	Kh	Kh	Kh	Kh	Kh	Kh	Kh	

The empty space at the intersection of the 6-Z19/Z44 row and the 5-26 column signals the fact that 5-26—Perle's "pentad X"—is the one basic set of the movement that is not a member of the subcomplex Kh or the complex K about 6-Z19/6-Z44. Note, nevertheless, that 5-26 is in either the K-relation or the Kh-relation with all the other basic pitch-structural components of the scene. It may be helpful to remind the reader that 5-26 is the set that appears at the opening of the First Exposition (Ex. 65, mm. 7–9), Second Exposition (Act II, mm. 60–63), and Recapitulation (Act II, mm. 128–30) both as a vertical structure and as the simultaneously unfolding melodic component of the first phrase of the "earrings" theme. Set 5-26 also figures in the Development as the result of interlocking forms of 4-19 and 4-27 in the five-note syllabic setting for Marie's "Bin ich ein schlecht Mensch?" (Ex. 39) and in the setting for her own subsequent answer to that question (Ex. 40). Finally, at the end of chapter 3 set 5-26 was presented as one of the links within the chain of inclusion-related sets that I have chosen to regard as the "family of origin" of sets that relate primarily to the central character Wozzeck and provide the fundamental pitch-structural matrix of the opera:

$$4\text{-}19 \subset \begin{matrix} 5\text{-}26 \\ 5\text{-}30 \end{matrix} \subset 6\text{-}34 \subset 8\text{-}24$$

At the end of chapter 3 I promised to show that the bonds between the members of Wozzeck's chain of sets are even stronger than those represented by " $\subset$ " above. I will now propose that the closely integrated occurrences of set 5-26 in the sonata movement as well as its non-membership in the subcomplex Kh about the nexus set of that movement points to the interaction of the subcomplex Kh(6-Z19,6-Z44) in Act II/Scene 1 with another subcomplex Kh suggested by Wozzeck's chain of sets. In fact all of the sets

represented in Wozzeck's chain are members of the subcomplex Kh about
the most pervasive of the "almost whole-tone" hexachords, one form of which
is Perle's "principal referential chord of the work as a whole" (see chapter
2)—set 6-34.

Of the 28 sets and their complements that are members of Kh(6-34), the
14 sets underlined below play significant roles as recurring components of
the harmonic language of *Wozzeck*:

members of Kh(6-34):

3-2; 3-3; 3-4; 3-5; 3-6; 3-7; 3-8; 3-9; 3-10;
3-11; 3-12
4-11; 4-12; 4-Z15; 4-16; 4-19; 4-21; 4-22;
4-24; 4-25; 4-27; 4-Z29
5-24; 5-26; 5-28; 5-30; 5-33; 5-34

First note that all the members of Wozzeck's "family of origin" chain—
4-19, 5-26, 5-30, and 8-24 (represented above by its complement 4-24)—
appear among the members of Kh(6-34). The reader might recall that a form
of set 5-30 was featured as the second of the two chords that announce the
beginning of the opera (Ex. 3). Among the other pentachords within the Kh-
family about 6-34, we naturally find the whole-tone pentachord 5-33. We
also find set 5-28, the pentachord that punctuates the end of the first phrase
of the opera (Ex. 3) and then assumes the role of the recurring cadential-
initial vertical structure at the intersections of each of the small dance forms
within the first scene (see chapter 2). The membership of 5-28 in Kh(6-34)
will not be surprising to the reader who remembers that the fixed form of this
set established at m. 6 in Act I/Scene 1 is the form that adumbrates and then
becomes absorbed within the final six-note cadential structure of the same
scene (Ex. 10)—the fixed "principal referential" form of 6-34 that returns as
a component of the fixed cadential 8-24 at the conclusion of each act. Like
the pentachords 5-30 and 5-28, and in fact like the nexus set 6-34 itself, the
tetrachord 4-12 appears at the very opening of the opera (see Ex. 3 and the
discussion at the end of chapter 2). Finally, the list of tetrachords in Kh
(6-34) also includes both of the Doctor's sets, 4-Z15 and 4-Z29 (Examples 1
and 2), and the only two tetrachords distinctively associated with Wozzeck—
4-19 and 4-21 (the whole-tone tetrachord 4-21 is featured in Wozzeck's second "entrance" theme, shown at Examples 17d and 65). Of primary interest
is the fact that of the six tetrachords that appear throughout the opera in close
association with Marie (4-16, 4-17, 4-18, 4-20, 4-23, and 4-27), only two—

4-27 and the "waiting" set 4-16—are members of Kh(6-34). I read the absence especially of Marie's most pervasive tetrachord—4-18—as an indication that a very special effort has been made to underscore Marie's individuality and her uniquely multifaceted role in the opera: whereas the Kh-family about the hexachords 6-Z19/Z44 brings Marie's 4-18 into structural bondage with Wozzeck's 4-19, Kh(6-34)—the operative subcomplex at the end of each act—releases Marie from that bond. In the closing 8-24 sonority (Ex. 69), Marie's 4-18—predominant at the beginning of the final scene, and contained in 8-24 two times—in the end becomes concealed to the extent that it cannot be distinguished; instead, the fixed oscillating tetrachords, eminently heard again and again above the ͵G♮-D♮͵ pedal point, are 4-27 and the embedded complement of the complete collection, 4-24; and unlike 4-18, these tetrachords are members of Kh(6-34).

So far the reader has learned that 4-18 qualifies for membership in Kh(6-Z19,6-Z44) but maintains independence in respect to the Kh-family about 6-34. For further evidence that Marie's 4-18 can be given a distinctive place in the hierarchy of fundamental pitch-structural components of the work, we need only examine the complete list of sets with which 4-18 shares the relation Kh. As with the membership list of Kh(6-34), the sets underlined below are those whose roles in *Wozzeck* have been carefully examined earlier; the sets not underlined do not have motivic significance in the work and therefore will not be discussed:

members of Kh(4-18):

3-3; 3-5; 3-10; 3-11
5-16; 5-Z18; 5-19; 5-22; 5-31; 5-32; 5-Z36;
5-Z38
6-5; 6-Z11/Z40; 6-Z13/Z42; 6-15;
6-Z17/Z43; 6-18; 6-Z19/Z44;
6-27; 6-Z28/Z49; 6-Z29/Z50; 6-30; 6-31

It is hoped that at this point the reader can consider himself adequately prepared to recognize that once again the relation Kh simply reinforces connections between pitch structures that have already been established in the context of specific musical events and dramatic issues. Among the underlined sets, the reader will find the "Komm, mein Bub!" set 3-3; the Drum Major's 5-Z18 and 5-Z38 (Ex. 56; Examples 53 and 54); the Z-related hexachords 6-Z17 and 6-Z43, whose appearances as literal pc complements coincide with the rising moon in the murder scene (Ex. 74); the "hallucination" chord 5-19 (Ex. 29); the "basic pentad" 5-22 and the nexus sets 6-Z19/Z44 of Act II/Scene 1, discussed above; the hexachord 6-Z28 and its subset 5-31, which was heard as the harmonic component of the first "Eia popeia" phrase in Marie's Act I/Scene 3 (Ex. 46) and then featured in the final scene (Examples 69 and 70); and finally, the hexachord 6-31, whose fixed form 7, 2, 9, 3, 6, 11 is vertically projected as a component of both the eight-note structure at the close of each act and the seven-note "Abgeblasen" collection sustained at mm. 317–23 of the Interlude preceding Act I/Scene 3 (Examples 11 and 60). The reader certainly will not forget that the trichord 3-3 demonstrates its inclusion relation to 4-18 at the opening of Marie's Lullaby tune (Ex. 46), and he will now also be reminded that in fact all of the 5- and 6-element sets underlined above have already been shown to contain at least one form of 4-18; in short, the K-relation between 4-18 and each of the underlined sets was implicitly established in chapter 4. And with advance knowledge of the requirements of Kh-membership, the fact that the same sets also hold the more restrictive Kh-relation with 4-18 might further have been predicted earlier in light of frequent references in examples to the complement of 4-18, 8-18. What should come as a surprise, however, is the remarkable fact that despite the membership in Kh(4-18) of the hexachords 6-Z19 and 6-Z44—sets whose own Kh-family contains an assortment of sets associated with both Wozzeck and Marie, Kh(4-18) contains not one set exclusively associated with Wozzeck. (Like the occurrences of Marie's 4-18 and the Drum Major's sets 5-Z18 and 5-Z38 in Leitsektionen from the open-field scene, the membership of the "hallucination" chords 5-19 and 6-Z43 in Kh(4-18) suggests a transmission by concealed pitch-structural means of the subliminal message in Wozzeck's visions that the actions of Marie will fulfill the prophecy of doom.)

The moment of reckoning has arrived. First, since many set-analytical observations about a large and complex work have been presented in the course of this study, it may astonish the reader to learn that of the 220 discrete pitch-class sets of 3 to 9 elements, only 36—not including complements—have been treated in this analysis as significant components of the harmonic language of *Wozzeck*. Second, only the calculative reader will expect to be informed that of those 36 pitch-class sets, all but 8 have been identified in this chapter as members of one or two of just three Kh-families—Kh(6-Z19, 6-Z44), Kh(6-34), and Kh(4-18). (The "Komm, mein Bub!" set 3-3 is in fact a family member of all three of these subcomplexes Kh.) For those who may otherwise withhold belief, a set-complex table that summarizes all K- and Kh-relations among the 36 carefully considered sets will be found in table 1.

To review the membership of sets in the three Kh-families mentioned above, the reader need only examine the rows and columns labeled 6-Z19/Z44, 6-34, and 4-18. The table further provides new information, to which I shall now call the reader's attention.

Let us first examine the eight sets on the table—4-14, 4-23, 5-15, 5-Z17, 5-20, 6-21, 6-22, and 6-Z47 (with its complement 6-Z25)—that are shown *not* to hold the Kh-relation with 6-Z19/Z44, 6-34, or 4-18:

1. By comparing the Kh-entries for the "almost whole-tone" hexachords 6-21 and 6-22 with those for the "almost whole-tone" hexachord 6-34, the reader will see that all of the members of the Kh-family about 6-34 are also members of either or both Kh(6-21) and Kh(6-22), though neither of these families is quite as large; note that whereas both 6-21 and 6-22 relate to Wozzeck's 4-19 by Kh, 6-21 holds the Kh-relation neither with Marie's "waiting" set 4-16 nor with Wozzeck's 5-30, and Kh(6-22) contains neither Marie's 4-27 nor the basic pentachords 5-26 and 5-28.

2. Among the eight sets isolated above, we find two of the three sets that appear in fixed forms as the "hallucination" chords of the open-field scene— 5-15 and 5-Z17. Set 5-15 holds the Kh-relation with only two other sets prominent in *Wozzeck*—4-16 and 6-22; note, however, that both 5-15 and 5-Z17 relate to Wozzeck's 4-19 by K, and in fact 5-Z17 further shares the Kh-relation with 4-19 and the K-relation with 6-Z19/Z44 (see Examples 28 and 29 and the corresponding discussion in chapter 3).

3. Three of the eight sets listed above—4-14, 4-23, and 6-Z47 (with its complement 6-Z25)—form a Kh-family of their own that is distinctively *diatonic*. The reader may recall that the hexachord 6-Z47 and its subset 4-23 are heard at the beginning of the opera in the form and shape of the Captain's theme (Ex. 3, m. 4). The "fourths-chord" 4-23 becomes the principal conveyor of folk elements in the opera, and its complement 8-23 results from the eight-note cycle-of-fifths (fourths) series that mocks the Captain's definition of "eternity" (Act I/Scene 1, mm. 33–35) and the Doctor's claim to immortal fame (Ex. 15f: Act I/Scene 4, mm. 620–23). The fixed form 10, 1, 4, 8, 3, 5 of set 6-Z47 becomes the basic hexachord of the drowning scene; its initial appearance in that scene is directly preceded by a presentation of its complement, 6-Z25 (Ex. 23). The remaining set in the "diatonic" family—4-14—is the set that takes the form of the D-minor triad with added ninth (2, 5, 9, 4) at the beginning and end of the final Interlude (Examples 16b and 70); three forms of 4-14 are also featured melodically in the dual *Thema* for Marie's Bible-reading scene, Act III/Scene 1 (Ex. 50), and one of these (5, 7, 8, 0) forecasts the F-minor tonal center (and key signature) for

Table 1. *Wozzeck*. Set-Complex

	3-3	3-12	4-12	4-14	4-Z15	4-16	4-17	4-18	4-19	4-20	4-21	4-23	4-24	4-27	4-Z29	5-15	5-Z17	5-Z18	5-19	5-20	5-21	5-22	5-26	5-28	5-30	5-31	5-33	5-Z38
4-12	Kh	K																										
4-14	K	K																										
4-Z15	Kh	K																										
4-16	K	K																										
4-17	K	K																										
4-18	K	K																										
4-19	Kh	Kh																										
4-20	K	K																										
4-21	K	K																										
4-23		Kh																										
4-24	Kh	K																										
4-27	K																											
4-Z29	K	K	K	K	Kh		K	K	K	K	K		K	K														
5-15	K	K	K	Kh	Kh	K	K	Kh	K	K			K	K	K													
5-Z17	Kh	Kh	Kh	K	Kh	Kh	Kh	Kh	Kh	K			K	K	Kh													
5-Z18	Kh	K	K	K	K	K	K	K	K	Kh	K		K	Kh	K													
5-19	Kh		Kh	K	K	Kh	K	Kh	K	Kh	Kh		K	K	K													
5-20	K		K	K	K	K	K	K	K	K	K		Kh	K	K													
5-21	Kh		Kh	Kh	Kh	K	Kh	K	Kh	K	K		K	K	Kh				K									
5-22	Kh		Kh	K	Kh	K	Kh	Kh	Kh	K			Kh	K	K													
5-26	Kh		K	Kh	K	K	K	K	K	K			K	Kh	K													
5-28	K		Kh	K	Kh	K	Kh	K	Kh		K		Kh	K	K													
5-30	Kh		Kh	Kh	K	K	K	Kh	K	K	K		K	K	K													
5-31	Kh		Kh	K	Kh	K	K		Kh				K	K	K													
5-33	K		K	K	K	K	Kh	Kh	K	Kh	Kh	Kh	Kh	K	Kh	K	K	K	Kh	K	K	Kh	Kh	K	K			
5-Z38	Kh		Kh	K	K	K	K	Kh	K	Kh	Kh		K	Kh	K		K	K	K	Kh	Kh		Kh	Kh	Kh	K	K	
6-Z17/Z43	Kh	Kh	Kh	K	Kh	Kh	Kh	Kh	Kh	Kh		K	Kh	Kh	Kh	Kh	Kh	Kh	Kh	Kh			Kh	Kh	Kh	Kh	Kh	Kh
6-Z19/Z44	Kh	Kh	Kh	K	Kh	K	K	Kh	Kh	Kh			Kh	Kh	Kh	Kh		K	Kh	K			Kh					
6-21	Kh	Kh	Kh	K	K	Kh	K	K	K	K	Kh		K	Kh	K		K		Kh		Kh	K	Kh	Kh	Kh		Kh	
6-22	Kh	Kh	Kh	Kh	Kh	Kh	Kh	Kh	Kh	Kh	Kh		Kh	Kh	Kh	Kh	Kh			K	K	Kh	Kh	K	Kh		Kh	
6-Z25/Z47	K	Kh	Kh	K	K	K	K	K	K	K	K	Kh	K	K	K		K		Kh	Kh	K	Kh	K	K	K	K		
6-Z28/Z49	Kh	Kh	Kh	K	Kh	Kh	Kh	Kh	Kh	Kh	Kh		K	Kh	Kh		Kh	Kh	Kh	Kh	Kh	Kh	Kh	Kh	Kh		Kh	
6-31	Kh	Kh	Kh	Kh	Kh	Kh	Kh	Kh	Kh	Kh	Kh		Kh	Kh	Kh		K	Kh	K	Kh	Kh	Kh	Kh	Kh	Kh		Kh	
6-34	Kh	Kh	Kh	Kh	Kh	Kh	Kh	Kh	Kh	Kh	Kh		Kh	Kh	Kh		Kh	Kh	Kh	Kh	Kh	Kh	Kh	Kh	Kh		Kh	Kh

variations 4 and 5 of that scene. The striking absence of Kh-ties between members of the "diatonic" Kh-family 4-14, 4-23, 6-Z25/Z47 and all the other prominent sets of the opera (note the many empty spaces in the 4-23 column) points to the potential of the "diatonic" family for providing contrast with the predominantly atonal materials of the work—a potential that is fully exploited by the composer.

4. Finally, the remaining set in the list of eight excluded from membership in Kh(6-Z19/Z44), Kh(6-34), and Kh(4-18) is none other than the set that appears as the first chord of the opera—5-20. In chapter 3 (note 8) I drew attention to the connection by inclusion between 5-20 and the final cadential structure, 8-24 (note the K at the intersection of the 4-24 column and the 5-20 row). In contrast with the second chord of the opera, whose set structure (5-30) becomes unequivocally associated with Wozzeck in the Aria (Ex. 24) and in subsequent appearances of his first "entrance" motive, the set structure of the opening chord acquires a specific association with Marie by virtue of its role as the pitch-structural component of the fixed harmonic progression 4-20; 4-16 (0, 4, 5, 9; 11, 4, 5, 9) featured in Marie's Act I/Scene 3 at mm. 412–25, the passage in which the adumbration of Marie's "waiting" motive gives way to the "waiting" motive proper (review Examples 48 and 28 and the reduction on p. 130).[1] Note, moreover, that set 5-20 holds K- and Kh-relations with a rich assortment of prominent sets that includes all of the fundamental tetrachords save 4-12 and the whole-tone tetrachord 4-21.

Thus far in this chapter greater stress has been placed on Kh-relations than on K-relations among *Wozzeck*-sets. It should now be noted that the extraordinary number of set-complex relations in general—K and Kh—suggests a morphological homogeneity among components of the language; this may seem incompatible with our appreciation of the complexity and tremendous diversity of the work until we remember that in a well-developed language, the range of expression depends not so much on the extent and limitations of the vocabulary as upon the degree to which components of the vocabulary can be ordered, combined, isolated, inflected, and, in general, transformed in an infinite number of ways. Note, for example, that among the tetrachords, Marie's 4-18, Wozzeck's 4-19, and Marie's 4-27 hold either the K-relation or the stronger Kh-relation with all but respectively four, three, and two of the larger sets of the work. Structural differences as well as the distinctive Kh ties held by each of these sets have been called into support of the position that 4-18 and 4-27 help to establish Marie's identity in distinction from Wozzeck. Once again, however, it must be stressed that structural differences and Kh-family ties *only reinforce* specific dramatic associations, established by textual, rhythmic, registral, orchestrative, and motivic means, and traced throughout the opera in chapters 2 through 4. Conversely, that the Doctor's sets 4-Z15 and 4-Z29 exhibit an even larger number of K- and Kh-relations with the other sets on the table than 4-18, 4-19, and 4-27 has less to do with the Doctor's importance to the opera as a whole than it has to do with (1) the fact that 4-Z15 and 4-Z29 are among those of the 29 discrete tetrachords with the largest Kh-families in general, and (2) the fact that these sets, though not as clearly distinguished in specific association with fundamental dramatic elements, nevertheless permeate the harmonic language as significant elements of the large design.

Similarly, the hexachord 6-31, whose number of Kh-relations with other sets on the table is greater than those of either 6-34 or 6-Z19/6-Z44, shares with sets 6-15 and 6-16 (not featured in *Wozzeck*) the distinction of having the largest Kh-family (31 sets) in comparison with the Kh-families of the other 4- to 6-element sets. Note that set 6-31 holds the Kh-relation not only with all of Marie's tetrachords but also with the Drum Major's 5-Z18, the Wozzeck-Marie associatives 3-3 and 5-26, and Wozzeck's own 4-19, 4-24, 5-21, and 5-30 (the Kh-relation of 6-31 with 4-19/8-19 and 7-21 is musically demonstrated at the "Abgeblasen" passage from the Interlude to Act I/Scene 3 shown at Example 60). In my opinion this wealth of inclusion relations, in sharp distinction to the dearth of discrete, thematically prominent appearances of set 6-31 in the opera, undermines Douglas Jarman's view that his "cadential chord *A*"—the fixed form of our set 6-31 as presented in the closing 8-element structure (see chapter 2, section II)—"is the main source of the material associated with Marie" (Jarman 1979, p. 60).

My closing statements rest, then, not on an assumption of the theoretical significance of K- and Kh-relations but rather on the simple fact that set-complex data reflect specific aspects of the work established without recourse to set-complex theory over the course of this analysis. On that basis alone I shall conclude with the following proposals. (1) The fundamental pitch-structural components of *Wozzeck* share complex interrelationships that can be formally summarized in terms of the interaction of just three subcomplex Kh-families—Kh(6-Z19/Z44), Kh(6-34), and Kh(4-18). (2) The most basic dramatic elements of the work are uniquely served by this organizational design: whereas the most pervasive and predominant pitch collections of the opera, established from the outset in straightforward association with the central character Wozzeck, unite as members of the Kh-family about the "almost whole-tone" hexachord 6-34, the fundamental tetrachord associated with Marie serves as the nexus about which a nearly independent and equally memorable collection of pitch structures helps to portray Marie's role as mother, her partnership with the Drum Major, and, in general, her determinative role in the drama. (3) Finally, the diverse collection of tetrachords that characterizes Marie's material is brought into inevitable union with Wozzeck's most fundamental pitch-structural representatives through the binding properties of the two complementary hexachords 6-Z19 and 6-Z44—hexachords whose outstanding role in the history of the Viennese atonal repertoire has just begun to be recognized.

APPENDIX: PRIME FORMS AND
VECTORS OF PITCH-CLASS SETS

Name	Pcs	Vector	Name	Pcs	Vector
3-1(12)	0,1,2	210000	9-1	0,1,2,3,4,5,6,7,8	876663
3-2	0,1,3	111000	9-2	0,1,2,3,4,5,6,7,9	777663
3-3	0,1,4	101100	9-3	0,1,2,3,4,5,6,8,9	767763
3-4	0,1,5	100110	9-4	0,1,2,3,4,5,7,8,9	766773
3-5	0,1,6	100011	9-5	0,1,2,3,4,6,7,8,9	766674
3-6(12)	0,2,4	020100	9-6	0,1,2,3,4,5,6,8,10	686763
3-7	0,2,5	011010	9-7	0,1,2,3,4,5,7,8,10	677673
3-8	0,2,6	010101	9-8	0,1,2,3,4,6,7,8,10	676764
3-9(12)	0,2,7	010020	9-9	0,1,2,3,5,6,7,8,10	676683
3-10(12)	0,3,6	002001	9-10	0,1,2,3,4,6,7,9,10	668664
3-11	0,3,7	001110	9-11	0,1,2,3,5,6,7,9,10	667773
3-12(4)	0,4,8	000300	9-12	0,1,2,4,5,6,8,9,10	666963
4-1(12)	0,1,2,3	321000	8-1	0,1,2,3,4,5,6,7	765442
4-2	0,1,2,4	221100	8-2	0,1,2,3,4,5,6,8	665542
4-3(12)	0,1,3,4	212100	8-3	0,1,2,3,4,5,6,9	656542
4-4	0,1,2,5	211110	8-4	0,1,2,3,4,5,7,8	655552
4-5	0,1,2,6	210111	8-5	0,1,2,3,4,6,7,8	654553
4-6(12)	0,1,2,7	210021	8-6	0,1,2,3,5,6,7,8	654463
4-7(12)	0,1,4,5	201210	8-7	0,1,2,3,4,5,8,9	645652
4-8(12)	0,1,5,6	200121	8-8	0,1,2,3,4,7,8,9	644563
4-9(6)	0,1,6,7	200022	8-9	0,1,2,3,6,7,8,9	644464
4-10(12)	0,2,3,5	122010	8-10	0,2,3,4,5,6,7,9	566452
4-11	0,1,3,5	121110	8-11	0,1,2,3,4,5,7,9	565552
4-12	0,2,3,6	112101	8-12	0,1,3,4,5,6,7,9	556543

Reprinted from *The Structure of Atonal Music*, by Allen Forte (New Haven and London, 1973), pp. 179–81, by permission of Yale University Press. Copyright 1973 by Yale University.

Name	Pcs	Vector	Name	Pcs	Vector
4-13	0,1,3,6	112011	8-13	0,1,2,3,4,6,7,9	556453
4-14	0,2,3,7	111120	8-14	0,1,2,4,5,6,7,9	555562
4-Z15	0,1,4,6	111111	8-Z15	0,1,2,3,4,6,8,9	555553
4-16	0,1,5,7	110121	8-16	0,1,2,3,5,7,8,9	554563
4-17(12)	0,3,4,7	102210	8-17	0,1,3,4,5,6,8,9	546652
4-18	0,1,4,7	102111	8-18	0,1,2,3,5,6,8,9	546553
4-19	0,1,4,8	101310	8-19	0,1,2,4,5,6,8,9	545752
4-20(12)	0,1,5,8	101220	8-20	0,1,2,4,5,7,8,9	545662
4-21(12)	0,2,4,6	030201	8-21	0,1,2,3,4,6,8,10	474643
4-22	0,2,4,7	021120	8-22	0,1,2,3,5,6,8,10	465562
4-23(12)	0,2,5,7	021030	8-23	0,1,2,3,5,7,8,10	465472
4-24(12)	0,2,4,8	020301	8-24	0,1,2,4,5,6,8,10	464743
4-25(6)	0,2,6,8	020202	8-25	0,1,2,4,6,7,8,10	464644
4-26(12)	0,3,5,8	012120	8-26	0,1,2,4,5,7,9,10	456562
4-27	0,2,5,8	012111	8-27	0,1,2,4,5,7,8,10	456553
4-28(3)	0,3,6,9	004002	8-28	0,1,3,4,6,7,9,10	448444
4-Z29	0,1,3,7	111111	8-Z29	0,1,2,3,5,6,7,9	555553
5-1(12)	0,1,2,3,4	432100	7-1	0,1,2,3,4,5,6	654321
5-2	0,1,2,3,5	332110	7-2	0,1,2,3,4,5,7	554331
5-3	0,1,2,4,5	322210	7-3	0,1,2,3,4,5,8	544431
5-4	0,1,2,3,6	322111	7-4	0,1,2,3,4,6,7	544332
5-5	0,1,2,3,7	321121	7-5	0,1,2,3,5,6,7	543342
5-6	0,1,2,5,6	311221	7-6	0,1,2,3,4,7,8	533442
5-7	0,1,2,6,7	310132	7-7	0,1,2,3,6,7,8	532353
5-8(12)	0,2,3,4,6	232201	7-8	0,2,3,4,5,6,8	454422
5-9	0,1,2,4,6	231211	7-9	0,1,2,3,4,6,8	453432
5-10	0,1,3,4,6	223111	7-10	0,1,2,3,4,6,9	445332
5-11	0,2,3,4,7	222220	7-11	0,1,3,4,5,6,8	444441
5-Z12(12)	0,1,3,5,6	222121	7-Z12	0,1,2,3,4,7,9	444342
5-13	0,1,2,4,8	221311	7-13	0,1,2,4,5,6,8	443532
5-14	0,1,2,5,7	221131	7-14	0,1,2,3,5,7,8	443352
5-15(12)	0,1,2,6,8	220222	7-15	0,1,2,4,6,7,8	442443
5-16	0,1,3,4,7	213211	7-16	0,1,2,3,5,6,9	435432
5-Z17(12)	0,1,3,4,8	212320	7-Z17	0,1,2,4,5,6,9	434541
5-Z18	0,1,4,5,7	212221	7-Z18	0,1,2,3,5,8,9	434442
5-19	0,1,3,6,7	212122	7-19	0,1,2,3,6,7,9	434343
5-20	0,1,3,7,8	211231	7-20	0,1,2,4,7, 8,9	433452
5-21	0,1,4,5,8	202420	7-21	0,1,2,4,5, 8,9	424641
5-22(12)	0,1,4,7,8	202321	7-22	0,1,2,5,6,8,9	424542
5-23	0,2,3,5,7	132130	7-23	0,2,3,4,5,7,9	354351
5-24	0,1,3,5,7	131221	7-24	0,1,2,3,5,7,9	353442

Name	Pcs	Vector	Name	Pcs	Vector
5-25	0,2,3,5,8	123121	7-25	0,2,3,4,6,7,9	345342
5-26	0,2,4,5,8	122311	7-26	0,1,3,4,5,7,9	344532
5-27	0,1,3,5,8	122230	7-27	0,1,2,4,5,7,9	344451
5-28	0,2,3,6,8	122212	7-28	0,1,3,5,6,7,9	344433
5-29	0,1,3,6,8	122131	7-29	0,1,2,4,6,7,9	344352
5-30	0,1,4,6,8	121321	7-30	0,1,2,4,6,8,9	343542
5-31	0,1,3,6,9	114112	7-31	0,1,3,4,6,7,9	336333
5-32	0,1,4,6,9	113221	7-32	0,1,3,4,6,8,9	335442
5-33(12)	0,2,4,6,8	040402	7-33	0,1,2,4,6,8,10	262623
5-34(12)	0,2,4,6,9	032221	7-34	0,1,3,4,6,8,10	254442
5-35(12)	0,2,4,7,9	032140	7-35	0,1,3,5,6,8,10	254361
5-Z36	0,1,2,4,7	222121	7-Z36	0,1,2,3,5,6,8	444342
5-Z37(12)	0,3,4,5,8	212320	7-Z37	0,1,3,4,5,7,8	434541
5-Z38	0,1,2,5,8	212221	7-Z38	0,1,2,4,5,7,8	434442
6-1(12)	0,1,2,3,4,5	543210			
6-2	0,1,2,3,4,6	443211			
6-Z3	0,1,2,3,5,6	433221	6-Z36	0,1,2,3,4,7	
6-Z4(12)	0,1,2,4,5,6	432321	6-Z37(12)	0,1,2,3,4,8	
6-5	0,1,2,3,6,7	422232			
6-Z6(12)	0,1,2,5,6,7	421242	6-Z38(12)	0,1,2,3,7,8	
6-7(6)	0,1,2,6,7,8	420243			
6-8(12)	0,2,3,4,5,7	343230			
6-9	0,1,2,3,5,7	342231			
6-Z10	0,1,3,4,5,7	333321	6-Z39	0,2,3,4,5,8	
6-Z11	0,1,2,4,5,7	333231	6-Z40	0,1,2,3,5,8	
6-Z12	0,1,2,4,6,7	332232	6-Z41	0,1,2,3,6,8	
6-Z13(12)	0,1,3,4,6,7	324222	6-Z42(12)	0,1,2,3,6,9	
6-14	0,1,3,4,5,8	323430			
6-15	0,1,2,4,5,8	323421			
6-16	0,1,4,5,6,8	322431			
6-Z17	0,1,2,4,7,8	322332	6-Z43	0,1,2,5,6,8	
6-18	0,1,2,5,7,8	322242			
6-Z19	0,1,3,4,7,8	313431	6-Z44	0,1,2,5,6,9	
6-20(4)	0,1,4,5,8,9	303630			
6-21	0,2,3,4,6,8	242412			
6-22	0,1,2,4,6,8	241422			
6-Z23(12)	0,2,3,5,6,8	234222	6-Z45(12)	0,2,3,4,6,9	
6-Z24	0,1,3,4,6,8	233331	6-Z46	0,1,2,4,6,9	
6-Z25	0,1,3,5,6,8	233241	6-Z47	0,1,2,4,7,9	
6-Z26(12)	0,1,3,5,7,8	232341	6-Z48(12)	0,1,2,5,7,9	
6-27	0,1,3,4,6,9	225222			

Name	Pcs	Vector	Name	Pcs	Vector
6-Z28(12)	0,1,3,5,6,9	224322	6-Z49(12)	0,1,3,4,7,9	
6-Z29(12)	0,1,3,6,8,9	224232	6-Z50(12)	0,1,4,6,7,9	
6-30(12)	0,1,3,6,7,9	224223			
6-31	0,1,3,5,8,9	223431			
6-32(12)	0,2,4,5,7,9	143250			
6-33	0,2,3,5,7,9	143241			
6-34	0,1,3,5,7,9	142422			
6-35(2)	0,2,4,6,8,10	060603			

NOTES

Chapter 1

1. See Forte 1974a for a summary of early contributions toward the systematic study of non-traditional pitch combinations, made by the following pioneers: Bernhard Ziehn (1845–1912) in 1888 undertook a systematic treatment of chromatic harmonies, in 1912 introduced the notion of symmetric inversion, and regarded the twelve-tone chromatic scale as a compositional unit; Hermann Schröder (1843–1909) in 1902 continued Ziehn's investigation of the inversion process and briefly examined transformations under inversion followed by transposition; Ferruccio Busoni (1866–1924) in 1907 constructed 113 new scales, which, like Georg Capellen (1869–1934) and, later, Schoenberg, he used as precompositional materials; Alois Hába (1893–1972) tried in 1927 to catalogue all the chords available in the twelve-pitch-class system. Forte's article includes the appropriate bibliographical data for the above; the data have not been duplicated in this work.

2. Rudolph Reti, who knew both Schoenberg and Hauer, reports that Hauer's theories first appeared in 1920 in a publication entitled *Vom Wesen des Musikalischen: Ein Lehrbuch der Zwölftonmusik* (Reti 1958, p. 61). In 1919 Hauer claimed to have discovered the "twelve-tone law," whereby twelve distinct pitches (pitch classes) are employed in a circulating fashion such that within a twelve-tone "circle" no pitch (class) can be repeated. He later classified forty-four unordered twelve-tone sets, called *tropes*, each of which he partitioned into complementary hexachords. These are discussed by Karl Eschman (1945) and have been compared by George Rochberg (1959) with Milton Babbitt's source sets and with characteristic Schoenberg rows; more recently Hauer's tropes have been matched with Forte's hexachord prime forms by Richmond Browne (1974). Whereas Schoenberg recommended the use of only one basic row (with its transformations) in a single composition, Hauer apparently placed no restrictions upon the number of different tropes that can be employed within the single work. For further information about Hauer, see Szmolyan (1965) and Perle (1962, pp. 5–7), who provides additional bibliography on the subject of which system, Schoenberg's or Hauer's, is entitled to chronological priority. The original texts of the first and second editions of Hauer's earliest work on twelve-tone music were edited by Victor Sokolowski in 1966 and published under the title *Vom Wesen des Musikalischen: Grundlagen der Zwölftonmusik* (see Hauer 1920).

3. Egon Wellesz (1958, pp. 7–9) claims that Schoenberg knew Hauer's ideas as early as 1916. Schoenberg's tenuous relationship with Hauer is documented by two letters from the former to the latter, dated December 1923 (Schoenberg 1965, letters

78 and 79, pp. 103–07); in these Schoenberg offers to prove the independence of his ideas from those of Hauer, confesses his preoccupation with the possibility of being charged with plagiarism, and accepts Hauer's suggestion that together they either create a school for the teaching of the twelve-tone method or hold a public discussion on the subject. Nothing came of these proposals.

Incipient aspects of Schoenberg's twelve-tone method were publicly described for the first time in an article by his pupil Erwin Stein, entitled "Neue Formprinzipien," that appeared in a special issue of the Viennese magazine *Musikblätter des Anbruch* honoring Schoenberg's fiftieth birthday in 1924; the same article also appeared in *Von neuer Musik*, 1925 (see Stein 1924). Stein's "Einige Bemerkungen zu Schönbergs Zwölftonreihen," published in *Anbruch* in 1926, complements his earlier article in that it treats Schoenberg's final step toward strict composition with twelve tones (see Stein 1926). Translations of the 1924 and 1926 articles are presented in Stein's *Orpheus in New Guises* (Stein 1953).

Schoenberg's only formal public statements about his twelve-tone method took the form of lectures delivered in 1934 at Princeton University, in 1935 at the University of Southern California, in 1941 and 1942 at the University of California at Los Angeles, and in 1946 at the University of Chicago. The Princeton lecture may have been presented three weeks earlier at the University of Chicago (10 February 1934). The 1941 lecture was published in 1950 (see Schoenberg 1950); a transcription of the drafts for the first lecture (at Princeton) appeared in 1974 (see Schoenberg 1974). An addendum to the 1946 lecture as well as a few hitherto unpublished essays and fragments from 1923 to 1947 are now also available in Schoenberg 1975.

Along with Schoenberg 1950, the standard early texts for the study of Schoenberg's twelve-tone method are Leibowitz 1949a and 1949b, and Rufer 1952. For a concise summary of the development of the twelve-tone technique, see Brian Fennelly 1974. A recent, penetrating study that gives a new view of Schoenberg's twelve-tone music is Martha MacLean Hyde's "Schoenberg's Concept of Multi-Dimensional Twelve-Tone Music: A Theoretical Study of the Music and Compositional Sketches" (Hyde 1977).

4. See Basart 1961 for a classified bibliography of writings on twelve-tone music. As of 1982 the Basart bibliography has not been updated; John D. Vander Weg's annotated bibliography covers the period 1955–80 but only includes articles on serialism published in major American journals (Weg 1979).

5. Cowell's *New Musical Resources* was completed in 1919 but not published until 1930. Cowell had probably read Schoenberg's theoretical explanation for new pitch combinations in the first edition of the *Harmonielehre*, published in 1911. Cowell most certainly did not invent "tone clusters"; Charles Ives had probably used them as early as 1911 (*Concord Sonata*, the "Hawthorne" movement) and even possibly as early as 1903 (see Ives 1972 for Ives's own comments about the genesis of the second movement of *Three Places in New England*; see also Elliott Carter's contribution to *Charles Ives Remembered* [Perlis 1974, pp. 131–46], in which Carter raises a few questions about the chronology of certain "avant-garde" elements in Ives's work).

6. Hindemith (1937) describes fewer than one-half of the 220 distinct pitch-class sets of 3 to 9 elements (to be discussed).

7. See Messiaen 1944, chapter 16 (pp. 51–56). Messiaen's "modes of limited transposition" constitute some but not all of those pitch-class sets for which some transpositional value will yield complete invariance (see Forte 1973a, p. 37).

8. A discussion of the special properties of the pitch structure described by Hauer,

Messiaen, and Slonimsky (Forte's set name is 6-30) may be found in Forte 1973a (p. 45) and also in Howe 1965 (p. 52, n. 27).

9. According to George Perle (1962, p. 2), Babbitt introduces the term *set* in "The Function of Set Structure in the Twelve-Tone System" (reproduced in typescript by Princeton University, Department of Music, 1946). Babbitt apparently chose to delay publication of this material until 1955, after which his ideas appeared in a series of articles extending over an eight-year period (see Babbitt 1955, 1960, 1961, and 1962). His delay seems to have caused considerable aggravation to others who were contemporaneously investigating aspects of twelve-tone theory. For example, see George Rochberg's comments about Babbitt in Rochberg 1959, p. 209.

10. Although Babbitt applies the term *set* to any twelve-tone series and to the complementary hexachords of which any series is comprised, he stresses that "the totality of twelve transposed sets associated with a given S" constitutes an instance of the mathematical structure called a *group* (Babbitt 1960, p. 249; see note 13 below). See Rothgeb 1966 (p. 211, n. 1) for a brief explanation of why the relationship of the mathematical group to the twelve-tone system has remained unclear; Rothgeb recognizes that the elements of the group are the twelve-tone operators rather than the twelve transpositions of the set itself, and that the binary group operation is composition of mappings.

11. "As a consequence of octave equivalence and enharmonic equivalence any notated pitch belongs to one and only one of 12 distinct pitch classes" (Forte 1973a, p. 2); thus the pitches C♮, D♭♭, and B♯ in any register are members of the same pitch class, which will be assigned the integer 0 (mod 12).

12. Lest David Lewin be misrepresented, I wish to stress that the quotation from Lewin cited in the text is from an article in which he rejects the by now customary method of labelling the twelve pitch classes by the numbers 0 through 11. Lewin's objections rest primarily upon the view that "the practice can lead to problems in conceptualizing the exact nature of the musical structure involved" (Lewin 1977, p. 30). He holds that "by labelling any one pc with the zero residue, we are implicitly (if only formally) attributing a tonic status to that pc, in exactly the sense that twelve o'clock enjoys a tonic status among the hours" (ibid.). Lewin demonstrates by means of algebraic formulas that "the system of transpositions and inversions on the total pc chromatic can be developed without having to label pitch-classes" (p. 32); his point of reference is the interval, which, unlike the pitch class, exhibits "algebraic behavior." Concerned with devising a "suggestive notation" for the analysis of a particular passage or piece, he limits his analytical choices in this article to serial works by Schoenberg, Webern, Stravinsky, and Boulez. Since the analytical method employed throughout my own work includes the labelling of pitch classes from 0 to 11 described above, I shall assert from the outset in response to Lewin that the assignment of the number 0 to C♮ is obviously in no way intended to suggest that I regard C♮ to have a "tonic status" in the opera *Wozzeck*.

13. "A 'group' is a system whose elements (denoted a, b, c, . . .), an operation (denoted *), and an equivalence relation (denoted =) satisfy the following properties:

1. Closure: If a, b are elements of the system, then a*b is an element of the system.

2. Associativity: If a, b, c are elements of the system, then $(a*b)*c = a*(b*c)$.

3. Existence of an identity: There is an element of the system, e, such that, for each element of the system (say, d), $d*e = e*d = d$.

4. Existence of an inverse: For each element of the system (say, d), there exists an element of the system, d−, such that $d*d- = d-*d = e$.

"In interpreting the twelve-tone system as a group, the elements of the group are twelve-tone sets, represented as permutations of pitch or order numbers; the operation is the multiplication of permutations. 'S' is the identity element. The 'order' of a group is the number of elements of the group.

"In addition, the groups presented here have the property of 'commutativity': if a, b are elements of the system, then a*b = b*a." [Babbitt 1960, p. 249, n. 3.]

14. By extension of the system the musical retrograde operation has been regarded along with addition mod 12 (transposition) and inversion as a twelve-tone operation. Recently, moreover, multiplication of pitch classes by 5 and 7 mod 12 has been included as a basic row operation. See Eimert 1954; Winham 1970; Howe 1965; Batstone 1972; Morris and Starr 1974; Morris 1977.

15. In many of the studies mentioned above, especially those that concern the relative frequency of specific structural types, large-scale tabulations have been made with the digital computer.

16. Hanson reduces the 12 distinct intervals to 6 interval classes, offering the intuitive justification that an interval and its inversion "perform the same function in a sonority" (Hanson 1960, p. 9). The same reduction is made by Martino (1961) and Forte (1964, 1973a). See the explanation later in this chapter.

17. Hanson uses the letters *pmnsdt* to represent, respectively, the perfect fifth, the major third, the minor third, the major second, the minor second, and the tritone; the interval content of the all-interval tetrachord will accordingly be represented as *pmnsdt*. Interval classes that are not represented in a sonority are not represented by their corresponding letter in the analysis; thus the interval content of the major triad and its inversion the minor triad is represented as *pmn*. If more than one representative of an interval class is present in a sonority, a numeric exponent is attached to the appropriate letter; thus the augmented triad is represented as m^3. For the sake of space in the diagram that accompanies Hanson's text, the letters are removed and only the integers remain, with the integer 0 substituting for an interval class that is not represented in the sonority. Now there is no difference in format between Hanson's "analysis" and Martino's array, except for the order of representation of interval classes; thus the augmented triad becomes [030,000] for Hanson (the comma separates intervals "commonly considered consonant" from intervals "commonly considered dissonant"), but reads [000300] for Martino and Forte, where array columns from left to right represent interval classes 1 through 6 respectively. See the step-by-step tabulation of total interval content on pp. 14–15.

18. "The second tetrad, p^2s^2, for example, may be analyzed as the simultaneous projection of two perfect fifths and two major seconds (p^2s^2); or as the projection of a perfect fifth above and below an axis tone, together with the projection of a minor third above or below the same axis ($p^2n^1 \updownarrow$); or, again, as the projection of a major second above and below an axis tone, together with the projection of a perfect fifth above *or* below the same axis (s^2p^1)" (Hanson 1960, p. 353). Note that confusion is heightened by the fact that after Hanson introduces the integer array, he continues to use the letter format, but only as a representation of the origin, or "analysis," of a sonority, and no longer as an accurate representation of its interval content. Hanson's p^2s^2 ($p^2n^1 \updownarrow$) is Forte's set 4-22: 0, 2, 4, 7 [021120].

19. Perle's chapter on "'Free' Atonality" has a special historical importance for the English-reading community in light of the dearth of detailed studies of non-serial atonal music prior to 1963. For example, in comparison with the number of analyses of Viennese twelve-tone compositions that had appeared in American publications by 1963, the selection of essays of an analytical nature in the form of articles written and published in English by this date on Viennese pre-serial atonal compositions is

small. Among those articles (not including translated essays by the three Viennese composers themselves and not including excerpts from survey texts by single authors on twentieth-century music), I mention the following for their historical as well as literary value and for their effort to give thoughtful, if only brief, attention to aspects of the pitch organization of specific pre-serial atonal Viennese works:

1. Gray 1922 (a strongly critical but sympathetic early survey of Schoenberg's major works predating his Op. 22)
2. Leichtentritt 1928 (a tonal-based analysis of Schoenberg's Op. 19, arising from a study of Schoenberg's Op. 11 in Leichtentritt's *Musikalische Formenlehre* [3d ed.] of 1927)
3. Jalowetz 1944 (this article includes brief analytical observations about Schoenberg's *Gurrelieder*, his Op. 6, Nos. 1 and 3, and his Op. 9)
4. Gradenwitz 1945 (a "motivic" and thematic analysis of Schoenberg's four string quartets)
5. Leibowitz 1948 (the first detailed study of Berg's *Altenberg Songs* Op. 4, including a piano reduction of the fifth song)
6. Craft 1955 (an expanded version of this article serves as the introductory essay in the booklet [ed. Kurt Stone] that accompanies Craft's 1957 recording of the complete works of Webern [Columbia K4L-232])
7. Goehr 1957 (a survey of Schoenberg's pre-serial works from the viewpoint of the historical development of German music toward the twelve-tone system; *Erwartung* is chosen for detailed analytical comment)
8. Maegaard 1961, 1962 (studies in which Webern's Op. 9, No. 4, and the chronology of Schoenberg's Op. 23–26 respectively figure)

In 1955, *Die Reihe* 1 (p. 62) announced the "first major study of Anton Webern to be published in German or English"—*Die Reihe* 2: *Anton Webern* (German ed., 1955; English trans., 1958); significantly, only two of the eleven analytical articles in this publication (see Pousseur 1958 and Metzger 1958) concern works by Webern that predate his twelve-tone compositions. Articles by Perle (1960), Albersheim (1960), and Stuckenschmidt (1963) present general discussions of the development of atonal music and point to the eventual general acceptance of the label "atonality" for the non-serial, non-tonal idiom. Allen Forte's article on Schoenberg's Op. 19 (Forte 1963) is a preliminary study in the application of set-theoretic concepts.

20. To my knowledge Perle was the first to use the term *set* to refer to unordered collections of fewer than twelve pitch classes.

21. The Doctor's theme first appears as an almost inaudible part of a complex contrapuntal texture at mm. 562–64 (see Ex. 34) and at mm. 573–75 of Act I/Scene 4—the scene that the Doctor dominates. In Act II/Scene 2, the Doctor's theme is developed in counterpoint with the Captain's theme and later becomes the second subject of a triple fugue.

22. Using a geometric, or spatial, model, Hanson describes forms of this pair of pitch combinations and others like it as *isometric sonorities*. Hanson's bias in favor of twentieth-century compositions whose harmonic language exhibits similarities to that of functional tonality is reflected in the fact that, for Hanson, pitch combinations of the twelve-pitch-class system group themselves into "sounds which have a preponderance" of one one of the six interval classes; thus, even though the pair of pitch combinations discussed above contains precisely one representative of *every* interval class, these tetrachords are introduced by Hanson as "projections of the minor third" (Hanson 1960, p. 101).

23. Forte's "normal order" is what Babbitt called "normal form." Babbitt's expla-

nation is incomplete: he simply recommends that hexachords under examination for inversional combinatoriality be ordered in "normal form, wherein the interval determined by the first p.c. - last p.c. is greater than any interval determined by successive p.cs" in the hexachord; he adds that "the further specification for 'normal form' when there is no such unique interval need not concern us here" (Babbitt 1961, p. 77). Martino (1961) uses the term "normal order" without definition.

24. Despite the fact that this change of definition was crucial in the development of Forte's theory, it is not mentioned by Richmond Browne (1974) in his review of *The Structure of Atonal Music*—a review in which Browne considers this text within the context of Forte's earlier work.

25. The textbook *Basic Atonal Theory* by John Rahn (1980) warrants a special category in relation to Forte's work. Rahn states that "acknowledgments for a book of this sort must be extended to the entire music-theoretical community"; he emphasizes in particular the contributions of Milton Babbitt as well as Benjamin Boretz and clarifies in his preliminary annotated bibliography that "much basic [atonal] theory appeared for the first time in book form in Part 1" of Forte's 1973a publication. Aiming "to induce an enjoyable understanding of atonal music, for listening, composing, or performing," Rahn offers a systematic introductory presentation of many fundamental and some very sophisticated aspects of atonal theory. My reader is referred to his chapters on "The Integer Model of Pitch," "Basic Operations," and "Set Types" for theorems and for much more detailed information about the set-theoretical concepts presented thus far in my work.

26. See Forte 1973a for his general observations about form (p. 124) and for specific comments about formal aspects of the following: Berg's *Four Pieces for Clarinet and Piano* (*Vier Stücke*) Op. 5 (pp. 32–33) and *Altenberg Songs* (pp. 139–44); Stravinsky's *Rite of Spring* (pp. 34, 76–77, 85–89, 144–62) and *Four Studies for Orchestra* No. 2 (pp. 130–39); Webern's *Four Pieces for Violin and Piano* (*Vier Stücke*) Op. 7, No. 3 (pp. 126–30).

27. In 1978 Forte published a comprehensive study of the pitch materials of a large and well-known twentieth-century work—*The Rite of Spring*.

28. " . . . stand ich, zumindest in harmonischer Hinsicht, vor einer neuen Aufgabe: Wie erreiche ich ohne diese bis dahin bewährten Mittel der Tonalität und ohne die auf ihr basierten formalen Gestaltungsmöglichkeiten dieselbe Geschlossenheit, dieselbe zwingende musikalische Einheitlichkeit? Und zwar eine Geschlossenheit nicht nur in den kleinen Formen der Szenen und Auftritte, . . . sondern auch, was ja das Schwierigere war, die Einheitlichkeit in den grossen Formen der einzelnen Akte, ja in der Gesamtarchitektonik des ganzen Werkes?"

29. "Jener Stil verzichtete auf die Tonalität und damit auf eines der stärksten und bewährtesten Mittel, kleine, aber auch ganz grosse Formen zu bilden."

30. " . . . jeder Akt dieser Oper auf ein und denselben Schlussakkord, quasi Kadenz bildend, zusteuert und, wie auf einer Tonika, dort verweilt."

31. Werner König's *Tonalitätsstrukturen in Alban Bergs Oper "Wozzeck"* (1974) is an attempt to show that each scene of the opera has its own "tonic," expressed by means of "cadence formulas" that may be recognized through the application of Hindemith's *Stufengang-Analyse* ("step-motion analysis") as presented in his *Unterweisung im Tonsatz* (1937). Hindemith's theory, like that of Rameau, permits König to determine the fundamental tone (*Grundton*) of a chord by choosing its so-called "best interval"; the actual bass tone (i.e., the lowest-sounding tone of the chord) need not be a component of the "best interval," and thus the relative influence of the bass tone as well as the interaction of other intervallic relationships within the chord

can be ignored. König's analysis is seriously flawed by his unwillingness to provide a definitional boundary for the concept of "tonal center" (*tonales Zentrum*) in relationship to his notion of "tonality structures" (*Tonalitätsstrukturen*), "tonic" (*Tonika*), and "key" (*Tonart*). In an article cited by König, George Perle (1967a) presents a thorough survey of the presence of "tone centers" associated with specific scenes, textual motifs, and characters in *Wozzeck*; unlike König, Perle is careful to make a distinction between "tonic functionality" and "pitch centricity," and he concurs with Arthur Berger that the presence of a tone center, that is, "pitch-class priority," is "not a sufficient condition of that music which is tonal" (Berger 1963, p. 11). As a response to König's position, the question of the formal and dramatic significance of specific pitch classes *in the absence of tonic functionality* will be probed in the present study (see especially chapter 2). ·

Chapter 2

1. For an excellent summary, with descriptive titles, of musical and verbal leitmotifs, *Leitsektionen*, and cross references in *Wozzeck*, see Perle 1971 (adapted as chapter 4 in Perle 1980). Except where shortened titles convey all that is necessary, descriptive titles used for motives and themes under discussion in this study conform in general with those used by Perle, Carner (1975), Jarman (1979), and earlier commentators.

2. With one exception (Ex. 50), all excerpts used as examples in this work have been reproduced from the piano-vocal score, made in 1922 by Berg's pupil Fritz Heinrich Klein under the composer's supervision (see acknowledgments). The choice of vocal score rather than full score by no means reflects a lack of concern for orchestration; the full score was used along with the vocal score in every stage of the analysis. In the end, the vocal score was chosen solely for the purpose of saving space and to facilitate the reading of pitch combinations at concert pitch.

3. In Ex. 3 as well as in most of the remaining examples in this study, set names for segments other than the ones under immediate discussion have been included for one or both of the following reasons: (1) their corresponding segments will be examined in due time; (2) these set names represent pitch structures of prominence elsewhere in the opera that will be discussed in detail later in the study.

A vast number of segments that will not be discussed were also examined in preparation for this essay. Limitations of space and the unsatisfying prospect of a cluttered score have ruled out the presentation of a "complete" set analysis for each example. Instead I have chosen to call attention only to those pitch structures that will play a significant role in my interpretation of the overall pitch organization. Since those pitch structures have themselves been chosen partly on the basis of numerous recurrences throughout the opera, that decision, though intended as a guideline for elimination, has nevertheless led to extensive annotation. Should the reader remain unconvinced of the choices made for discussion, he is strongly encouraged to examine unlabeled segments on his own; this is his alternative to trusting that those segments omitted from discussion have been eliminated only after careful consideration for their importance relative to immediate context, to networks of relationships, and to the context of the work as a whole.

4. In Forte's 1964 article (n. 11, p. 180), the "greater than" (>) symbols were misprinted to read "less than" (<).

5. In order to facilitate examination of this and all other examples where the musical segment under discussion is a simultaneity, or "vertical" (an unarpeggiated

chord), integers representing pitch classes will be read from "bottom" to "top," that is, the integer representing the lowest-sounding pitch will be presented first. Pc integers for segments that are melodic statements will be presented in the order of the appearance of pitch classes within the statement rather than in normal order unless otherwise indicated.

6. Note that this final statement of Act I is a rhythmic-motivic transformation of the fundamental "seduction" idea, heard at the beginning of the Prelude to Scene 5 (Ex. 17b). The cadential idea at Ex. 9 is even more closely linked to the material heard at m. 662 of the Prelude (Ex. 57) and restated again just before the descent of the curtain. All of these passages feature the pedal point ⌐G♮-D♮⌐.

7. I do not imply that the composer's choice of first pitch was made arbitrarily. As upbeat to the fundamental pitch structure, set 6-34, the opening C♮ initiates the series of ascending perfect fifths that is featured by the specific linear ordering chosen for the fundamental structure, a series that will be reiterated in descent at the end of the Prelude (see Ex. 65 and the corresponding discussion). Note that the motivically-important perfect fifth ⌐G♮-D♮⌐, now both approached and left by the same interval, falls on the strong beat. The opening perfect-fifths tetrachord (pc set 4-23) resulting from the addition of the C♮ is an important motivic component of the opera (see chapter 4), associated with folk elements and with Marie (see her Lullaby [Ex. 46] and her Gypsy Song in Act II/Scene 1 [Ex. 62]); Marie will dominate the first scene of Act II until Wozzeck's entrance at m. 93.

8. These are the set structures that would have been formed in combination with the other six possible choices:

1. (5, 9, 11, 0, 3) + 8: 6-Z49   4. (5, 9, 11, 0, 3) + 1: 6-21
2. (5, 9, 11, 0, 3) + 10: 6-Z41   5. (5, 9, 11, 0, 3) + 4: 6-Z43
3. (5, 9, 11, 0, 3) + 2: 6-Z23   6. (5, 9, 11, 0, 3) + 6: 6-30

Of these sets, the first three listed do not figure predominantly elsewhere in the opera. As will be discussed below, set 6-21 is an important set, but its most prominent appearances take the form of melodic rather than vertical statements. Set 6-Z43 will be introduced as a component of the Doctor's passacaglia theme (Ex. 33) and a component of Wozzeck's "hallucination" material (Examples 29, 49). Set 6-30 is in fact represented in the passage under discussion when the F♯ (pc6) appears as an upbeat to the vocal climax-pitch G♮.

9. The purpose of the long beamed stems added in Examples 15 through 17 will be explained in chapter 3. The italicized pc integers and the asterisks after pc integers will be explained shortly.

10. I follow Blaukopf (1954), Redlich (1957), Perle (1971), Carner (1975), and probably others in mentioning that the theme shown at Example 17e is most likely the theme to which Berg refers in a letter from Trahütten (7 August 1917) to his wife. In the following, Berg describes his return home alone after seeing her off on a visit to Alma Mahler:

> I myself went uphill very slowly, rested frequently "according to regulations," and eventually, as I proceeded with heavy steps, there occurred to me—though I wasn't planning to work—a long-sought idea for one of Wozzeck's entrances. (Ich selbst ging äusserst langsam bergaufwärts, rastete "vorschriftsmässig" des öfteren und schliesslich, wie ich so mit schweren Schritten vor mich hin ging, kam mir sogar—ohne dass ich zu arbeiten beabsichtigte—ein langgesuchter Ausdruck für einen Auftritt Wozzecks.) [Berg 1965.]

In the same letter Berg speaks of his identification with the character Wozzeck:

There is a piece of me in his character, since I have been spending these war years just as dependent upon hateful people, sick, unfree, resigned, even humiliated. (Steckt doch auch ein Stück von mir in seiner Figur, seit ich ebenso abhängig von verhassten Menschen, gebunden, kränklich, unfrei, resigniert, ja gedemütigt, diese Kriegsjahre verbringe.) [Ibid.]

(Translations based on Grun's [Berg 1971, p. 229] and Perle's [Perle 1971, n. 4, p. 282].)

11. Repetition, durational preponderance, and prominence at registral and temporal boundaries, as outlined by George Perle, constitute some of the means by which C#/Db is given priority in the examples cited above. Perle observes that in the Captain's theme, itself repeated frequently throughout the scene, the priority of C#/Db is established by its exposed position as highest note, lowest note, last note, repeated note, and longest note. He also notices that C#/Db is the pitch class that serves as the lowest note of the entire scene (Ex. 21, mm. 35ff) and the highest note of the second half of the scene (m. 147). [Perle 1967a, pp. 205–07.]

12. Perle recognizes that "the dyad B-F is frequently associated with the rise or fall of the curtain" (Perle 1967a, pp. 213–14). Recall the discussion of Examples 3 and 10 above. See also the openings of Act I/Scene 3 (Ex. 58, m. 330), Act I/Scene 5 (Ex. 56, mm. 665–66), and Act III/Scene 2 (Ex. 73, m. 73) as well as the closing of Act II/Scene 1 (m. 139). Larger pitch structures featured at Examples 3, 56, 58, and 73 will be investigated later.

13. "H-F ist das Schicksalsintervall, das Intervall der gequälten Kreatur."*

---

*"Diese Tonbeziehung kann auf eine musikgeschichtliche Tradition zurückblicken (mi contra fa est diabolus in musica)."

14. With this observation, *not* made by Werner König, I lend support to König's assertion that "in several cases one recognizes the intention to allow the relationships of the characters to be reflected in the interval relationships" ("in einigen Fällen lässt sich die Absicht erkennen, in den Intervallverhältnissen die Verhältnisse der Personen sich spiegeln zu lassen"). [König 1974, p. 110.] König's own examples, with only a few exceptions, depend upon his reading of virtually all sections of the opera in terms of "key centers," or "tonics."

15. The two mutually related "seduction" themes from the *Andante affettuoso* (Examples 17b and 57) are recalled in Act II/Scene 3 (mm. 388–91), where Marie thinks of the Drum Major while trying to counter Wozzeck's accusations, and also later in Act II/Scene 4 (mm. 529–36), where Wozzeck sees the Drum Major and Marie dancing together. The dyad ⌐G♮-D♮⌐ is held as a pedal point not only throughout these passages but also throughout the variation in Act II/Scene 3 (mm. 392–94) of Marie's Trio from the Military March (Ex. 64: Act I, mm. 346–50).

16. It must be stressed that the "tonal" aspects of the first phrase of Andres's Song by no means obliterate specific "whole-tonal" and "atonal" features. As shown at Ex. 16a, the structure that forms the first complete phrase of the Song is set 6-22, a set that appears in atonal (non-tonal) contexts elsewhere throughout the opera (e.g., see Act I, m. 9: all instruments, second and third beats; Act III, m. 102: all instruments excluding bassoons; Act III, m. 73 [Ex. 73], last simultaneity including the voice and the grace notes). The subset 5-33—the whole-tone pentachord—is made prominent after the upbeat. Beneath the vocal part, a tremolo on ⌐Db-Eb⌐ in the solo flute signals Wozzeck's distracted presence. (The reader will recall that the pitch class Db is associated with Wozzeck in Act I/Scene 1; the tremolo originates here as a component of the first of the three five-note chords that control the scene [see

chapter 3].) The composite pitch structure formed by (*a*) Andres's first phrase excluding upbeat (pcs 7, 9, 11, 1, 3), (*b*) the tremolo figure (pcs 1, 3) and (*c*) the horn echo (pcs 1, 6) is represented by the set name 6-34 (discussed above), whose importance in the large-scale pitch organization of the opera will become even more evident as we proceed.

17. In a recent monograph study of *Wozzeck*, Ernst Hilmar (1975), who has examined hitherto inaccessible sketches of the opera (until recently these sketches were in the possession of Berg's wife Helene), describes two large sketch sheets containing "pitch models" (*Tonmodelle*) connected with a "fixed rhythmic plan" (*ein bestimmtes rhythmisches Schema*), all pertaining to the finale of the Tavern scene. According to Hilmar (1975, p. 41), Berg carefully planned the gradual build-up toward climax for this section by means of a series of a fixed (odd) number of pitches, to be repeated for a precise number of measures, then to be replaced by a series of a larger (odd) number of pitches, to be repeated for a larger number of measures as follows:

3 pitches—5 measures (mm. 692–96); 5 pitches—7 measures (mm. 697–703); 7 pitches—9 measures (mm. 704–12); 9 pitches—11 measures (mm. 713–23); 11 pitches—13 measures (mm. 724–36)

"Longwindedness" (*Langatmigkeit*) was to be prevented by the insertion of eighth-rests at regular intervals but on different parts of the beat from measure to measure; these would create a continuous rhythmic displacement within successive statements of each series of pitches. Thus "Model III," as presented by Hilmar (p. 41), appears as follows:

Note that although the number of distinct pitches in "Model III" is three, the placement of eighth-rests divides the pitches into groups of four such that no two successive groups will begin with the same pitch. In his final version Berg used this scheme throughout the entire finale, such that, for instance, in the section dominated by the five eighth-notes in ostinato (Ex. 19, mm. 697f), the eighth-rest will appear after every sixth rather than fifth eighth-note value.

It is unclear whether Berg specified his choice of pitch classes for each group in the series of from three to eleven pitches. Hilmar does not account for the fact that in the realization of the composer's plan only ten rather than eleven different pitch classes are used for the final ostinato figure (mm. 724–36); nor does he acknowledge the straightforward complement relation between the five-note and the seven-note figure discussed in my text. He does call our attention, however, to abundant evidence that Berg's constructivist tendencies come into play even when his dramatic intention is to create the effect of "orgy" (Berg's own word, as indicated in the sketches).

18. Note also that the pitch structure (represented by the set name 6-Z47) of the complete melodic statement shared by double bass and 'cello in Example 20, mm. 15–16, is the same as that formed by the first six pitches of the Captain's theme (Ex. 3, m. 4), a detail about which I shall make further comment below.

19. Perle (1967a, p. 240), who wishes to stress only the whole-tone and twelve-tone aspects of this excerpt, simply does not include the "wrong" upbeat C♮ of m. 36 and downbeat G♮ of m. 39 in his reproduction of the passage.

20. Although only one further reference to a pitch specially notated for *Sprechstimme* ("speech-song") treatment (♪, ♪) will be made in this study (see Ex.

28), I take the opportunity provided by Ex. 22 to stress that Berg's choices for notated Sprechstimme pitches are not only made with concern for speech inflection and dramatic gesture but are also determined by the supporting motivic and pitch-structural design. Any Sprechstimme passage from the opera might be chosen in support of this view; the following will suffice:

1. As shown in Example 54 from Act I/Scene 2 (mm. 274–76), Wozzeck's Sprechstimme pitches for "Hörst Du, es wandert was mit uns da unten!" ("Do you hear, there's something moving with us down there!") double the oscillating G♮-A♮ pedal point in timpani, harp, 'cellos, and double basses.

2. In the same scene (Act I/Scene 2), at mm. 290–91, the notated Sprechstimme pitches for Wozzeck's "Das fährt von der Erde" ("It rises from the earth")—pcs 9, 11, 5, 3, 2—produce a form of set 5-28, the set whose outstanding role in the first scene of the opera has been discussed at length; at mm. 292–93, the "fateful" tritone F♮-B♮ provides the Sprechstimme setting for Wozzeck's climactic "Himmel" ("heaven").

3. At mm. 232–34 of the drowning scene (Act III/Scene 4), the B♮-F♮ tritone again appears at Wozzeck's Sprechstimme "Tot! Mörder! Mörder!" ("Dead! Murder!").

4. See the F-minor variation 5 in Marie's Bible-reading scene (Act III/Scene 1): here Marie's Sprechstimme pitches for "Es war einmal ein armes Kind und hatt' keinen Vater und keine Mutter" ("Once upon a time there was a poor child who had no father and no mother") are entirely doubled in the orchestral accompaniment, and priority is given to the ascending F-minor arpeggiation A♭-C♮-F♮ (the repeated A♭ and the F♮ constitute respectively the first and last pitches of the line, and the C♮ is given metric stress on the downbeat of m. 35).

5. Marie's Sprechstimme opening statement in the central third scene of Act II— "Guten Tag, Franz" (m. 374)—is set to the pitch-class collection 2, 1, 7, 10, a form of Marie's own set 4-18 (see chapter 4). As shown at m. 432 in Ex. 28, the same collection is *sung* by Marie at the words "Was hast Du, Franz?" ("What's the matter with you, Franz?") in Act I/Scene 3. At the beginning of Act II/Scene 1 (Ex. 65, mm. 18–19), Marie again sings the same collection at the words "Was sind's für welche?" ("What kind are they?")—a reference to the earrings.

Evidence in support of the view that Sprechstimme pitches play a pitch-structural role in the opera entirely conforms with Berg's own instructions for the performance of Sprechstimme: in his preface to the full score, Berg says that the performer has the task of changing the "special notes" into a "spoken melody *while taking into account the pitch of the notes . . .* : in singing the performer stays on the note without change; in speaking he strikes the note but leaves it immediately by rising or falling in pitch, *but always bringing out the relative pitches of the notes*." [Emphasis my own.]

Chapter 3

1. It will now be useful to mention that the set names for the Z-related all-interval tetrachords examined in association with the Doctor at Examples 1 and 2 in chapter 1 are respectively 4-Z29 (prime form: 0, 1, 3, 7) and 4-Z15 (prime form: 0, 1, 4, 6).

2. At first inspired, then tremendously disillusioned by the ideas of the French Revolution, Georg Büchner (1813–1837) was a politically committed rebel. At the

age of twenty-one he wrote a pamphlet urging Hessian peasants to rebel against their autocratic rulers; when the revolt backfired and the cause was betrayed, he was forced to retreat to his father's home in Darmstadt, where in five weeks, under constant fear of arrest, he completed his first play, *Danton's Death*. In March 1835, Büchner fled Germany for Strasbourg, France, never to return home. In the remaining two years of his life, Büchner wrote the novella *Lenz*, completed a Ph.D. thesis in French on the nervous system of the barbel fish, gave lectures in natural philosophy as a permanent member of the Zurich faculty, completed a second play (*Leonce and Lena*) and possibly a third (a lost play about Pietro Aretino) as well as two translations (of the dramas *Lucretia Borgia* and *Maria Tudor* by Victor Hugo), and began work on *Woyzeck*. At the start of a brilliant career in medicine, Büchner apparently burned himself out by overworking. In 1837 he contracted typhoid fever. "Then, after a beginning more remarkable in its promise than Schiller's or even Goethe's, he was dead at twenty-three. One cannot help but wonder what course German and European literature might have taken, had he lived longer" (Richards 1977, p. 200).

Büchner did not become widely known and appreciated in Germany or elsewhere until after the turn of the century. A collection of his writings including excerpts from his letters was published by his brother in 1850, but *Woyzeck* was omitted, partly because the manuscripts were found to be written in a miniscule and nearly illegible shorthand that could not be easily deciphered. In 1879 *Woyzeck* was finally included in an edition of Büchner's complete works by Karl Emil Franzos. Although Franzos's "discovery" of the masterpiece must be gratefully acknowledged, several aspects of his work subsequently contributed toward widespread confusion about the play: first, Franzos almost destroyed the manuscript with the chemicals he used in order to read the fading ink; second, where the text could not be read or the dramatic logic ascertained, Franzos, a novelist, took it upon himself to fill in the gaps with his own ideas (see note 8 below); and finally, confusing a "y" for the nearly identical "z" in German script, Franzos misread the title of the play, for which reason Germanists know the work as *Woyzeck* but musicians call it *Wozzeck* (see note 3 below).

3. The real Woyzeck, an impoverished ex-barber and ex-soldier, was publicly beheaded at Leipzig in 1824, having stabbed to death his unfaithful mistress. Like Büchner's Woyzeck, the real Woyzeck was known to have visions and claimed to hear voices; his plea of insanity was, however, not upheld in a diagnosis by the Saxon court physician Johann Christian August Clarus, whose moralistic report raised a storm of controversy and was subsequently published in *The Journal of State Pharmaceutics*. Büchner's father, a well-known doctor and one-time staff member of that journal, owned a complete set of issues. Without question Büchner carefully studied his father's copy of the Clarus report and found in it not only the story for his drama but also explicit verbal motifs and a philosophical position to which his play would be a strongly negative response; whereas Clarus, like the Doctor in *Woyzeck*, maintained that man must "become better so that conditions may improve," Büchner would show that man is not capable of improvement until conditions have changed (see Schmidt 1969, pp. 103, 106).

The historical precedent for Büchner's *Woyzeck* was discovered as late as 1914 by Hugo Bieber, whose report appeared in *Literarisches Echo* 16 a few weeks after the Vienna première. It was brought to George Perle's attention that Berg knew Bieber's report and considered calling his opera *Woyzeck*; Perle suggests that in the end Berg stuck to the name *Wozzeck* for vocal reasons (Perle 1967b, p. 212). It is of significance that in Büchner's *Woyzeck* (Lehmann's reconstruction [1967], Scene 1) as in Berg's opera (Act I/Scene 2) Wozzeck and Andres are seen cutting branches in the bushes. In the nineteenth-century German army, cutting firewood was regarded as the lowliest task.

4. Büchner regarded the earlier *Sturm und Drang* movement and, within this, the dramatist J. M. R. Lenz as "all[ies] in the struggle against classicism" (Benn 1976, pp. 88–89); Büchner was moreover the "first dramatist to take serious note of Lenz's work" (see William E. Yuill in Lenz 1972, p. xxiii), and without question he modeled certain characters and motifs in *Woyzeck* on Lenz's drama *Die Soldaten* (1775). Beyond this, the issue of the relationship of *Die Soldaten* to *Woyzeck* is complex. Lenz's reaction against the early idealistic classicism of the European Enlightenment takes the form in *Die Soldaten* of a sympathetic and realistic but also didactic and moralizing portrayal of social problems of the middle classes. In his reaction against the later classicism of Schiller, Büchner radicalizes the tradition of "demanding truth to nature and sympathy for humble people" initiated by Lenz: he "dared to choose as his hero a proletarian outcast, and so became the first dramatist of Europe to write a working-class tragedy" (Benn 1976, pp. 206, 217). In a recent review of Bernd Alois Zimmermann's opera *Die Soldaten* (1965), based on an adaptation of Lenz's play, Andrew Porter holds that "with its short scenes, ellipses, 'jump cuts,' and ta'azieh-like techniques for bridging space and time, [Lenz's *Die Soldaten*] seems more advanced than Büchner's 'Woyzeck' and Wedekind's 'Lulu' plays—on which it plainly left a mark—and than most of Brecht's dramas" (Porter 1982, p. 114). In respect to *Woyzeck* this view is not generally shared by Germanists, nor does it ring true upon careful readings of both plays. While it is clear that Lenz's above-mentioned formal innovations strongly influenced Büchner, their integration in *Woyzeck* yields a new form that is "free of the moralizing, the prolixity of Lenz's work; . . . spare, concentrated, economical; in its powerful directness extraordinarily modern" (Benn 1976, p. 263). For further information about the influence of Lenz on Büchner, see McInnes 1977 (pp. 124–28) and Klotz 1960.

5. See Büchner's letter of 28 July 1835 to his family (Büchner 1971 [Lehmann's Hamburg edition], pp. 443–45; translated by Schmidt in Büchner 1969a, pp. 126–27).

6. Berg lost a touch of the explicitly harsh circus atmosphere of the play when he chose not to use Büchner's carnival scene. Here Marie and Woyzeck are naively taken in by a satirical showman who puts a horse through his tricks, proclaiming him "a member of all learned societies . . . a professor at our university with whom the students learn to ride and fight." ("Yes, that is no dumb animal, that's a person! A human being, a beastly human being, but still an animal, *une bête*. . . . he can add. . . . He simply can't express himself, explain himself" [translated by Schmidt in Büchner 1969a, pp. 31–32].) The horse "behaves improperly" while on stage, just as Woyzeck does later in the street (Berg changes the phrase "pissing on the wall" to "coughing"). Henry Schmidt discusses the "multilayered parody" succinctly: "The satiric technique of debasing a man to an animal becomes more ambivalent through the transformation of an animal to resemble a man, since we cannot be sure whether the animal itself is being elevated or debased in this process" (Schmidt 1969, pp. 110–11).

7. Though inspired by Büchner's Scene 15 in the Lehmann reconstruction, the final scene used by Berg is largely the creation of Franzos (see note 2), who, having also added the stage direction " . . . ertrinkt" (" . . . drowns") to the scene where Woyzeck goes into the pond in search of the knife, could not logically use any of Büchner's possible choices for the final scene, since all of these contain a "living" Woyzeck. Franzos is entirely responsible for one of the most shattering lines of the opera: "Du! Dein' Mutter ist tot!" ("You! Your mother is dead!"). He did not, how-

ever, invent the reference to "Ring-around-a-Rosy" or to the child's "Hopp, hopp!" refrain; he simply lifted these from other scenes (Lehmann's Scenes 19 and 27 respectively). Some Germanists appear to have accepted Lehmann's decision to use the scene in which Woyzeck's child rejects him as the last scene. In a more recent reconstruction, Lothar Bornscheuer (Büchner 1972) has the play end with Woyzeck at the pond; Bornscheuer refuses to speculate about Woyzeck's fate after this scene, concluding that the manuscript leaves the question open. Although the majority opinion among German scholars today is that there is no warrant for believing Büchner intended to have Woyzeck drown at the end, devotees of Berg's opera defend Franzos's " . . . ertrinkt" and agree that Berg's setting of Franzos's final scene constitutes one of the most powerful moments of the work (e.g., see Perle 1967b, Stein 1972, Schmidt 1969). The final scene of the opera will be discussed at length in chapter 4.

8. In his 1929 lecture on *Wozzeck*, Berg played the final scene of the opera and then said:

> With this the opera ends. However, although here again the music clearly moves toward a cadence on the final chord, it almost seems as if it would go on. And it does go on! In fact the opening bars of the opera could immediately link up with these closing bars, and with that the circle would be closed.
>
> (Damit schliesst die Oper. Aber obwohl hier wiederum deutlich zu dem Schlussakkord kadenziert wurde, hat es fast den Anschein, als ginge es weiter. Es geht ja auch weiter! Tatsächlich würden die Anfangstakte der Oper an diese Endtakte ohne weiteres anschliessen, womit der Kreis geschlossen wäre.) [In Redlich 1957a, p. 313.]

Berg then played the last bar of the opera followed immediately by the first three bars from Act I, adding:

> But that was not intentional, just as indeed much of what I am relating to you here has only now, as I look back after ten and more years, become clear to me in a theoretical sense.
>
> (Das war aber nicht Absicht, wie ja überhaupt vieles, was ich Ihnen hier erzähle, erst jetzt, wo ich nach zehn und mehr Jahren zurückblicke, mir theoretisch klar wurde.) [Ibid., p. 314.]

While it is possible that this demonstration was made in part as an appeal to concurrent popular interest in cyclical concepts, Berg's own predilection for arch forms and palindromes is amply demonstrated elsewhere—for example, in his *Altenberg Songs* Op. 4 (Mark DeVoto shows that "the *Bogenform* property is in fact common to all five of the songs" and to the cycle as a whole [DeVoto 1966, p. 39]); in the *Lyric Suite* (the third movement [*Allegro misterioso*] is a Scherzo with Trio after which the Scherzo is recapitulated in retrograde); in the film music for *Lulu* (as outlined by Perle [1964, pp. 187–88], the second half of the film music is a retrograde of the first half); in *Der Wein* (the setting for the last of the three songs recapitulates the setting for the first song within an expanded sonata plan, and the second song is a palindrome); and in the very first scene of *Wozzeck* (the reader will recall the retrograde recapitulation of the Prelude). For a detailed discussion of Berg's apparent obsession with circular and symmetrical designs, as manifested especially by the inclusion of palindromic and retrograde formal structures in virtually all his major works after Op. 5, see Jarman 1979 (chapters 5 and 6).

The reader is invited to try Berg's demonstration on his own. He will discover that the demonstration works on a superficial level because the tempo indications for the end of Act III and the beginning of Act I are almost the same (Act III, m. 389 to the end: $\downarrow.$ = ca 52 in 12/8; Act I, opening: $\downarrow$ = 60 in 2/4). Several more fundamental harmonic relationships between the ending and the beginning of the opera can be stated as follows:

1. The final 8-element figure shares no fewer than seven pitch classes in common with the opening 10-element chord-pair; the common subset is 7-33 (1, 2, 3, 5, 7, 9, 11), and this collection itself contains the "odd-numbered" whole-tone hexachord. Note that two components of that hexachord—the pitch classes F♮ and A♮—are held in common between the final tetrachord of the opera (B♮-F♮-A♮-C♯) and the first chord of the opera. Possibly Berg's demonstration was made with the expectation that his listeners would hear this common-tone connection as well as the chromatic voice-leading in contrary motion with register transfer that connects the apex C♯ and lowest tone B♮ of the final tetrachord to the apex D♮ and the B♭ of the opening chord.
2. Whereas the opening vertical structure (set 5-20) is related by inclusion to the final set 8-24, the second vertical structure (set 5-30) shares the special inclusion relation Kh with the final set, a relation that will be the subject of our discussion in chapter 5.

9. Except for several excisions and alterations as well as a few bowdlerizations (i.e., see note 6 above), Berg's libretto is a courageously faithful setting of Büchner's blunt, sometimes obscene text as Berg knew it. George Perle (1968) and Gerd Ploebsch (1968) have independently shown beyond doubt that Berg used not only the Franzos edition (1879) but also the edition by Landau (1909), whose wording is exactly the same as Franzos's but whose ordering of the scenes is different and in fact corresponds exactly with Berg's (i.e., aside from the omission of scenes Berg chose not to use, Berg's sequence of scenes exactly follows Landau's).

Until recently, the Bergemann edition (published in 1922, after Berg had completed the opera) was considered the last word in Büchner scholarship. In 1969 Henry J. Schmidt, whose translation of Lehmann's reconstruction of *Woyzeck* has been cited above, considered Lehmann's edition of the play to be definitive (Schmidt 1969, p. 81); however, in a comparative review of Lehmann's work and Bornscheuer's *Kritische Lese- und Arbeitsausgabe* (1972), Schmidt later finds problems with both editions and concedes that "an edition of *Woyzeck* is, in a way, an exercise in futility" (Schmidt 1973, p. 425). For an up-to-date and straightforward comparative study of editions of *Woyzeck* and textual problems, see Hinderer 1977. For further information on the question of editions used by Berg and in general on the relationship of *Wozzeck* to *Woyzeck*, see Schäfke 1926, Perle 1967b, Ploebsch 1968, Schmidt 1969, and Stein 1972.

10. "Schon die Notwendigkeit, von den 26 losen, teils fragmentarischen Szenen Büchners eine Auswahl für mein Opernbuch zu treffen, hiebei [sic] Wiederholungen, soweit sie musikalisch nicht variationsfähig waren, zu vermeiden, weiter diese Szenen eventuell zusammenzuziehen und aneinanderzureihen und sie gruppenweise in Akte zusammenzufassen, stellte mich—ob ich wollte oder nicht—vor eine mehr musikalische als literarische Aufgabe, also vor eine Aufgabe, die nur mit den Gesetzen der musikalischen Architektonik zu lösen war und nicht mit denen der Dramaturgie."

11. "Und selbst als es gelungen war, eine dreiaktige Anordnung zu finden, die in dreimal fünf Szenen Exposition, Peripetie und Katastrophe des Dramas deutlich auseinanderhielt und damit die Einheit der *Handlung*, die dramatische Geschlossenheit erzwang, war noch keinesfalls die *musikalische* Einheit und Geschlossenheit gegeben."

12. See Büchner 1967 (Lehmann edition), Schmidt 1969, Bornscheuer 1972, Benn 1976, and Richards 1977.

13. Significantly, the "Wir arme Leut!" motive is one of the few "leitmotifs, or better, . . . reminiscence-motives" ("Leit- oder, besser gesagt, . . . Erinnerungs-Motive") to which Berg calls attention in his 1929 lecture; Berg describes the "Wir arme Leut!" motive as a "reminiscence-motive that is transmitted throughout the piece" ("durch das ganze Stück gehenden Erinnerungsmotivs"). [In Redlich 1957a, pp. 318, 320.]

14. The traditional names for these two inversionally equivalent forms of set 4-19 are supplied only to facilitate identification. Among those tonal theorists who have classified these seventh-chord formations, common terms have not been agreed upon; in many recent texts labels have been discarded in recognition that within the so-called common-practice period these seventh-chord formations arise from suspension, passing, and neighbor motions and are hence dependent upon the consonant structures they prolong.

In the chapter of his *Harmonielehre* (1911) entitled "'Harmoniefremde' Töne" ("'Nonharmonic' Tones"), Schoenberg may have been the first to call attention in print to a chord that in set-theoretical terms is represented by the name 4-19 (pcs 7, 8, 3, 11). In defense of the composer's right to employ chords that theorist-aestheticians have not permitted, Schoenberg presents this musical example with the following comments:

For a similar case, there is 'that Mozart,' who writes the following chord in the G-minor Symphony (233a). To be sure, in this context (233b), but still, without any preparation (Da ist ja gleich 'dieser Mozart,' der in der G-Mollsymphonie folgenden Akkord schreibt (233a). Allerdings in diesem Zusammenhang (233b), aber doch ohne jede Vorbereitung). [Schoenberg 1911, p. 363; 3d ed. (1922), p. 392.]

15. Wozzeck's correlation of cash and morality in the Aria found reverberation almost one hundred years later in Macheath's "Erst kommt das Fressen, dann kommt die Moral" ("First comes the grub, then come the morals"), from Bertolt Brecht's libretto for Kurt Weill's *Dreigroschenoper* (*Three-Penny Opera*). *Die Dreigroschenoper* was first performed in 1928. For information on fundamental relationships between Brecht and Büchner, the reader might begin with Brustein's *The Theatre of Revolt* (1962).

16. Of added interest in reference to the passage shown at Ex. 25 is the fact that the complete melodic unit comprising the fundamental bass line (1, 0, 9, 8, 4, 5, 11, 7)—marked N⁻ for *Nebenstimme* ("subordinate voice") in the full score—provides a form of the complement of 4-19, set 8-19. This large 8-element structure will assume greater importance in association with Wozzeck as we proceed. For a second preliminary example, return to Example 17f, where the entire pitch content of the passage in which Wozzeck utters his "Einer nach dem Andern" constitutes another form of set 8-19 (normal order: 8, 9, 10, 0, 1, 2, 4, 5).

17. In Woyzeck's time as well as in the earlier period portrayed in Lenz's *Die Soldaten* (1775), army men were not permitted to marry. In *Die Soldaten* this fact serves as the focal point for Lenz's attack on middle-class social conditions. The relevance of army celibacy to the estranged relationship between Woyzeck and Marie reveals the futility of Lenz's earlier efforts toward reform and points to one of several areas in which Büchner's *Woyzeck* and Lenz's *Die Soldaten* share important concerns.

18. "Um wieder zu jenem Largo zurückzukehren: Die Art, wie es eingeführt wird und ausklingt, wäre auch wieder ein Beispiel dafür, wie eine Geschlossenheit, die sonst nur durch Wiederkehr zur Haupttonart möglich war, durch andere Mittel erreicht wurde. Die aus der fugierten Thematik der vorhergehenden Szene gleichsam verrinnenden Klarinettenfiguren leiten zum Einsatz dieses Largo über, dort—indem diese Figuren gleichsam stillstehen—die erste harmonische Grundlage des Largo-Themas bildend.

Der Ausgang dieses Largo mündet auf derselben Harmonie, die—wieder in Bewegung umgesetzt—rückläufig dieselben Klarinettenfiguren bildet, aus denen dieser Akkord herausgewachsen war."

19. For a detailed set-structural analysis of the complete Interlude preceding Act II/Scene 3 (mm. 367–74), see Forte 1973a (pp. 119–23). Forte treats this passage in the context of an introduction to the interpretation of small-scale sections of larger works in set-complex terms (see my chapter 5). To avoid confusion, it should be mentioned that some of Forte's references to associations between particular characters of the opera and specific pc sets are not supported by examples and do not coincide with views expressed in this study.

20. Douglas Jarman (1979, pp. 54–55) draws attention to the fact that the total pitch content of Wozzeck's vocal statement from m. 668 ("Blut?") to m. 676 in the passage under discussion consists of three of the four pitch classes that compose the first of the two tetrachords (Jarman's "'blood' chord") in the ostinato brass figure—pcs 6, 2, 3. Of added significance is that these three pitch classes combine to produce a form of set 3-3—the subset of set 4-19, whose outstanding importance as Marie's "Komm, mein Bub!" set was alluded to earlier (see section IV of this chapter) and will be discussed at length in chapter 4. See Jarman (ibid., pp. 55–56) for a summary of other appearances of the "'blood' chord" (i.e., appearances of the fixed form ⌊3, 6, 10, 2⌋ of set 4-19).

21. The reader will recall that the Z-correspondents 6-Z19 and 6-Z44 multiply contain Wozzeck's 4-19 and Marie's most prominent tetrachord, 4-18 (see chapter 4). My interpretation of these hexachords as representative of the fatal bond between Wozzeck and Marie is based not only on the preeminent role of these sets in scenes where Marie and Wozzeck are shown together (we have yet to examine Act II/Scene 1 in this respect; see chapter 4), but also on the outstanding presentation of one of those hexachords at the precise moment when Wozzeck makes contact with Marie for the last time. As shown in Example 43, the stabbing coincides with a sixteenth-note triplet figure—triple forte in trumpets, oboes, and harp—whose set structure is none other than 6-Z19.

22. Note that the first eight discrete pitch classes of Wozzeck's vocal line at Ex. 44 (1, 3, 7, 2, 11, 6, 5, 10) form the complement of Wozzeck's 4-19, 8-19. The last five pcs of the complete phrase (10, 1, 2, 4, 8) provide yet another statement of set 5-28—the set whose importance throughout the first scene of the opera and as a component of the final 8-element structure was established in chapter 2.

Chapter 4

1. Several additional set structures that play outstanding roles in *Wozzeck* figure prominently in the opening phrase of the Sonata Op. 1:

1. The initial 4-element segment of the opening melodic phrase features the same inverted form of set 4-18 (7, 0, 6, 3) that will be heard in the same register as a segment of the soprano line at the beginning of Marie's Trio from the Military March (Ex. 64).

2. The initial soprano statement of set 4-18 in the Sonata interlocks with a form of set 4-19 and proceeds to its conclusion with the following set-structural results:

$$
\begin{array}{l}
\overline{\hspace{0.5em} 7\text{-}6 \hspace{3.5em}} \\
\hspace{1em}\overline{\hspace{0.3em} 4\text{-}19 \hspace{2.2em}} \\
7\ 0\ 6\ 7\ 3\ 11\ 2\ 1 \\
\underline{\hspace{0.3em} 4\text{-}18 \hspace{0.8em}} \\
\underline{\hspace{0.3em} 5\text{-}22 \hspace{1.4em}} \\
\underline{\hspace{0.3em} 6\text{-}Z19 \hspace{2.2em}}
\end{array}
$$

The reader may turn ahead to Examples 59 and 61 for two prominent melodic statements in the opera in which set 6-Z19 likewise results from interlocking presentations of sets 4-18 and 4-19. In the discussion that accompanies Ex. 59, I point to the fact that set 6-Z19 can be generated by juxtaposing two semitone-related major or two semitone-related minor triads. This observation has particular relevance with respect to the Sonata theme: the two semitone-related triads unfolded in the theme are $,0, 3, 7,$ and $,11, 2, 6,$; the second of these represents the B-minor tonal center of the work, embedded within the theme itself and confirmed by the V-i cadence at the end of the opening phrase.

3. Set 4-18 again appears as the vertical harmony on the last metric beat of m. 2 of the Sonata; here the set functions as a suspension chord whose resolution provides the cadential dominant on its way to the tonic.

4. Finally, note the metrically stressed vertical statements of the whole-tone tetrachords 4-24 and 4-25 in mm. 1 and 2.

Although a study of the works of Berg that precede the composition of *Wozzeck* does not fall within the scope of this work, I am prepared to demonstrate in greater detail elsewhere (1) that set structures that play a prominent role in the language of *Wozzeck* are sets for which Berg exhibits a strong predilection throughout his creative work, and (2) that many of the sets that appear in atonal contexts in *Wozzeck* originate with Berg and other early twentieth-century composers as the result of dissonant voice-leading procedures within the late nineteenth-century tonal idiom. In the transition from tonality to atonality, the change of language can be described, then, not so accurately in terms of the choice of pitch combinations as by the measure of autonomy dissonant pitch combinations are given by such means as extended duration, repetitions that ensure closure, irregular resolutions, and absence or near absence of resolution to consonance. In respect to bodies of works by early twentieth-century composers other than Berg, an examination of these points has currently become an important concern. See, for example, James Baker's work on Scriabin (Baker 1977) and Allen Forte's most recent article on Schoenberg (Forte 1978b).

2. To the discussion of set 6-Z43 that follows, it can be added that the comple-

mentary hexachords that comprise the Doctor's ordered twelve-tone passacaglia theme are the Z-related sets 6-Z17/6-Z43. At the end of this chapter we shall examine one additional outstanding presentation of the complementary hexachords 6-Z17 and 6-Z43 in the murder scene (Ex. 74).

3. "Das andere Ergebnis meiner jetzigen Untersuchungen ist die Art, wie ich der Notwendigkeit, Volkstümlich-Liedmässiges zu bringen, also der Notwendigkeit, innerhalb meiner Oper ein Verhältnis zwischen Kunst-Musik und Volks-Musik herzustellen, gerecht wurde; etwas, was in der tonalen Musik eine ganz selbstverständliche Sache ist. Es war nicht leicht, auch in dieser sogenannt atonalen Harmonik jenen Niveau-Unterschied deutlich zu machen. Ich glaube, es ist mir dadurch gelungen, dass ich alles was musikalisch in die Sphäre des Volkstümlichen reicht, mit einer auch innerhalb der atonalen Harmonik anwendbaren, leicht fasslichen Primitivität erfüllte. Als da sind: Bevorzugung von symmetrischem Bau der Perioden und Sätze, Heranziehung von Terzen- und namentlich Quarten-Harmonik, ja von einer Melodik, in der die Ganztonskala und die reine Quart eine grosse Rolle spielen, während sonst ja, in der atonalen Musik der Wiener Schule, die verminderten und übermässigen Intervalle vorherrschen."

Berg is entirely justified in describing the inclusion of folk elements in his opera as a "necessity"; in fact had he not taken this position, he would have neglected a most important element of Büchner's play: "Nowhere in Büchner's work do songs appear with such profusion as in *Woyzeck.* . . . no serious German drama before *Woyzeck* shows them with such frequency. . . . If the songs which fill the play serve in one sense to render that 'fullness of life' which Büchner so evidently prizes [see Büchner's *Lenz* (Lehmann edition, 1967), pp. 84–85], through the irony they express they work no less to evaluate and define the life which he attempted to record in the play" (Lindenberger 1964, p. 90).

4. Set 8-23 (prime form: 0, 1, 2, 3, 5, 7, 8, 10) is the "mother" tonal set in that it contains two discrete forms of the seven-note set (7-35: 0, 1, 3, 5, 6, 8, 10) to which the diatonic major (or natural minor) scale reduces. The only other 8-element sets that contain set 7-35 are 8-22 and 8-26, and these contain only one form each.

5. Of general importance in this discussion is that Berg gives preference to the "fourths-chord" set 4-23 rather than to the triad as his harmonic means of conveying folk elements. Berg's interest in "fourths chords" was undoubtedly nurtured by Schoenberg, who devoted a chapter to "fourths chords" (*Quarten-Akkorden*) in his *Harmonielehre* (1911), a work for which Berg prepared the index and proofread the galleys (see translations of Berg's letters to Schoenberg from 1911 in Harris 1977). Schoenberg shows the horn passage from the last movement of Beethoven's Pastorale Symphony and the opening of the second act of *Tristan*; he then proposes that "everything that modern composers have written in the sphere of fourths harmonies . . . certain successions of fourths in Mahler, the Jochanaan theme in *Salome*, the fourths chords of Debussy and Dukas can all be traced back to the peculiar freshness" that "emanates from these two passages" (Schoenberg 1911 [3d ed., 1922], p. 482). Schoenberg stresses that he himself had used fourths chords in his *Pelleas und Melisande* and in his *Kammersymphonie* (Op. 9) before having "got to know" Debussy's or Dukas's music. In the *Kammersymphonie* the fourths chords "do not appear here merely as melody or as a purely impressionistic chord effect; rather their unique character permeates the complete harmonic structure,—they are chords like all others" (ibid., p. 484). Berg published thematic analyses of Schoenberg's *Kammersymphonie* Op. 9 in 1913 and of his *Pelleas und Melisande* in 1920; in each of these he called particular attention to Schoenberg's fourths chords.

6. In a broader sense the "hallucination" passage under discussion can be re-garded as a Leitsektion from the very moment it first appears in Act I/Scene 2 (Ex. 54): the passage is a varied quotation from the last movement (*Marsch*) of Berg's *Drei Orchesterstücke* Op. 6 (the *Marsch* was completed in 1914). While many have noted that the Hauptstimme in the double basses at mm. 79–83 of the *Marsch* be-comes the "hallucination" melody in the horns at the passage shown in Ex. 54, to my knowledge no one has clarified the fact that the other distinguishing features of this Leitsektion in *Wozzeck*—the ⌊G♮-A♮⌋ pedal point, the chromatically ascending vertical statements of set 5-Z38, the crescendo, and the accelerando—are also all present in the passage from the earlier work.

7. The undated letter (of 1925 or 1926) from Berg to Schoenberg that concerns the *Lyric Suite* was published for the first time in the article "Berg's Notes for the *Lyric Suite*," by Mark DeVoto and Donald Harris, in *The International Alban Berg Society Newsletter* 2, January 1971.

8. Set 4-18 is the *only* tetrachord contained in both 5-Z18 and 5-Z38.

9. In fact two discrete inversionally related forms of set 3-3 are contained in set 4-17. In the vertical structure at the downbeat of m. 365 in Act I/Scene 3 (1, 6, 9, 10), set 3-3 is represented by the collections ⌊6, 9, 10⌋ and ⌊9, 10, 1⌋; the first of these trichords is made more prominent inasmuch as it is presented in contiguity with the soprano B♭ pedal point. See my comments about set 4-17 in section VIII of this chapter.

10. Set 5-31 plays a significant role in the closing portion of Richard Strauss's *Salome*, a work that Berg first heard in 1906 and attended no fewer than six times in 1907 (see Carner 1975, p. 6; Berg later became critical of both *Salome* and its com-poser). In the vertical form ⌊0, 3, 6, 7, 9⌋, set 5-31 provides the final sustained chord that marks the end of Salome's well-known "Und das Geheimnis der Liebe ist grösser als das Geheimnis des Todes" (rehearsal 349 to 350 + 3: "And the secret of love is greater than the secret of death"). At rehearsal 355 the set reappears in the vertical form ⌊1, 4, 7, 8, 10⌋ as a pedal point sustained for seventeen measures against the A♮-B♭ trill in flutes and clarinets while Salome contemplates having kissed the head of Jochanaan. (Here the set form is identical to the form shown in m. 370 of Ex. 46 from *Wozzeck*; the coincidence is curious, especially in light of the fact that Berg chooses the same form of the set for reiteration at the end of the final Interlude [Ex. 70] and does not feature the set elsewhere in the opera except in the final scene.) These "non-traditional" 5-31 formations are adumbrated earlier throughout *Salome* in the form of dominant-seventh chords with added minor ninth, a structure that also reduces to set 5-31. See, for example, the first strong cadence into D minor at re-hearsal 4 (mm. 27–29); Salome's climactic "Jochanaan" after rehearsal 332; the downbeat vertical structures in the *stringendo* at rehearsal 346 + 1 and in the follow-ing sequence.

11. For information about the special role of set 6-Z19 in the works of Schoenberg that are representative of his transition from tonality to atonality, see Forte 1978b; especially note the settings given to set 6-Z19 in Forte's Examples 7 and 9, respec-tively from Schoenberg's "Mädchenlied" Op. 6/3, and from his *Kammersymphonie* Op. 9.

Berg's creative output is much smaller than Schoenberg's; and among his pub-lished works, only those that preceded the String Quartet Op. 3 of 1910—namely, the songs "Schliesse mir die Augen beide" (first version, 1907) and "An Leukon" (1907), the *Seven Early Songs* (1905–08), the Piano Sonata Op. 1 (1908), and the *Four Songs for Voice and Piano* Op. 2 (1909)—can be regarded as transitional in his path from tonality to atonality. Among these, we have already noted the appearance of set 6-Z19 in the fundamental opening melodic idea of the Sonata Op. 1. Although Berg employs set 6-Z19 much less frequently than Schoenberg, two additional examples can be cited: (1) see the penultimate measure of Berg's "Liebesode" from the *Seven Early Songs*; (2) in the third of the *Four Songs* Op. 2 ("Nun ich der Riesen Stärksten überwand"), the opening vocal line exhibits the following set structures, all of which play an important role in *Wozzeck*:

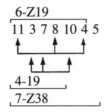

As in the Sonata theme, one of the two semitone-related triads (see the brackets with arrows above) that together form set 6-Z19 is the ultimate tonic of the song, E

major; in the penultimate measure, the final resolution to that tonic yields a second form of 6-Z19:

$$
\begin{array}{c}
2 \frown 3 \\
11 \frown 10 \\
8 \smile 7 \\
3 \smile 3 \\
\hline
6\text{-}Z19 \\
\end{array}
$$

12. In general the systematic sequential extraction of subcomponents of a configuration is a type of segmentation procedure that has been called *imbrication* (see Gilbert 1970a; Forte 1973a, pp. 83–84). Our treatment of the descending line in Ex. 60 is an instance of *linear imbrication*.

13. In fact set 8-26 contains 6-Z47 twice. The two forms represented in the final vertical sonority at the end of the Prelude (Ex. 65, m. 6) are ⎣7, 9, 3, 6, 11, 4⎦ and ⎣0, 7, 2, 9, 3, 4⎦. Neither of these forms is the fixed form that serves as the pitch-structural matrix of the drowning scene.

Chapter 5

1. The associations of the first and second chords of the opera with Marie and Wozzeck respectively have been superbly demonstrated by Douglas Jarman (1979, pp. 64–67). Jarman supports these associations with the following observations: (1) the presentations of Marie's "waiting" motive followed immediately by Wozzeck's (first) "entrance" motive in Act I/Scene 3 (mm. 412–27; see Examples 48 and 28), Act II/Scene 3 (mm. 373–74), and Act III/Scene 2 (mm. 106–08) repeat in an extended fashion the motivic pattern represented by the progression from the first to the second chord of the opera; (2) the "pitch relation" between Marie's "waiting" motive and Wozzeck's "entrance" motive at each of these three points is the same as the "pitch relation" between the first and the second chord. In respect, for example,

to Act I/Scene 3, mm. 412–27, Jarman's "pitch relation" (shown by him in musical notation) can be demonstrated set-theoretically as follows:

$$t=7 \quad \begin{array}{l} \overset{\text{5-20}}{\text{A: } \overline{4,10,5,9,2}} \\ \text{A}': 11,5,0,4,9 \end{array} \qquad \begin{array}{l} \overset{\text{5-30}}{\text{B: } \overline{7,8,11,1,3}} \\ \text{B}': 2,3,6,8,10 \end{array}$$

As indicated above, there is some value of t, namely 7, that, when added to each integer of sets A and B yields sets A' and B', where A and B represent respectively the first and second chords of the opera (Ex. 3), A' represents the collection projected by the harmonic progression from "adumbration"-chord to "waiting"-chord in Act I/Scene 3 (see chapter 4), and B' represents the collection that constitutes the pitch-structural component of Wozzeck's "entrance" motive in the same scene (Ex. 28). See Jarman for several additional well-placed appearances in the opera of the collection labelled A' above—appearances that lend further support to the association of the first chord of the opera with Marie.

BIBLIOGRAPHY

Adorno, Theodor W.
1968   *Berg: Der Meister des kleinsten Übergangs*. Österreichische Komponisten des XX. Jahrhunderts, vol. 15. Vienna: Elisabeth Lafite; Österreichischer Bundesverlag.

Albersheim, Gerhard Ludwig.
1960   "The Sense of Space in Tonal and Atonal Music." *Journal of Aesthetics
and Art Criticism* 19, pp. 17–30.

Alphonce, Bo.
1974   "The Invariance Matrix." Ph.D. dissertation, Yale University.

Archibald, Bruce.
1968   "The Harmony of Berg's 'Reigen'." *Perspectives of New Music* 6:2,
pp. 73–91.

Babbitt, Milton.
1955   "Some Aspects of Twelve-Tone Composition." *The Score and I.M.A.
Magazine* 12, pp. 53–61. (Reprinted, with addenda by Gerald War-
field, in *Twentieth-Century Views of Music History*, edited by William
Mays, pp. 359–72. New York: Charles Scribner's Sons, 1972.)

1960   "Twelve-Tone Invariants as Compositional Determinants." *Musical
Quarterly* 46:2, pp. 246–59. (Reprinted in *Problems of Modern Music*,
edited by Paul Henry Lang, pp. 108–21. New York: W. W. Norton &
Co., 1962.)

1961   "Set Structure as a Compositional Determinant." *Journal of Music Theory*
5:2, pp. 72–94. (Reprinted in *Perspectives on Contemporary Music
Theory*, edited by Benjamin Boretz and Edward T. Cone, pp. 129–47.
New York: W. W. Norton & Co., 1972.)

1962   "Twelve-Tone Rhythmic Structure and the Electronic Medium." *Perspectives of New Music* 1:1, pp. 49–79. (Reprinted in *Perspectives on
Contemporary Music Theory*, pp. 148–79.)

1973–74   "Since Schoenberg." *Perspectives of New Music* 12:1–2, pp. 3–28.

1976   "Responses: A First Approximation." *Perspectives of New Music* 14:2
and 15:1 (double issue), pp. 3–23.

Baker, James.
1977   "Alexander Scriabin: The Transition from Tonality to Atonality." Ph.D.
dissertation, Yale University.

Basart, Ann.
1961   *Serial Music: A Classified Bibliography of Writings on Twelve-Tone
            and Electronic Music.* Berkeley and Los Angeles: University of Cali-
            fornia Press. (Reprinted in 1976.)
Batstone, Philip N.
1972   "Multiple Order Functions in Twelve-Tone Music." *Perspectives of New
            Music* 10:2, pp. 60–71, and 11:1, pp. 92–111.
Bauer-Mengelberg, Stefan, and Ferentz, Melvin.
1965   "On Eleven-Interval Twelve-Tone Rows." *Perspectives of New Music*
            3:2, pp. 93–103.
Beach, David W.
1979   "Pitch Structure and the Analytic Process in Atonal Music: An Inter-
            pretation of the Theory of Sets." *Music Theory Spectrum* 1, pp. 7–22.
Benjamin, William E.
1974   *"The Structure of Atonal Music* by Allen Forte." *Perspectives of New
            Music* 13:1, pp. 170–90.
1979   "Ideas of Order in Motivic Music." *Music Theory Spectrum* 1, pp. 23–
            34.
Benn, Maurice B.
1976   *The Drama of Revolt: A Critical Study of Georg Büchner.* Anglica
            Germanica Series 2. Edited by Leonard Froster, S. S. Prawer, and A. T.
            Hatto. Cambridge: Cambridge University Press.
Berg, Alban.
1913a   *Arnold Schoenberg: Gurrelieder, Führer* [Guide]. Vienna: Universal
            Edition No. 3695. (Shortened edition, Universal Edition No. 52577.)
1913b   *Arnold Schoenberg: Kammersymphonie Op. 9, thematische Analyse.*
            Vienna: Universal Edition No. 6140.
1920   *Arnold Schoenberg: Pelleas und Melisande, kurze thematische Ana-
            lyse.* Vienna: Universal Edition No. 6268.
1924   "Die musikalischen Formen in meiner Oper 'Wozzeck.'" *Die Musik*
            16:8 (May), pp. 587ff.
1928   "Das 'Opernproblem'." Stuttgart: *Neue Musik-Zeitung* 49:9, pp. 285–
            87. (A somewhat altered and abbreviated version of the essay appeared
            in translation as "A Word About *Wozzeck*" in *Modern Music* 5:1 [No-
            vember 1927], pp. 22–24. "A Word about *Wozzeck*" was reprinted in
            Musical Quarterly 38:1 [January 1952], pp. 20–21. A translation of
            "Das 'Opernproblem'" by Henry J. Schmidt will be found in Georg
            Büchner's *Woyzeck*; New York: Bard Books/Avon, 1969 [see Büchner
            1969a].)
1929   *"Wozzeck"-Vortrag* [Lecture on *Wozzeck*] (first delivered in Olden-
            burg, Germany). In *Alban Berg: Versuch einer Würdigung*, by Hans
            Ferdinand Redlich. Vienna: Universal Edition, 1957. (Translation in
            Alban Berg: The Man and His Music, by H. F. Redlich. London: John
            Calder, 1957.)
1936   "Was ist atonal?" *23* (Vienna; edited by Willi Reich), No. 26/27 (8

June 1936). (Transcription of a radio talk on Vienna Rundfunk, 23 April 1930. Translated by M. D. Herder Norton in *Music Since 1900*, by Nicolas Slonimsky. 3d ed. New York: Coleman-Ross, 1949.)

1937   "Praktische Anweisungen zur Einstudierung des *Wozzeck*." In *Alban Berg*, by Willi Reich. Vienna: Verlag Herbert Reichner. (Translated by George Perle as "The Preparation and Staging of *Wozzeck*" in *Musical Times* 109 [June 1968], pp. 518–21.)

1965   *Alban Berg: Briefe an seine Frau*. Munich and Vienna: Langen Müller Verlag.

1971   *Alban Berg: Letters to his Wife*. Edited, translated, and annotated by Bernard Grun. New York: St. Martin's Press.

Berger, Arthur.

1963   "Problems of Pitch Organization in Stravinsky." *Perspectives of New Music* 2:1, pp. 11–42.

Blaukopf, Kurt.

1953   "New Light on *Wozzeck*." *Saturday Review* 26 (September 1953).

1954   "Autobiographische Elemente in Alban Bergs 'Wozzeck'." *Österreichische Musikzeitschrift* 9, pp. 155–58.

Browne, Richmond.

1974   Review of *The Structure of Atonal Music*, by Allen Forte. *Journal of Music Theory* 18:2, pp. 390–415.

Brustein, Robert.

1962   *The Theatre of Revolt: An Approach to the Modern Drama*. Boston: Little, Brown, & Co. in association with the Atlantic Monthly Press.

Büchner, Georg.

1879   *Sämtliche Werke und handschriftlicher Nachlass*. Edited by Karl Emil Franzos. Frankfurt am Main: J. D. Sauerländer.

1909   *Georg Büchners Gesammelte Schriften*. 2 vols. Edited by Paul Landau. Berlin: Paul Cassirer.

1922   *Sämtliche Werke und Briefe*. Edited by Fritz Bergemann. Leipzig: Insel. 9th ed., Frankfurt am Main: Insel, 1962; Munich: Deutscher Taschenbuch Verlag, 1968.

1967   *Sämtliche Werke und Briefe: Historisch-kritische Ausgabe mit Kommentar*. Vol. 1: *Dichtungen und Übersetzungen, mit Dokumentationen zur Stoffgeschichte*. Edited by Werner R. Lehmann. Hamburg: Christian Wegner Verlag. 2d ed., Munich: Carl Hanser Verlag, 1974.

1969a   *Woyzeck*. Translation with notes and supplementary material by Henry J. Schmidt; based on the Werner R. Lehmann reconstruction (Hamburg edition; see Büchner 1967). Introductory notes by Richard Schechner. New York: Bard Books/Avon.

1969b   *Woyzeck: Texte und Dokumente*. Edited by Egon Krause. Frankfurt am Main: Insel.

1971   *Sämtliche Werke und Briefe: Historisch-kritische Ausgabe mit Kommentar*. Vol. 2: *Vermischte Schriften und Briefe*. Edited by Werner R. Lehmann. Hamburg: Christian Wegner Verlag.

1972   *Woyzeck: Kritische Lese- und Arbeitsausgabe.* Edited by Lothar Bornscheuer. Stuttgart: Reclam.

Carner, Mosco.
1975   *Alban Berg: The Man and His Work.* London: Duckworth.

Chapman, Alan.
1978   "A Theory of Harmonic Structures for Non-Tonal Music." Ph.D. dissertation, Yale University.

1981   "Some Intervallic Aspects of Pitch-Class Set Relations." *Journal of
Music Theory* 25:2, pp. 275–90.

Chittum, Donald.
1967   "The Triple Fugue in Berg's *Wozzeck*." *Music Review* 28:1, pp. 52–62.

Chrisman, Richard.
1969   "A Theory of Axis-Tonality for Twentieth-Century Music." Ph.D. dissertation, Yale University.

1971   "Identification and Correlation of Pitch-Sets." *Journal of Music Theory*
15:1 and 2, pp. 58–83.

1977   "Describing Structural Aspects of Pitch-Sets Using Successive-Interval
Arrays." *Journal of Music Theory* 21:1, pp. 1–28.

1979   "Anton Webern's 'Six Bagatelles for String Quartet,' Op. 9: The Unfolding of Intervallic Successions." *Journal of Music Theory* 23:1, pp.
81–122.

Clough, John.
1965   "Pitch-Set Equivalence and Inclusion (A Comment on Forte's Theory
of Set-Complexes)." *Journal of Music Theory* 9:1, pp. 163–71.

Cohen, David.
1972–73 "A Re-examination of All-Interval Rows." *Proceedings of the American Society of University Composers* 7:8.

Cowell, Henry.
1930   *New Musical Resources.* New York: A. A. Knopf.

Craft, Robert.
1955   "Anton Webern." *Score* 13 (September 1955), pp. 9–22. (Adapted in
the booklet [ed. Kurt Stone] that accompanies the recording *The Complete Music of Anton Webern*, Columbia K4L-232, 1957.)

DeVoto, Mark.
1966   "Some Notes on the Unknown *Altenberg Lieder*." *Perspectives of New
Music* 5:1, pp. 37–74.

DeVoto, Mark, and Harris, Donald.
1971   "Berg's Notes for the *Lyric Suite*." *International Alban Berg Society
Newsletter* 2 (January 1971).

Eimert, Herbert.
1954   *Lehrbuch der Zwölftontechnik.* 3d ed. Wiesbaden: Breitkopf und Härtel.

Eschman, Karl.
1945   *Changing Forms in Modern Music.* 2d ed., Boston: E. C. Schirmer
Music Co., 1968.

Fennelly, Brian.
1974   "Twelve-Tone Techniques." In *Dictionary of Contemporary Music*, pp. 771–80. Edited by John Vinton. New York: E. P. Dutton & Co.
Forte, Allen.
1963   "Context and Continuity in an Atonal Work: A Set-Theoretic Approach." *Perspectives of New Music* 1:2, pp. 72–82.
1964   "A Theory of Set-Complexes for Music." *Journal of Music Theory* 8:2, pp. 136–83.
1965   "The Domain and Relations of Set-Complex Theory." *Journal of Music Theory* 9:1, pp. 173–80.
1972   "Sets and Nonsets in Schoenberg's Atonal Music." *Perspectives of New Music* 11:2, pp. 43–64.
1973a   *The Structure of Atonal Music*. New Haven: Yale University Press.
1973b   "The Basic Interval Patterns." *Journal of Music Theory* 17:2, pp. 234–72.
1974a   "Theory." In *Dictionary of Contemporary Music*. Edited by John Vinton. New York: E. P. Dutton & Co.
1974b   "Analysis Symposium: Webern, Orchestral Pieces (1913), Movement I ('Bewegt')." *Journal of Music Theory* 18:1, pp. 13–43.
1978a   *The Harmonic Organization of "The Rite of Spring."* New Haven: Yale University Press.
1978b   "Schoenberg's Creative Evolution: The Path to Atonality." *Musical Quarterly* 64:2, pp. 133–76.
1980   "Aspects of Rhythm in Webern's Atonal Music." *Music Theory Spectrum* 2, pp. 90–109.
Gilbert, Steven E.
1970a   "The Trichord: An Analytic Outlook for Twentieth-Century Music." Ph.D. dissertation, Yale University.
1970b   "The 'Twelve-Tone System' of Carl Ruggles: A Study of the *Evocations for Piano*." *Journal of Music Theory* 14:1, pp. 68–91.
1974   "An Introduction to Trichordal Analysis." *Journal of Music Theory* 18:2, pp. 338–62.
Goehr, Walter and Alexander.
1957   "Arnold Schönberg's Development Towards the Twelve-Note System." In *European Music in the Twentieth Century*, pp. 76–93. Edited by Howard Hartog. London: Routledge and Paul. (Reprinted by Greenwood Press, Westport, Ct., 1976.)
Gradenwitz, Peter.
1945   "The Idiom and Development in Schoenberg's Quartets." *Music and Letters* 26:3 (July 1945), pp. 123–42.
Gray, Cecil.
1922   "Arnold Schönberg—A Critical Study." *Music and Letters* 3:1 (January 1922), pp. 73–89.
Hanson, Howard.
1960   *Harmonic Materials of Modern Music: Resources of the Tempered Scale.*

New York: Appleton-Century-Crofts.

Harris, Donald.
1977   "Some Thoughts on the Teacher-Student Relationship Between Arnold Schoenberg and Alban Berg." *Perspectives of New Music* 15:2, pp. 133–44.

Hauer, Josef Matthias.
1920   *Vom Wesen des Musikalischen: Grundlagen der Zwölftonmusik.* Leipzig and Vienna: Waldheim-Eberle. 2d ed., Berlin-Lichterfelde: Robert Lienau, 1923. New ed. by Victor Sokolowski, Berlin-Lichterfelde: Robert Lienau, 1966.
1925   *Vom Melos zur Pauke: Eine Einführung in die Zwölftonmusik.* Vienna: Universal Edition.
1926   *Zwölftontechnik: Die Lehre von die Tropen.* Vienna: Universal Edition.

Hilmar, Ernst.
1975   *Wozzeck von Alban Berg: Entstehung, erste Erfolge, Repressionen.* Vienna: Universal Edition.

Hindemith, Paul.
1937   *Unterweisung im Tonsatz I: Theoretischer Teil.* 2d rev. ed., Mainz: B. Schott's Söhne, 1940. (English translation by Arthur Mendel as *The Craft of Musical Composition I: Theoretical Part.* New York: Associated Music Publishers; London: Schott & Co., 1942. Rev. ed. 1945.)

Hinderer, Walter.
1977   *Büchner: Kommentar zum dichterischen Werk.* Munich: Winkler.

Howe, Hubert S., Jr.
1965   "Some Combinational Properties of Pitch Structures." *Perspectives of New Music* 4:1, pp. 45–61.
1974–75   Review of *The Structure of Atonal Music*, by Allen Forte. *Proceedings of the American Society of University Composers* 9–10, pp. 118–24.

Hyde, Martha [Macmillan] MacLean
1977   "Schoenberg's Concept of Multi-Dimensional Twelve-Tone Music: A Theoretical Study." Ph.D. dissertation, Yale University. (Submitted under the name Martha Macmillan MacLean.)
1980a   "The Roots of Form in Schoenberg's Sketches." *Journal of Music Theory* 24:1, pp. 1–36.
1980b   "The Telltale Sketches: Harmonic Structure in Schoenberg's Twelve-Tone Method." *Musical Quarterly* 66:4, pp. 560–80.
1981   Review of *The Operas of Alban Berg, Vol. I: "Wozzeck"*, by George Perle. *Journal of the American Musicological Society* 34:3, pp. 573–87.

Ives, Charles.
1972   *Charles Ives: Memos.* Edited by John Kirkpatrick. New York: W. W. Norton & Co.

Jalowetz, Heinrich.
1944   "On the Spontaneity of Schoenberg's Music." *Musical Quarterly* 30:4, pp. 385–408.

Jarman, Douglas.
1979   *The Music of Alban Berg*. Berkeley and Los Angeles: University of California Press.

Johnson, Peter.
1978   "Symmetrical Sets in Webern's Op. 10, No. 4." *Perspectives of New Music* 17:1, pp. 219–29.

Jouve, Pierre Jean, and Fano, Michel.
1953   *Wozzeck d'Alban Berg*. Preceded by a translation of the libretto into French by Pierre Jean Jouve. Paris: Plon. (Reprinted in 1964.)

Klotz, Volker.
1960   *Geschlossene und offene Form im Drama*. Literatur als Kunst: Eine Schriftenreihe. Edited by Kurt May and Walter Höllerer. Munich: Carl Hanser Verlag.

Knight, Arthur H. J.
1951   *Georg Büchner*. Oxford: Basil Blackwell.

König, Werner.
1974   *Tonalitätsstrukturen in Alban Bergs Oper "Wozzeck."* Tutzing: Hans Schneider.

Kolleritsch, Otto, ed.
1978   *50 Jahre Wozzeck von Alban Berg: Vorgeschichte und Auswirkungen in der Opernästhetik*. Studien zur Wertungsforschung, vol. 10. Graz: Universal Edition.

Krenek, Ernst.
1937   *Ueber neue Musik*. Vienna: Verlag der Ringbuchhandlung.
1939   *Music Here and Now*. Translated by Barthold Fles. New York: W. W. Norton & Co.
1940   *Studies in Counterpoint: Based on the Twelve-Tone Technique*. New York: G. Schirmer. (German ed. as *Zwölfton-Kontrapunkt-Studien*; Mainz, 1952.)
1943   "New Developments of the Twelve-Tone Technique." *Music Review* 4, pp. 81–97.
1960   "Extents and Limits of Serial Techniques." *Musical Quarterly* 46, pp. 210–32.

Leibowitz, René.
1948   "Alban Berg's *Five Orchestral Songs After Postcard Texts by Peter Altenberg*, Op. 4." *Musical Quarterly* 34:4, pp. 487–511.
1949a   *Schoenberg and His School*. Translated by Dika Newlin from the French ed. (pub. 1947). New York: Philosophical Library. (Reprinted in paperback ed. by Da Capo Press, New York, 1949.)
1949b   *Introduction à la musique de douze sons*. Paris: L'Arche.

Leichtentritt, Hugo.
1928   "Schönberg and Tonality." *Modern Music* 5:4 (May-June 1928), pp. 3–10. (Adapted in chapter 22 of the author's *Musical Form* [Cambridge: Harvard University Press, 1951], a translation of *Musikalische Formenlehre* [Berlin: Breitkopf und Härtel (3d ed.), 1927].)

Lenz, Jakob Michael Reinhold.
1972   *The Tutor* and *The Soldiers*. Translated and with an Introduction by William E. Yuill. German Literary Classics in Translation. General Editor: Kenneth J. Northcott. Chicago: University of Chicago Press.
Lewin, David.
1959   "Re: Intervallic Relations Between Two Collections of Notes." *Journal of Music Theory* 3:2, pp. 298–301.
1960   "Re: The Intervallic Content of a Collection of Notes, . . . Pieces." *Journal of Music Theory* 4:1, pp. 98–101.
1962   "A Theory of Segmental Association in Twelve-Tone Music." *Perspectives of New Music* 1:1, pp. 89–116. (Reprinted in *Perspectives on Contemporary Theory*, edited by Benjamin Boretz and Edward T. Cone, pp. 180–207. New York: W. W. Norton & Co., 1972.)
1966   "On Certain Techniques of Re-ordering in Serial Music." *Journal of Music Theory* 10:2, pp. 276–87.
1968   "Inversional Balance as an Organizing Force in Schoenberg's Music and Thought." *Perspectives of New Music* 6:2, pp. 1–21.
1977a   "A Label-Free Development for 12-Pitch-Class Systems." *Journal of Music Theory* 21:1, pp. 29–48.
1977b   "Forte's Interval Vector, My Interval Function, and Regener's Common-Note Function." *Journal of Music Theory* 21:2, pp. 194–237.
1979–80a "Some New Constructs Involving Abstract PCsets, and Probabilistic Applications." *Perspectives of New Music* 18:1–2, pp. 433–44.
1979–80b "A Response to a Response: On PCset Relatedness." *Perspectives of New Music* 18:1–2, pp. 498–502.
1980   "On Generalized Intervals and Transformations." *Journal of Music Theory* 24:2, pp. 243–51.
Lindenberger, Herbert Samuel.
1964   *Georg Büchner.* Carbondale: Southern Illinois University Press.
Lord, Charles.
1981   "Intervallic Similarity Relations in Atonal Set Analysis." *Journal of Music Theory* 25:1, pp. 91–111.
McInnes, Edward.
1977   *J. M. R. Lenz—"Die Soldaten": Text, Materialien, Kommentar.* Reihe Hanser: Literatur-Kommentare, vol. 8. Edited by Wolfgang Frühwald. Munich: Carl Hanser Verlag.
Maegaard, Jan.
1961   "Some Formal Devices in Expressionistic Works." *Dansk Aarbog for Musikforskning* 1, pp. 69–75.
1962   "A Study in the Chronology of Op. 23–26 by Arnold Schoenberg." *Dansk Aarbog for Musikforskning* 2, pp. 93–115.
1972   *Studien zur Entwicklung des dodekaphonen Satzes bei Arnold Schönberg.* 2 vols. Copenhagen: Wilhelm Hansen.
Martino, Donald.
1961   "The Source Set and its Aggregate Formations." *Journal of Music Theory* 5:2, pp. 224–73.

Messiaen, Olivier.
1944   *Technique de mon langage musical.* Paris: A. Leduc. (English transla-
        tion by John Satterfield as *The Technique of My Musical Language*;
        Paris: A. Leduc, 1956.)
Metzger, Heinz-Klaus.
1958   "Analysis of the Sacred Song, Op. 15 No. 4." *Die Reihe 2: Anton
        Webern*, pp. 75–80. (German ed., 1955.)
Morris, Robert.
1977   "On the Generation of Multiple-Order-Function Twelve-Tone Rows."
        Journal of Music Theory 21:2, pp. 238–62.
1979–80 "A Similarity Index for Pitch-Class Sets." *Perspectives of New Music*
        18:1–2, pp. 445–60.
Morris, Robert, and Starr, Daniel.
1974   "The Structure of All-Interval Series." *Journal of Music Theory* 18:2,
        pp. 364–89.
1977   "A General Theory of Combinatoriality and the Aggregate (Part I)."
        Perspectives of New Music 16:1, pp. 3–35.
1978   "A General Theory of Combinatoriality and the Aggregate (Part II)."
        Perspectives of New Music 16:2, pp. 50–84.
Neumeyer, David.
1976   "Counterpoint and Pitch Structure in the Early Music of Hindemith."
        Ph.D. dissertation, Yale University.
Parks, Richard S.
1980   "Pitch Organization in Debussy: Unordered Sets in 'Brouillards.'" *Mu-
        sic Theory Spectrum* 2, pp. 119–34.
1981   "Harmonic Resources in Bartók's 'Fourths.'" *Journal of Music Theory*
        25:2, pp. 245–74.
Perle, George.
1954   "The Possible Chords in Twelve-Tone Music." *The Score and I.M.A.
        Magazine* 9, pp. 54–58.
1955   "Symmetrical Formations in the String Quartets of Bela Bartók." *Mu-
        sic Review* 16, pp. 300–12.
1960   "Atonality and the Twelve-Tone System in the United States." *Score*
        27 (July 1960), pp. 51–66.
1962   *Serial Composition and Atonality: An Introduction to the Music of
        Schoenberg, Berg, and Webern.* 2d rev. and enl. ed., 1968; 3d rev.
        and enl. ed., 1972; 4th rev. ed., 1977. Berkeley and Los Angeles:
        University of California Press.
1964   "*Lulu*: The Formal Design." *Journal of the American Musicological
        Society* 17:2, pp. 179–92.
1967a   "The Musical Language of *Wozzeck*." In *The Music Forum* 1, edited by
        William J. Mitchell and Felix Salzer. New York: Columbia University
        Press. (Adapted as chap. 5 in Perle 1980.)
1967b   "Woyzeck and Wozzeck." *Musical Quarterly* 53:2, pp. 206–19. (Adapted
        as chap. 2 in Perle 1980.)
1968   "'Wozzeck.' Ein zweiter Blick auf das Libretto." *Neue Zeitschrift für*

Musik 129:5, pp. 218ff.

1971   "Representation and Symbol in the Music of *Wozzeck*." *Music Review* 32:4, pp. 281–308. (Adapted as chap. 4 in Perle 1980.)

1977a   "Berg's Master Array of the Interval Cycles." *Musical Quarterly* 63:1, pp. 1–30.

1977b   "The Secret Program of the *Lyric Suite*." *International Alban Berg Society Newsletter* 5 (April 1977), pp. 4–12. (A slightly expanded version of the same article will be found in *Musical Times* 118 [August–October 1977], pp. 629–32; 709–13; 809–13.)

1977c   *Twelve-Tone Tonality.* Berkeley and Los Angeles: University of California Press.

1980   *The Operas of Alban Berg, Vol. I: "Wozzeck."* Berkeley and Los Angeles: University of California Press. (The following have been adapted from the above-listed articles: chap. 2, from Perle 1967b; chap. 4, from Perle 1971; chap. 5, from Perle 1967a.)

Perlis, Vivian.

1974   *Charles Ives Remembered: An Oral History.* New Haven: Yale University Press.

Ploebsch, Gerd.

1968   *Alban Bergs "Wozzeck": Dramaturgie und musikalischer Aufbau.* Sammlung Musikwissenschaftlicher Abhandlungen, vol. 48. Strasbourg: Verlag Heitz.

Pohlmann, Peter.

1960   "Harmonische Gesetzmässigkeiten im atonalen Bereich." *Musikforschung* 13:3, pp. 257–67.

Porter, Andrew.

1982   "Soldiers [review of Bernd Alois Zimmermann's opera *Die Soldaten*]." *New Yorker*, 1 March 1982, pp. 114–16.

Pousseur, Henri.

1958   "Webern's Organic Chromaticism." *Die Reihe* 2: *Anton Webern*, pp. 51–60. (German ed., 1955.)

Rahn, John.

1979–80   "Relating Sets." *Perspectives of New Music* 18:1–2, pp. 483–98.

1980   *Basic Atonal Theory.* New York: Longman.

Redlich, Hans Ferdinand.

1957a   *Alban Berg: Versuch einer Würdigung.* Vienna: Universal Edition.

1957b   *Alban Berg: The Man and His Music.* London: John Calder. (A transcription and condensation of Redlich 1957a.)

Regener, Eric.

1974   "On Allen Forte's Theory of Chords." *Perspectives of New Music* 13:1, pp. 191–212.

Reich, Willi.

1931   *A Guide to Alban Berg's Opera "Wozzeck."* Translated by Adolph Weiss. Modern Music Monographs. New York: The League of Composers. 2d ed., New York: G. Schirmer, 1952. (Reprinted as "A Guide to *Wozzeck*" in *Musical Quarterly* 38:1 [January 1952], pp. 1–20.)

1937 *Alban Berg: Mit Bergs eigenen Schriften und Beiträgen von Theodor Wiesengrund-Adorno und Ernst Krenek.* Vienna: Verlag Herbert Reichner.

1959 *Alban Berg: Bildnis im Wort: Selbstzeugnisse und Aussagen der Freunde, mit Photos und Musikdokumenten.* Zurich: Verlag 'Die Arche.'

1963 *Alban Berg: Leben und Werk.* Zurich: Atlantis Verlag AG. English translation by Cornelius Cardew; London: Thames and Hudson, 1965. (Reprinted in paperback by Vienna House, New York, 1974.)

Reti, Rudolph.

1958 *Tonality, Atonality, and Pantonality: A Study of Some Trends in Twentieth-Century Music.* London: Rockliff. (Reprinted by Greenwood Press, Westport, Ct., 1978.)

Richards, David G.

1977 *Georg Büchner and the Birth of the Modern Drama.* Albany: State University of New York Press.

Rochberg, George.

1955 *The Hexachord and Its Relation to the Twelve-Tone Row.* Bryn Mawr: Theodore Presser Co.

1959 "The Harmonic Tendency of the Hexachord." *Journal of Music Theory* 3:2, pp. 208–30.

Rothgeb, John.

1966 "Some Uses of Mathematical Concepts in Theories of Music." *Journal of Music Theory* 10:2, pp. 200–15.

1967 "Some Ordering Relationships in the Twelve-Tone System." *Journal of Music Theory* 11:2, pp. 176–97.

Rufer, Josef.

1952 *Die Komposition mit zwölf Tönen.* Berlin: Max Hesses Verlag. (English translation as *Composition with Twelve Notes* by Humphrey Searle; New York: Macmillan Co., 1954.)

Schäfke, Rudolf.

1926 "Alban Bergs Oper *Wozzeck.*" *Melos* 5, pp. 267–83.

Schechner, Richard.

1969 "Notes Toward an Imaginary Production." In Henry J. Schmidt's translation of Georg Büchner's *Woyzeck* (see Büchner 1969a), pp. 11–23. New York: Bard Books/Avon.

Schmidt, Henry J.

1969 "Notes on *Woyzeck.*" In Henry J. Schmidt's translation of Georg Büchner's *Woyzeck* (see Büchner 1969a), pp. 79–116. New York: Bard Books/Avon.

1970 *Satire, Caricature and Perspectivism in the Works of Georg Büchner.* Stanford Studies in Germanics and Slavics, vol. 8. The Hague: Mouton.

1973 Review of *Georg Büchner: "Woyzeck": Kritische Lese- und Arbeitsausgabe*, edited by Lothar Bornscheuer; *Georg Büchner: Erläuterungen und Dokumente*, edited by Lothar Bornscheuer; and *Wortindex zu Georg Büchner: Dichtungen und Übersetzungen*, compiled by Monika Rössing-Hager and edited by Ludwig Erich Schmitt. *Monatshefte* 65, pp. 425–29.

Schoenberg, Arnold.

1911   *Harmonielehre*. 3d rev. and enl. ed., Vienna: Universal Edition, 1922. Translation as *Theory of Harmony* by Roy E. Carter; London: Faber, 1978.

1950   *Style and Idea*. Edited with some translations by Dika Newlin. New York: Philosophical Library. (See Schoenberg 1975 below.)

1965   *Arnold Schoenberg: Letters*. Selected and edited by Erwin Stein. Translated by Eithne Wilkins and Ernst Kaiser. New York: St. Martin's Press.

1974   "Vortrag / 12 T K / Princeton." Edited by Claudio Spies. *Perspectives of New Music* 13:1, pp. 58–136.

1975   *Style and Idea*. Enl. ed. Edited by Leonard Stein, with translations by Leo Black. New York: St. Martin's Press.

Schweizer, Klaus.

1970   *Die Sonatensatzform im Schaffen Alban Bergs*. Stuttgart: Musikwissenschaftliche Verlags Gesellschaft.

Slonimsky, Nicolas.

1947   *Thesaurus of Scales and Melodic Patterns*. New York: Coleman-Ross.

Stein, Erwin.

1924   "Neue Formprinzipien." In *Arnold Schoenberg zum fünfzigsten Geburtstage*. *Musikblätter des Anbruch* 6: 8–9 (13 September 1924), special issue. (Also published in *Von neuer Musik*, edited by H. Grues, E. Kruttge, and E. Thalheimer. Cologne: Marcan, 1925. Translated by Hans Keller in Stein 1953, pp. 57–77.)

1926   "Einige Bemerkungen zu Schoenbergs Zwölftonreihen." *Musikblätter des Anbruch* 8:6. (Translated by Hans Keller in Stein 1953, pp. 78–81.)

1953   *Orpheus in New Guises*. London: Rockliff.

Stein, Jack M.

1972   "From *Woyzeck* to *Wozzeck*: Alban Berg's Adaptation of Büchner." *Germanic Review* 47:3, pp. 168–80.

Stroh, Wolfgang Martin.

1968   "Alban Berg's 'Constructive Rhythm.'" *Perspectives of New Music* 7:1, pp. 18–31.

Stuckenschmidt, H. H.

1963   "Contemporary Techniques in Music." *Musical Quarterly* 49:1, pp. 1–16.

1969   *Twentieth Century Music*. Translated by Richard Deveson. New York: World University Library; McGraw-Hill Book Co.

Szmolyan, Walter.

1965   *Josef Matthias Hauer*. Österreichische Komponisten des XX. Jahrhunderts, vol. 6. Vienna: Elizabeth Lafite (Österreichische Musikzeitschrift); Österreichischer Bundesverlag.

Teitelbaum, Richard.
1965   "Intervallic Relations in Atonal Music." *Journal of Music Theory* 9:1, pp. 72–127.

Treitler, Leo.
1959   "Harmonic Procedure in the Fourth Quartet of Bela Bartók." *Journal of Music Theory* 3:2, pp. 292–98.
1976   "*Wozzeck* and the Apocalypse: An Essay in Historical Criticism." *Critical Inquiry* (Winter–Spring 1976). (Also published as "'Wozzeck' et l'Apocalypse" in *Schweizerische Musikzeitung/Revue musicale suisse* 116:4 [July–August 1976], pp. 249ff.)

Webern, Anton.
1963   *The Path to the New Music*. Edited by Willi Reich; translated by Leo Black. Bryn Mawr, Pa.: Theodore Presser Co., in association with Universal Edition.

Weg, John D. Vander
1979   "An Annotated Bibliography of Articles on Serialism: 1955–1980." *In Theory Only* 5:1, pp. iii–36.

Wellesz, Egon.
1958   *The Origins of Schoenberg's Twelve-Tone System*. Separate printing of a lecture. Washington, D.C.: Library of Congress.

Winham, Godfrey.
1970   "Composition with Arrays." *Perspectives of New Music* 9:1, pp. 43–67.

Wittlich, Gary E.
1974   "Interval Set Structure in Schoenberg's Op. 11, No. 1." *Perspectives of New Music* 13:1, pp. 41–55.
1975   "Sets and Ordering Procedures in Twentieth-Century Music." In *Aspects of Twentieth-Century Music*, pp. 388–476. By Richard Delone et al.; Gary E. Wittlich, coordinating editor. Englewood Cliffs, N.J.: Prentice-Hall.

Wuorinen, Charles.
1979   *Simple Composition*. New York and London: Longman.

INDEX